T0287964

My Great Arab Melancholy

My Great Arab Melancholy

by Lamia Ziadé

Translated by Emma Ramadan

First published by P.O.L. éditeur as *Ma très grande mélancholie arabe*, 2017
English language edition first published 2024 by Pluto Press
New Wing, Somerset House, Strand, London WC2R 1LA
and Pluto Press, Inc.
1930 Village Center Circle, 3-834, Las Vegas, NV 89134

www.plutobooks.com

Copyright © P.O.L. Editeur, 2017, 2024; English translation © Emma Ramadan 2023

Cet ouvrage a bénéficié du soutien du Programme d'aide à la publication de l'Institut français

This book has been selected to receive financial assistance from English PEN's PEN Translates programme, supported by Arts Council England. English PEN exists to promote literature and our understanding of it, to uphold writers' freedoms around the world, to campaign against the persecution and imprisonment of writers for stating their views, and to promote the friendly cooperation of writers and the free exchange of ideas. www.englishpen.org

Supported using public funding by
**ARTS COUNCIL
ENGLAND**

The translator would like to express her deep gratitude to Lamia Ziadé, and to the National Endowment for the Arts for its translation fellowship.

The right of Lamia Ziadé to be identified as the author of this work has been asserted in accordance with the Copyright, Designs and Patents Act 1988.

British Library Cataloguing in Publication Data
A catalogue record for this book is available from the British Library

ISBN 978 0 7453 4815 5 Paperback
ISBN 978 0 7453 4817 9 PDF
ISBN 978 0 7453 4816 2 EPUB

This book is printed on paper suitable for recycling and made from fully managed and sustained forest sources. Logging, pulping and manufacturing processes are expected to conform to the environmental standards of the country of origin.

Typeset by Squareart Ltd, London

Printed by Short Run Press, Exeter, Devon

He is neither botanist, nor crop specialist, nor landscape gardener,
and nothing in the garden belongs to him personally.
But this is where he lives with people he cares about,
and everything which might affect this land matters greatly to him.

Amin Maalouf[*]

* Amin Maalouf, *Disordered World: Setting a New Course for the Twenty-First Century*, translated by George Miller (London: Bloomsbury, 2011), xxiii.

For Barth, for Lola

Contents

Part One: Headed South

PART ONE

HEADED SOUTH

الجنوب
حتى التحرير

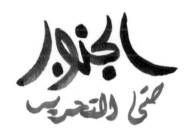

Flags and banners, palms trees, banana trees, and minarets on the road south

The Road to the South

The Opel Astra heads south. South Lebanon, the land of martyrs, ruins, and passion. You are the only passenger. You decided to go to Tyre just the night before; while sitting in a bar in Hamra, a stranger told you that in this part of Lebanon, you should never put off until tomorrow what you can do today. A drunken decision, but here you are anyway in this taxi that's just passed Saida. On both sides, banners with scenes from the Battle of Karbala alternate with Hezbollah flags.[1] On the houses and cinderblock frameworks constructed between banana trees, other flags depict different versions of Karbala, Husayn, Ali, Zulfiqar[2]... It's been three days since the Ashura festival, the commemoration of the famous battle. They are magnificent to see, all these banners. "I've traveled the Mediterranean and Mesopotamia, Ur to Volubilis, but nowhere compares to the magic of Tyre," the stranger told you the night before. You want to verify that nothing has changed, that the charm is still there, among these ruins. But really, you're heading south because you want to photograph a certain cemetery.

It's a sunlit cemetery that slopes gently toward the sea, at the tip of Tyre, between two fields of ancient ruins. A cemetery where reeds, fig, laurel, pomegranate and palm trees grow in anarchy, among the Roman columns and their capitals. There, the tombs of martyrs fallen in combat or of entire families mowed down in Israeli bombings bloom. It's a paradisiacal cemetery, gay, joyous, wrapped in ribbons.

The stranger told you: "If you like the melancholy of cemeteries, there's plenty more of that to be found." He had no idea how right he was. Your voyage into mourning and destruction has only just begun. It will be funereal and marvelous. You are entering the history of the Middle East.

---

1   The foundational event of the Shii branch of Islam and its martyrology.
2   Muhammad's double-bladed sword, which he gave to his son-in-law Ali.

Portraits of Hassan Nasrallah,
of Husayn and Ali, of Imam Musa al-Sadr

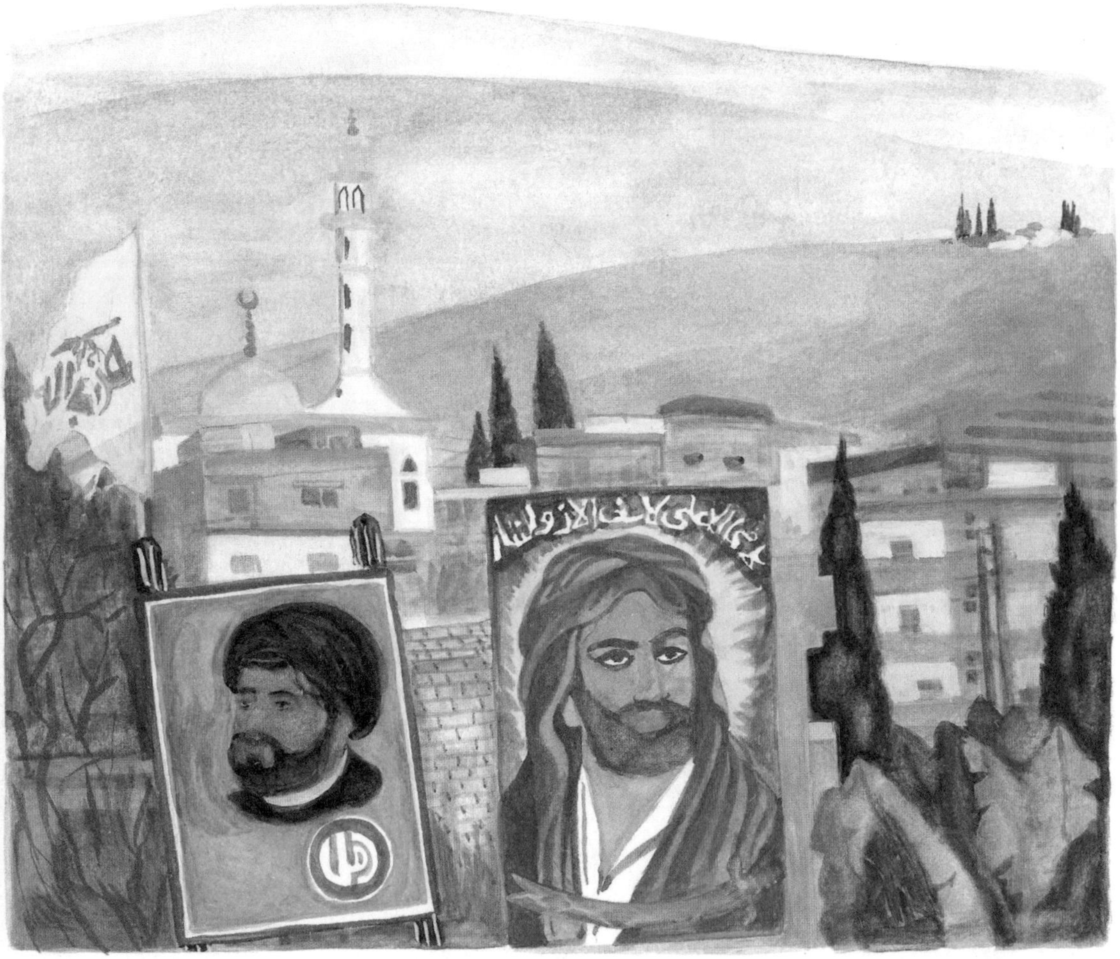

On every piece of land in South Lebanon, on every pylon, on every barn...

...reminders of the legendary imam still loom, forty years after his mysterious disappearance

A pit stop for a refreshing Pepsi

The Battle of Karbala

A pit stop at Nabatieh, an important Hezbollah stronghold renowned for its Ashura celebrations, gives you a chance to enjoy the vestiges of the festival. As soon as you enter the village, you see giant portraits of Khomeini and soldiers who have died recently in Syria. In the town center, the market is bustling. Girls in chadors walk arm in arm with girls in jeans and clingy T-shirts, their hair flying in the wind. You move between the stalls of fruit, vegetables, spices. You buy fresh dates and a magnificent flag from a merchant who still has some leftover stock from Ashura. You're intrigued: the young, graceful man who looks like Jesus is Husayn. The one with the double-bladed sword is Ali. But who is the one with the helmet and wounded eye, and why does he have water in his hands? That's Abbas, says the merchant, amused by your ignorance. And he tells you the story of the Battle of Karbala like you've never heard it before. Listen up...

A magnificent flag

Husayn, Ali, Abbas, and Zulfiqar

Upon Muhammad's death, the majority of believers align themselves with Abu Bakr al-Siddiq, his oldest friend and one of the first believers. The Prophet's companions appoint him as caliph (caliph, the successor of the messenger of God). Other Muslims support Ali ibn Abi Talib, cousin of Muhammad and husband of Fatima Zahra, his favorite daughter. Ali also has the privilege of being the father of the Prophet's only two grandsons, Hassan and Husayn. He is said to have been designated as his successor by the archangel Gabriel himself, who had conveyed the verses of the Quran to the Prophet a few years prior. The Sunnis are the followers of Abu Bakr, the Shia the followers of Ali and a succession that would remain in the Prophet's family... The first imam of the Shia, Ali is elected the fourth caliph of all Muslims a few years later. The reconciliation of believers seems possible then, but the hatred others feel for him, especially Aisha, one of Muhammad's wives and the daughter of Abu Bakr, stains his caliphate with violence, and he is assassinated. Muawiyah, founder of the Umayyad dynasty in Damascus, succeeds him as caliph.

O Husayn! O martyr!

Ali's eldest son, Hassan, in retirement in Medina, renounces his claim to power. In 680, Husayn, Ali's second son, refuses to pledge his allegiance to the new Umayyad caliph Yazid, son of Muawiyah, reputedly a false believer. Answering the call of the inhabitants of Kufa (in present-day Iraq), where Ali had been murdered a few years before, he leaves Mecca with seventy-two people, unaware of the trap Yazid has laid for him. The small group is defeated in Karbala, not long before reaching Kufa. The troops sent from Damas act with extreme barbarity, even decapitating Husayn, the grandson of their Prophet. His head is brought back to Damas on the end of a spear and presented to the caliph, who freezes in horror. The martyrdom of Husayn will be transformed, like the passion of Christ, into a redeeming sacrifice. Today, the Battle of Karbala is commemorated down to the minutest detail by all Shia, for ten days each year. These are the rites of Muharram. The faithful recreate each event as they mourn the martyrs. On the tenth day is the Ashura festival, mourning Husayn's death; the believers flagellate their backs in the streets until they bleed and slash their heads with very sharp blades.

Abbas on the bank of the Euphrates

The story of the battle is a colorful epic comprising numerous characters who share the spotlight with Husayn. One of the most popular is the loyal Abbas. Ali's son through a second marriage, he is Husayn's half-brother and his most faithful companion. They say that when he was born, he didn't open his eyes until Husayn took him in his arms. Not only brave in combat, Abbas is also the small troop's standard-bearer. When they are surrounded by the Umayyads who bar his access to the Euphrates, thirst takes hold of his followers, especially the children. After a few days, Abbas succeeds in penetrating the blockade in order to bring back water for Husayn and the youngest. He fills his goatskin and heads back down the path to the camp without drinking a single drop, despite his overwhelming thirst.

Husayn crying over his brother, the loyal Abbas

An enemy soldier surprises him and strikes him with a blow that severs his arm. Another strike amputates his second arm. Abbas continues on, clutching his goatskin between his teeth. Then he is targeted by a swarm of arrows. The goatskin is pierced and his eye is wounded. He falls from his horse and collapses to the ground, crying: "O, my brother!" He will be buried at the exact site of his fall. A mausoleum will be constructed around his tomb, and a mosque around the mausoleum, which is visited each year by millions of Shia.

Fresh dates at the Nabatieh market

The logo of the Lebanese National Resistance Front,
an association of several parties in opposition to the Israeli occupation

Martyrs

The Battle of Karbala gave rise to the cult of the martyr, of mourning, and the suicide attacks that terrorize us today. They say it's never so simple in this part of the world: How many people know that some of the first female kamikazes of the Middle East were Christian? Suicide missions actually originated in Lebanon in the 1980s before going on to inspire Palestinians and Iraqis fifteen years later, but then they were organized by secular leftist parties as well as by Hezbollah. These were not terrorist attacks that targeted civilians but acts of resistance directed against the Israeli occupation army and the SLA.[3]

---

3   The SLA (South Lebanon Army) were a Christian militia allied with and supported by Israel.

Sana'a posing in front of the SSNP flag

Sana'a Mehaidli was the first. On April 1985 at eleven in the morning, she drives a Peugeot 504 filled with 200kg of TNT, which she crashes into an Israeli army convoy on the road to Jezzine. She is sixteen years old. She is a Shia and member of the SSNP.[4] They call her the bride of the South. The ramifications of this operation are felt all the way to Palestine, and photos of Sana'a are posted in shop windows on Saladin Street in Jerusalem.

---

4   The Syrian Social Nationalist Party is a secular party founded in Beirut in 1932 by Antoun Saadeh.

Sana'a at sixteen

Sana'a will become an inspiration for other young women. The occupation of South Lebanon continues. Oppression, humiliation, and degradation are a daily reality for the area's inhabitants. Villages under blockade, houses blown up, arrests, confiscations, raids, destruction, curfews, incarcerations, beatings, torture, assassinations. Not to mention the decades of Israeli bombings and attacks this region has been subjected to long before the start of the war.

البطلة وفاء نور الدين

استشهدت في عملية بطولية في ٩/٥/١٩٨٥ ضد قوات الإحتلال الإسرائيلي وأعلائه

"Wafaa Noureddine died a martyr after a heroic operation on September 5, 1985, against the Israeli occupying forces and their collaborators"

Norma Abu Hassan was Christian, had a degree in social science, and was a professor in Zgharta.
She was twenty-six years old when she crashed a vehicle full of explosives into
a patrol of Israeli and SLA forces

شهيدة جبهة المقاومة الوطنية اللبنانية
لؤلؤة البقاع لولا الياس عبود

Loula Abboud, "the pearl of the Bekaa," is nineteen. She is a member of the Communist Party and comes from a militant Christian family that includes a long line of combatants who have died as martyrs. She blows herself up during a clash between her team and an Israeli patrol. Surrounded by soldiers and about to be captured, she waits for them to draw near and then triggers the detonator. At her funeral, amid tears and ululations, the women of the family cry out the names of her brothers and cousins who have also died for the homeland: "Tell Nicolas we say hi, Loula! Say hi to Khaled and Marwan, too!"

But the most revered member of the family is Loula's cousin, Souha Bechara, celebrated for shooting the leader of the SLA in an attempted assassination a few years later when she is twenty-one years old, which earns her ten years in the notoriously hellish Khiam prison.

The young future martyr writing her will and testament with her own blood

This photo of Wafa Idris was circulated widely after the attack

The Brief Life of Wafa Idris

Wafa Idris is born in the Al-Amʻari refugee camp in Ramallah and is still living there with her sick mother on that day in January 2002 when, at twenty-six years old, she triggers a detonator placed in her backpack in the center of Jerusalem, killing one man and wounding a few dozen others.

This act will turn her into an icon as the first female Palestinian kamikaze, nearly twenty years after Sana'a, who was the first female Lebanese kamikaze. She is trained as a nurse and works as an ambulance driver for the Palestinian Red Crescent. She is very proud of this. A framed photo of her in her graduation cap and gown holding her diploma hangs in one of the three rooms of the hovel where she lives with her mother, her brother, her sister-in-law, and their five children. As an ambulance driver in Jerusalem, the atrocities she witnesses every day end up breaking her. It is the beginning of the Second Intifada, there are too many victims to count. A wounded person missing their legs, a skull rolling on the asphalt, dead children... "The children especially were unbearable for Wafa," her brother recounted. "Wafa was joyous, vibrant, she loved to joke around. But inside her was a large black hole. Every morning she knew that a new day of humiliation and suffering was about to begin. The hopelessness spurred her to give the occupier a taste of his own medicine."

When we talk about suicide attacks, sometimes we forget about the word suicide. The suffering, the hopelessness, and the lack of faith in the future are generally what push a young person toward suicide. It's no different in Palestine, where the feeling of being trampled, immured alive, at the bottom of a chasm with no way out, is probably more intense than anywhere else...

Wafa's mother posing for journalists with the portrait of her daughter

Wafa and her mother during a family celebration a few months earlier

A scene from Patrick Chauvel's film Kamikaze 47...

By an incredible coincidence, Wafa had been filmed extensively by a French journalist a few months before her death. It was for a reportage on the Palestinian Red Crescent Society. Wafa is full of joy, her radiant smile and magnetic personality irresistibly draw in the journalist's camera, despite the numerous paramedics on the premises that day.

...filmed a few weeks before the attack

The camera witnesses a troubling scene. The young woman's expression suddenly changes as she stares at the television suspended from the room's ceiling. Her smile disappears and a veil of sadness and gravity cloud her face. She stands up and leaves the room, keeping her eyes fixed on the television screen. The journalist's camera then pans to the screen broadcasting a video testament of a young martyr who has carried out an attack that very day.

يا سيدتنا مريم وطار الياس
تشفعوا لأجلنا

The Virgin Mary and Saint Elias, on a narrow street not far from the port

The Port of Tyre and the Virgin Mary

The road from Nabatieh to Tyre is still decorated with images of Husayn, Nasrallah,[5] martyrs, and always with Musa al-Sadr. But more on the legendary imam later. Now you arrive in Tyre, welcomed by a triumphal arch in honor of Hezbollah. Your hotel is located under the lighthouse, on the edge of the old Christian neighborhood at the tip of Tyre. You walk to the port, two minutes away. After many kilometers of Shii imagery—minarets, turbans, veils, imams, and ayatollahs—now the Virgin Marys flourish in the alleys of the old neighborhood, in window displays or alcoves carved into the walls. On a pontoon right in the middle of the small port is an elegant blue-and-white mausoleum, and you hear the call to prayer from the neighboring mosques. You sit on a café terrace to have a beer and a plate of *foul*.

---

5   Hassan Nasrallah, leader of Hezbollah.

You photograph the young waiter making hummus in the back of the café

The young waiter is busy helping a couple of foreigners, probably affiliated with an NGO, visibly astonished by the omnipresence of the Virgin Mary in this region dominated by Hezbollah. As though entrusted with a mission, the waiter takes it upon himself to promote Lebanon, land of tolerance and cohabitation, as though he were addressing the General Assembly of the United Nations. He explains that here, in Lebanon, communities are never in conflict for religious reasons.

For other reasons, certainly. Economic, political, social, or military reasons, but not religious. Here, the only people who have destroyed Christian houses, churches, and convents are the Israelis. The Lebanese model of coexistence among communities, the founding principal of our National Pact, is the antithesis of the Zionist model, in which Palestine is reserved only for the "chosen people."[6]

---

6   A power-sharing agreement between Lebanon's religious communities signed in 1943 by Bechara El Khoury and Riad Al Solh, president of the republic and prime minister, Christian and Muslim, respectively.

A beer, foul, sunshine, and the chant of the muezzin

The Virgin Mary and Saint Elias on a pontoon in the middle of the port

Our neighbors have tried to destroy this principle of coexistence in Lebanon by pitting Christians against Muslims. But we are still here, together, still the only country in the world governed by Muslims and Christians together. I noticed you were surprised by the Virgin Mary. But Muslims also worship Mary who, in the Quran, is the only woman referred to by name and mentioned several times; an entire sura is even dedicated to her. I am Muslim and my mother goes twice a year to Maghdouché to pray to the Virgin.[7] Maghdouché is really something! It's not just a place of the Virgin's apparition, but where she actually stayed! She slept there while waiting for Jesus, who had gone to Saida to preach. And Lebanon is the only country in the world where the day of the Annunciation has been officially decreed a national Islamic–Christian celebration, since 2010. They want to divide us in the name of religion, but thanks to Mary, they won't succeed! Can I get you another beer?

---

7   Maghdouché is a village overlooking Saida.

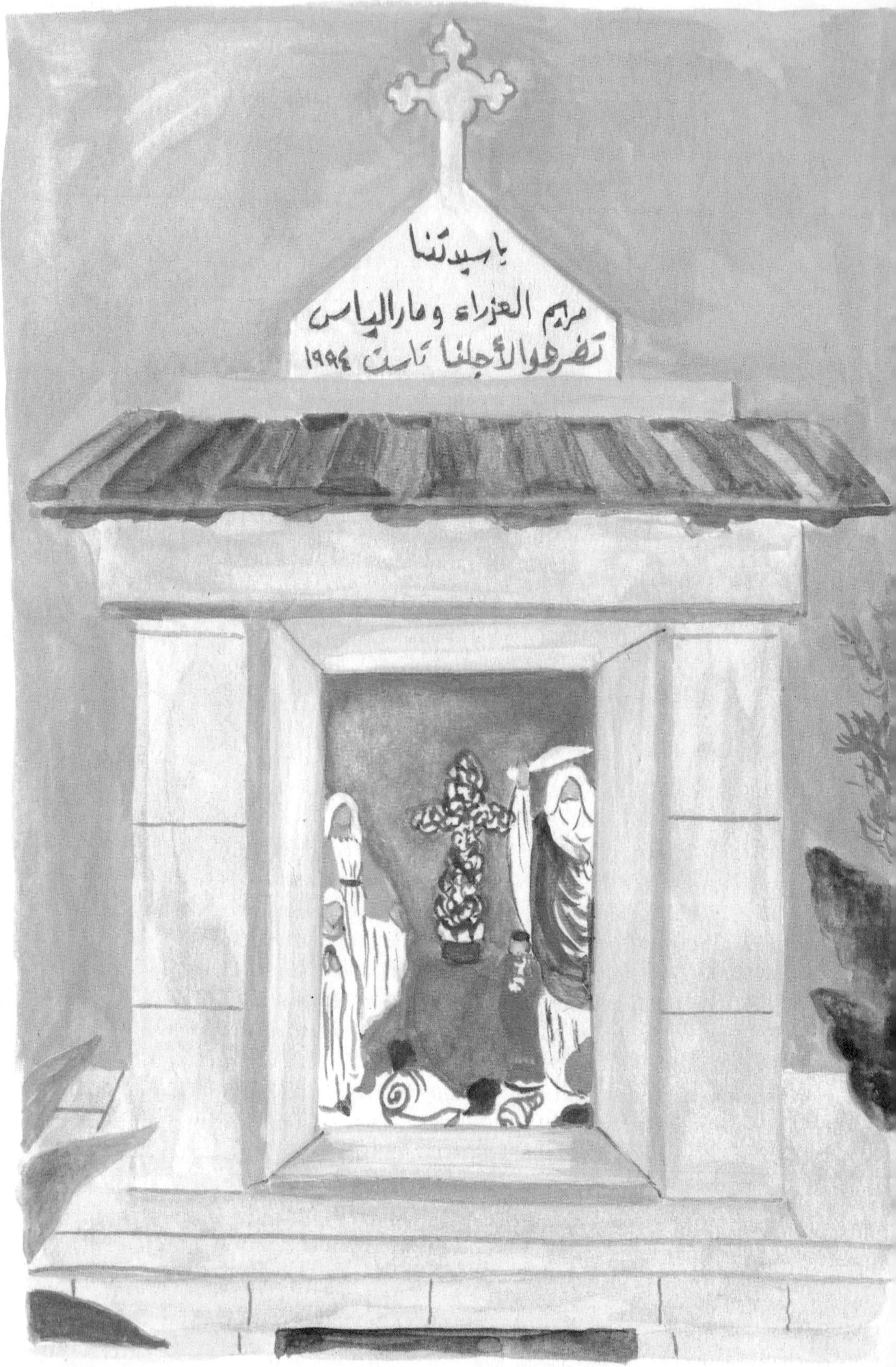

ياسيدتنا
مريم العزراء ومارالياس
تضرعوا لأجلنا تاسست ١٩٩٤

A photograph of Ahmad and his little brother

The Heroic Feat of Ahmad Qassir

Although the young female kamikazes were often leftists or Christians, the first suicide mission in South Lebanon was in fact carried out by a young Hezbollah resistance fighter in Tyre on November 11, 1982. His act turned November 11 into Martyrs' Day, still celebrated today. Ahmad Qassir was born and raised in a religious family in a village in the south. He is a calm, thoughtful, conscientious, and loving little boy. He has been involved in a few resistance operations against the Israeli occupying force but, on this day, at nineteen years old, he carries out the most formidable suicide attack the Israeli army had ever faced. This audacious and meticulously planned attack would inaugurate the era of martyr resistance operations, which will ultimately lead to Israel's retreat from Lebanon after twenty years of occupation. The name of the attacker would not be revealed until three years later, when Hezbollah, until then a secret organization, reveals its own existence.

A poster celebrating Ahmad Qassir's feat

It's 6:50 in the morning when Ahmad drives a vehicle loaded with 400kg of explosives at full speed into the seven-story building serving as the headquarters for the Israeli occupation army in Tyre. The impact is terrifying, the explosion extraordinary, the building completely collapses, a blaze erupts, the ammunition reserves explode. The operation results in approximately 140 deaths, including several high-ranking officers. There are practically no survivors. It is the greatest loss in the history of the Israeli army.

Above a child's tomb:

My child
don't go
don't leave me
don't abandon me,
I lost you,
light of my life,

your absence
will kill me,
and the tears
spring from my eyes.
I will not forget you
my child,

you will accompany me
for the rest of my life,
gleam of my cheek
my heart calls you
you will live within it
for the rest of my years.

The Cemetery Paradise

The cemetery you want to photograph is three minutes from the hotel; Tyre is not a big city. At the entrance is a large Hezbollah flag and another for Amal, honoring several of their combatants who died as martyrs.[8] In this large garden, a paradise on earth populated with the dead, the birds chirp, the butterflies flutter, and you can hear crickets and the sound of the sea. The flags of both parties are very present, along with other pennants, wreaths and ribbons of all kinds—it's very joyous. Often there is a photo of the combatants on their grave. There are entire families who died during the bombings, too. This cemetery contains a frightening number of tiny graves and people who died on the same date.

---

8   Amal is another Shii militia, today allied with Hezbollah.

An entire family killed on July 16, 2006: two women, a young girl, and five children. 2006, a deadly year...

You photographed two young men chanting and singing heartbreaking Shii laments, sheltered by a parasol among a cluster of Hezbollah martyrs. In the background of the photo, the entrance to the Christian cemetery

You stroll between the graves. The Roman road with the famous colonnade is separated from the tombs only by a swath of bushes, reeds, and wild laurel trees in bloom... This scenery of ancient ruins adds to the paradisiacal atmosphere of the place. Beyond the columns, the Lebanese coast stretches toward the south... A young man wearing a Hezbollah cap approaches you. Pointing at the shore, he says with a large smile, anticipating your question: "Palestine begins on the other side of that rocky point." The word Israel is never used here, you won't hear it for another two days. People speak of Palestine or Occupied Palestine.

Two young men from Hezbollah who died at eighteen years old

A tomb covered in flowers

Then the young man explains to you that, after the invasions of 1978 and 1982, the Zionists took with them a number of column capitals, busts, and bas-reliefs. He tells you proudly that it was the Greek Catholic bishop of Tyre who saved the town from destruction in 1982 by standing with his cross in front of the enemy tanks. Your guide leads you from grave to grave, recounting in detail the death of each victim of 2006. Cluster bombs, shells, shrapnel, explosive shells, incendiary shells, under the rubble of a house, of a school, of a hospital…

Yew trees, palm trees, bougainvilleas, oleander trees, fig trees...

...a paradisical cemetery

41

The Charm of the Ruins of Tyre

After the cemetery, the ruins. Here, the same vegetation, rose bushes, oleanders, and palm, pomegranate, fig, and olive trees... You are the only visitor. Perhaps the only visitor all day? All week? This certainly adds to the incredible voluptuousness of the site... with its state of magnificent neglect: not a single panel offering an archeological explanation, not an arrow, not a pictogram, no toilets, no trash cans, no caretakers except at the entrance, not a single flowerbed or lawn or bench, everywhere wild grass and lawless vegetation. How romantic! You must see the ruins of Tyre to understand what the word charm means. Tyre existed 2,700 years before Christ, and all the greatest names of antiquity and the Bible passed through here at some point. Nebuchadnezzar, Alexander the Great, Jesus, Saint Paul... And at the end of the second century, a diocese was established. Princess Europa, who gave her name to the continent, was born here. She was the daughter of Agenor, King of Tyre. She was abducted by Zeus disguised as a bull on the beach of Saida.

The colonnade along the Roman road and the coast that stretches to the south, toward Palestine

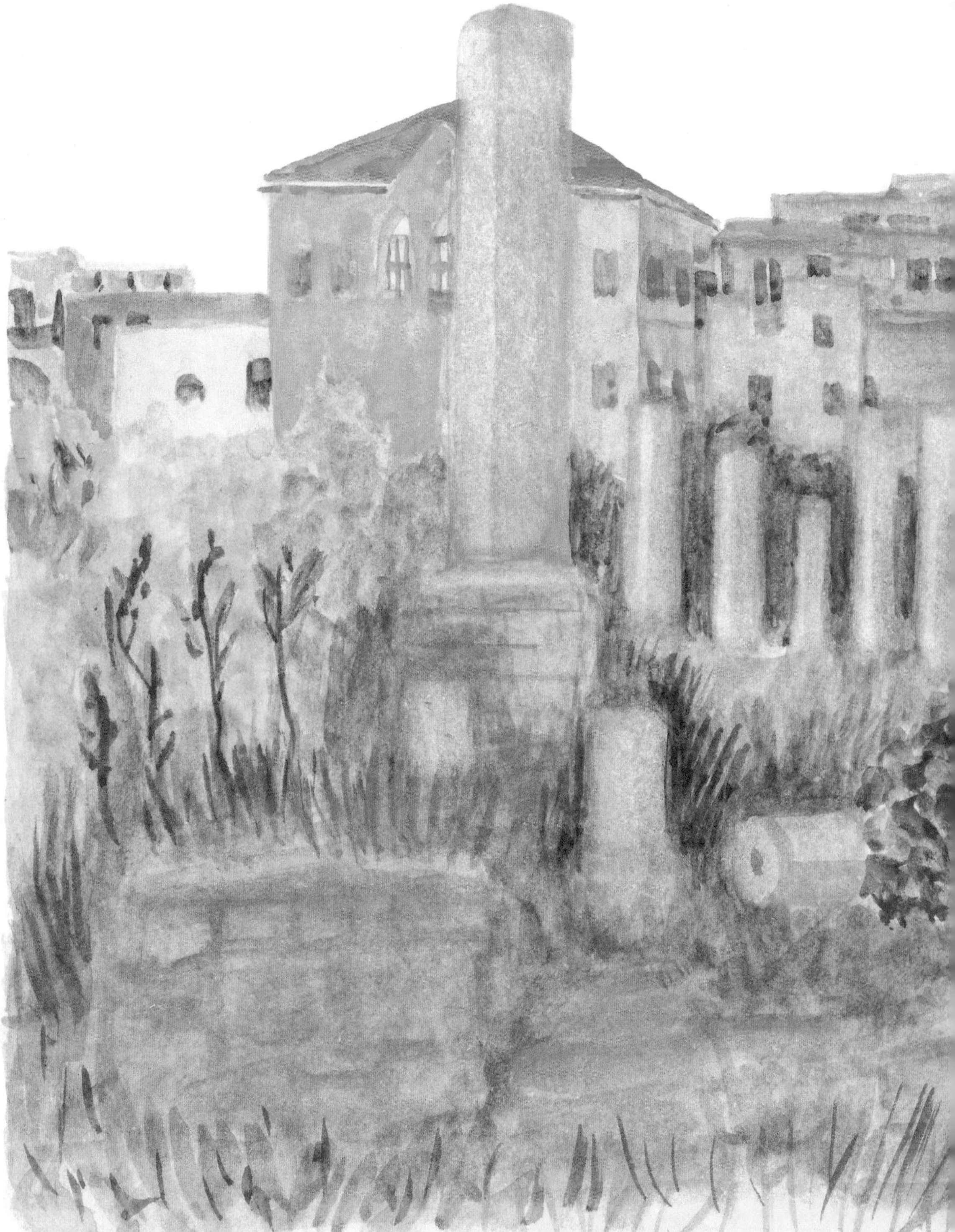

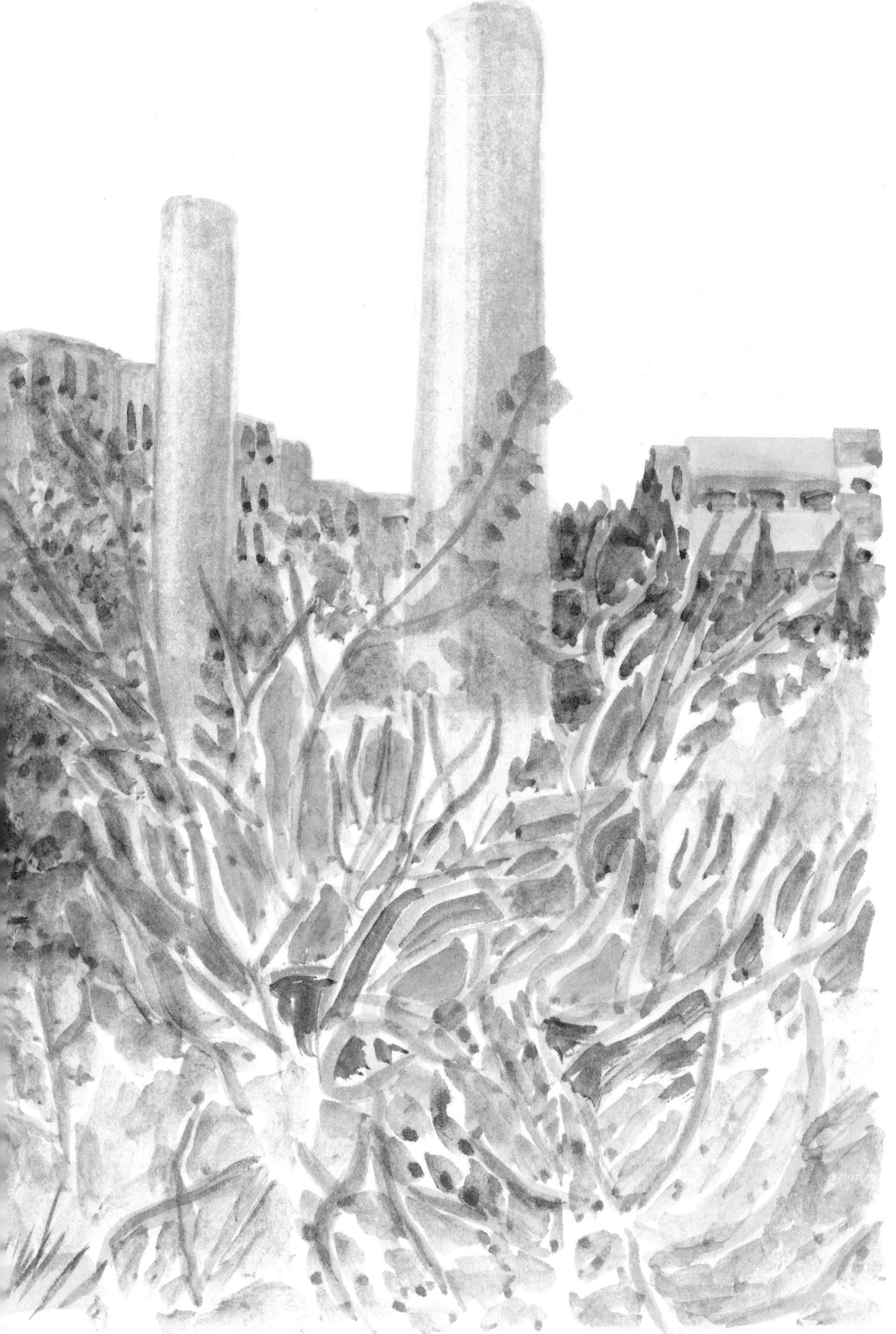

The ruins, the city

Since the nineteenth century, Lebanon's antique vestiges have been continually pillaged. In the museums of Istanbul or Paris, there are exceptional pieces from South Lebanon and Byblos. But the Ottoman sultans and French archeologists were not the only pillagers in the region. Moshe Dayan's magnificent collection didn't cost him much; it is comprised solely of masterpieces that he stole during his invasions of Palestine, Sinai, and Lebanon. Now with the publication of articles and books by Israeli journalists on this subject, it is public knowledge that he took everything he could, even deploying battalions of the Israeli army to locate and reap pieces for his collection, brazenly carrying off steles, busts, sarcophagi, and monumental capitals in the army's helicopters.

The Phoenician necropolis...

In the Phoenician necropolis, at the other end of the city, incredible sarcophagi disappear beneath abundant vegetation. The sight transports you for a moment to the museum in Beirut where other marvelous, exceptional sarcophagi have in former times escaped the fury of the war under the most extraordinary circumstances. There is a man to whom Lebanon owes its eternal gratitude. The exceptional archeological patrimony and immense cultural heritage of this small country have survived the ravages of fifteen years of madness thanks to him: Emir Maurice Chehab.

The site of the Phoenician necropolis and of the Roman hippodrome in Tyre.

Emir Maurice Chehab and the National Museum

Maurice Chehab is the director of antiquities when the war breaks out in 1975. He is over seventy years old but would prove to be a genius whom people would praise for many years to come for having protected the unique treasures held in the National Museum of Beirut from the hands of militiamen and the impact of shellfire. From the very first days of the war, the museum is in the heart of the battle. It is even situated on the "Rue de Damas" itself, the famous line of demarcation that separates East and West Beirut, the epicenter of combat and preferred spot of snipers on both sides—in other words, a death trap for anyone who ventures into the vicinity. Maurice Chehab takes advantage of the first brief moment of ceasefire to go to the museum with a few workers. They remove the small objects, statuettes, ceramics, pottery, and jewels from their cases and store them in an underground room whose entrance they conceal with a double concrete wall. Another wall is constructed in front of the twenty-seven recumbent effigies that make up the world's most beautiful collection of anthropoid sarcophagi dating from the fifth century BC, shielding them from prying eyes. The emir then circulates the rumor that everything the museum considers precious was sent abroad on the first day of combat. But his real stroke of genius is something else entirely.

The emir had personally supervised the excavations of Tyre in the 1950s and 1960s

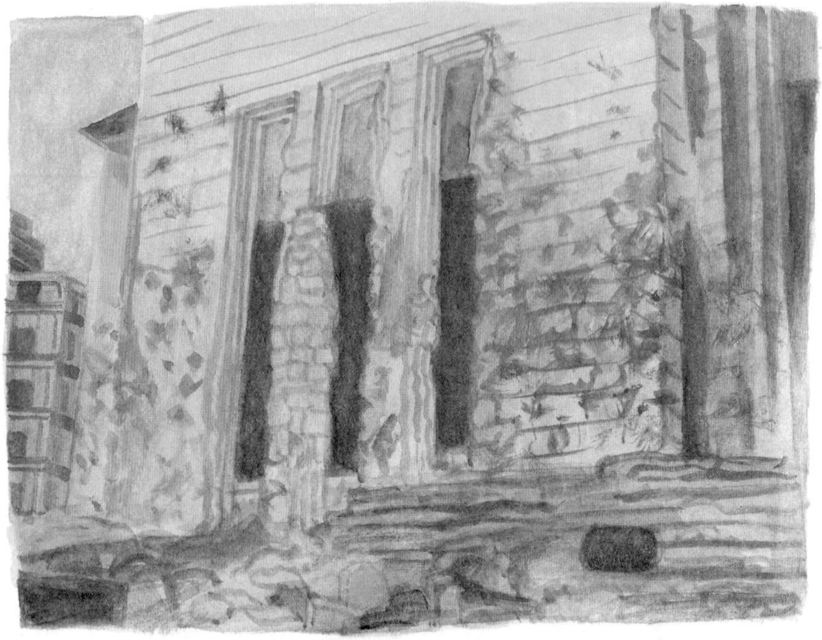

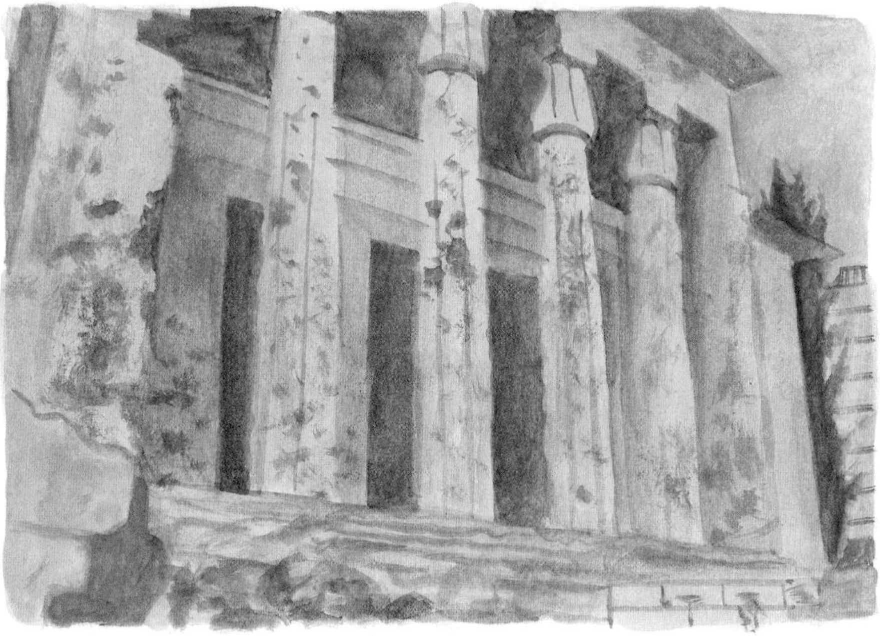

All kinds of damage

The museum at the end of the war

These slabs of reinforced concrete harbor great splendors…

Protecting the monumental and priceless sarcophagi that reside in the museum's large main room is another affair. Untransportable, they need to be sheltered *in situ*. Maurice Chehab comes up with the incredible idea to pour reinforced concrete over these marvels. This is how the famous sarcophagus of King Ahiram of Byblos, which bears the most ancient inscription in the Phoenician alphabet, was saved from theft, vandalism, and destruction, as well as the magnificent sarcophagus from Tyre covered in Ionic columns and nymphs performing bacchic dances.

...that they will protect for fifteen long years

The emir tackles each problem separately and finds the solution best suited for each. He covers the extremely rare floor mosaics with thick, large plastic tarps which are then covered in cement.

The sculptures they did not have time to protect are subjected to vandalism and destruction

The museum building, because of its location, is terribly damaged by the end of the war, having received its share of mortar shells, shrapnel, and missiles from both sides of Beirut. Occupied by different militias in turn, it also bears the trace of close combat, Kalashnikovs, grenades, and graffiti on every available surface. "When we entered the museum after the war, we discovered a devastated room with ninety-four imposing slabs of concrete," the museum curator at the time recounted. "When we dismantled them, even though we knew exactly what was inside, it was very emotional each time. In the basement, too, when we destroyed the first concrete wall and then the second, the treasures we found intact overwhelmed us." Maurice Chehab, alas, never saw them again; he had died a few years earlier.

After the end of the war, the concrete coffers are dismantled

Amid the clamor and the dust…

...treasures are revealed

The plastic tarps covered with cement that protected the floor mosaics are removed

Today, the museum has been restored. There is a room that bears the name Maurice Chehab. At the end of the war, the exterior wall of that room was pierced by a bullet hole that offered an unobscured view of the bustle of the square and the surrounding streets. It served as a loophole for snipers throughout those years of conflict. During the restoration, all the openings and chips that ravaged the building were filled back in, but they decided to keep that particular hole in memory of those dark years. It had perforated a mosaic from the fifth century embedded in the wall of the museum depicting a shepherd carrying a lamb on his shoulders—the Mosaic of the Good Shepherd.

The sniper hideout, made from tins, sheet metal, and tires.
The Mosaic of the Good Shepherd, and its hole

Some of the marvels from the National Museum of Beirut...
Victory, Tyre, Roman Period

Head of Dionysus, marble, Tyre, Roman Period

Long side of a sarcophagus depicting a scene from the legend of Icarus,
marble, Beirut, Roman Period (64 BC–AD 395)

Murex shells and purple-dyed fabric
The murex was discovered on a beach in Tyre in 1400 BC, earning Phoenicia global prestige for its
Tyrian purple color. It is mentioned in texts such as the Old Testament and the works of Homer

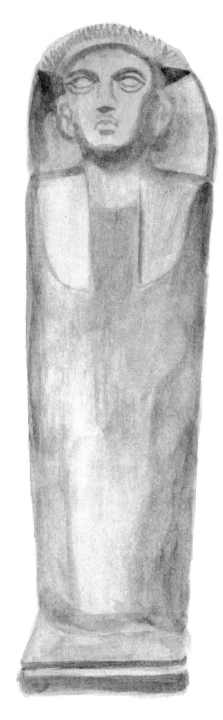

An anthropoid sarcophagus with an Egyptian-style head.
Most of the others have Greek heads

In 1960, during an official visit to Lebanon, Nehru was welcomed by Maurice Chehab at the National Museum, where he saw the anthropoid sarcophagi

Dinner at Le Phénicien

You have dinner at Le Phénicien, at the Port of Tyre. You order a mezze that is frugal by national standards. Neglecting the book you brought, you let yourself be absorbed in thought. You can't help but relive a memorable evening from April 2013, as if it happened yesterday. You were here, at this same table, with two Egyptian friends. Actually, you didn't know them very well; you had met them a few days prior at Cairo airport and had offered to help them during their stay in Lebanon. One of them was there to find his father, whom he had never met, and the other was accompanying him. His research had led him to believe that his father was living with a Palestinian woman in a village in South Lebanon, not far from Qana, the town where Jesus is said to have performed his first miracle, and where it is known that the Israeli army "accidentally" caused two massacres.[9] The night is unfurling pleasantly. Two-thirds of the way through dinner, with the help of the whiskey, Sami, the Egyptian looking for his father, makes a confession. He recounts his story in a detached and lighthearted manner, or at least tries to. His father left before he was born, his mother never spoke to Sami about him, nor did anyone else, and Sami never asked questions. He grew up in Cairo with his mother and two sisters who weren't much older than him. For years nothing special happened, until a bombshell dropped unexpectedly. He's having dinner at home with his mother and one of his sisters, Taheya, who shows them a video of Umm Kulthum recently posted on the internet, then another of Samia Gamal. They watch one video after another, drifting farther and farther from their initial subject, as often happens. The trend of retro and nostalgic videos from the golden age of the Arab world is in full swing, including those of Abdel Nasser. They watch two short clips of Nasser mostly attacking the kings of Arabia. They laugh a lot, the president had a great sense of humor, and knew how to talk. Then they watch a rare video, a brief reportage on the seizing of the Suez Canal and the Alexandria speech, then, naturally, Nasser's famous resignation speech on June 9, 1967, following the Naksa, which fills them with sadness.[10] Those videos, depicting two of the most significant events in the history of the Arab world in the twentieth century, are short. Then Sami's mother clicks on a long—a very long—video, which people typically avoid in a group setting,

---

9   The Qana massacre of April 18, 1996 and the 2006 Qana massacre.
10   The Naksa ("setback" in Arabic) or the "Six-Day War", refers to the Arab–Israeli war of June 5–10, 1967.

but they can't look away. They watch in silence, a lump in their throats. This is Nasser's funeral, recently uploaded in a full-length restored version. They don't know it yet, but in a few minutes Sami and Taheya's existences will be completely upended.

On the terrace of Le Phénicien:
whiskey, pistachios, and cigarettes...

The videos of the president's speeches, historic and captivating, make a splash on the internet

Other videos are compilations of photos in homage to Nasser. It is rare to find one where he doesn't have a cigarette in his hand

Family photos, previously unpublished...

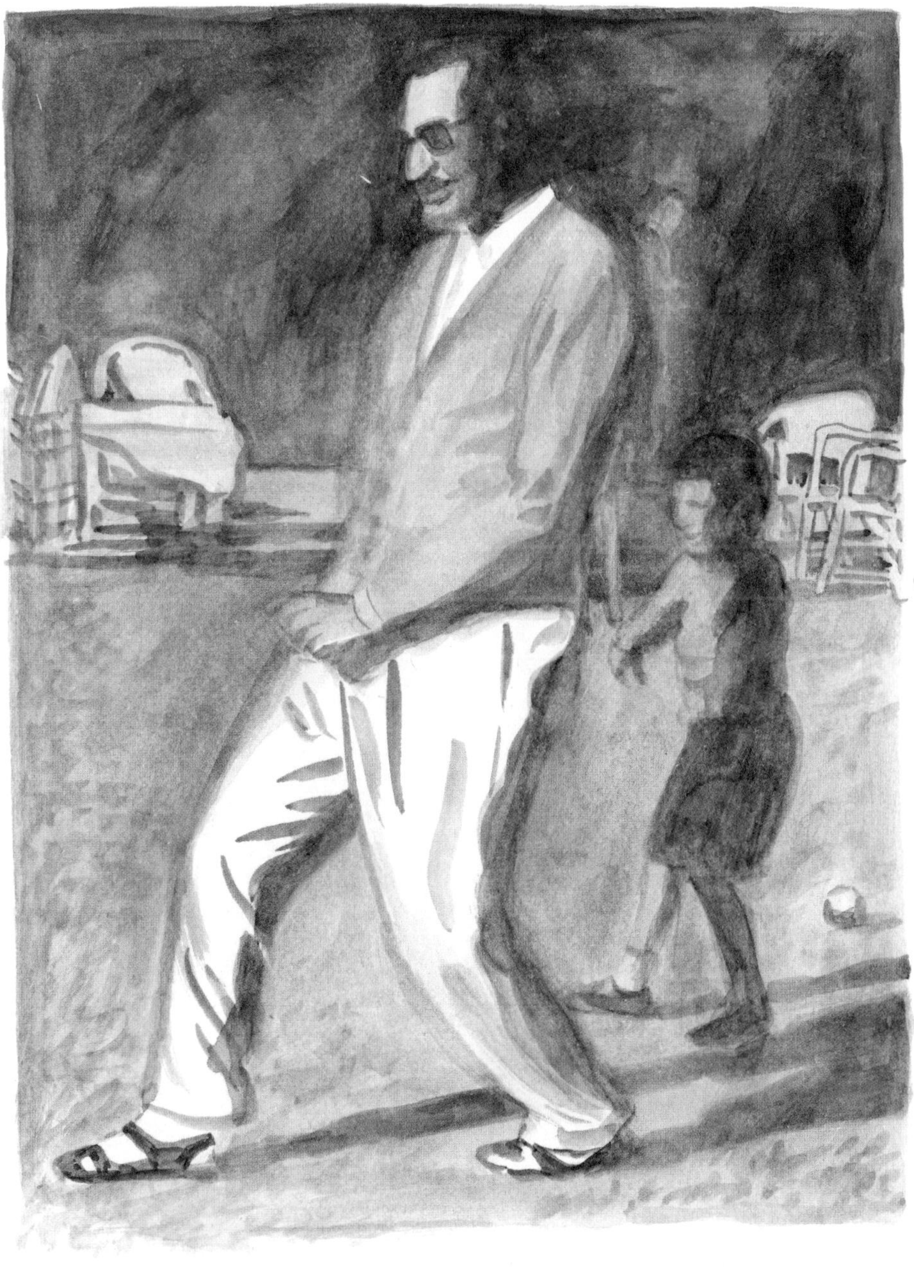

...are also released

With his wife Taheya, on a beach in Ras El Bar

He was passionate about photography and cinema

Color photos are rare and popular on the internet, as are magazines
and newspapers from that bygone era

You found this small book on the Suez Crisis at a second-hand bookstore in Hamra

A short and surprising film clip, depicting Nasser alongside Khrushchev...

...during a relaxing moment on Lake Nasser; recently made available online

77

Nasser Seizes the Canal

A short reportage about the seizing of the Suez Canal on the internet revives this exceptional and forgotten moment.

July 26, 1956. It's hot, it's stifling; Gamal Abdel Nasser is about to address the Egyptian people in Alexandria on the fourth anniversary of King Farouk's exile. This broadcast speech promises to be "sensational." For two or three days, it's all anyone talks about—the press, politicians, diplomats. Everyone awaits the president's response to the humiliating blow inflicted one week earlier by the Americans.[11] Everyone is waiting, but no one, absolutely no one, has any idea what's in store. "This is the Voice of the Arabs, live from Alexandria..." "...President Gamal Abdel Nasser appears... in a suit and tie... grabs the microphone..." A huge crowd is gathered on Muhammed Ali Square; everyone applauds the president. He begins his speech. This one is never-ending. Long, very long, delivered in a conversational tone, calm but full of rage, with notes of humor despite the gravity. He catalogues the centuries of exploitation and humiliation that the Arab world has suffered at the hands of the West, he mocks those countries, leaders of the "free world" who wrote the Declaration of the Rights of Man and the Charter of the United Nations and then besmirch them every day. He recounts his disagreements with the American emissaries, the World Bank; he hits his stride. Suddenly his tone changes, he starts talking about the Suez Canal as he has spoken about a thousand things before, but something is different. Finally, he utters these incredible words: "And I am here to announce that today, in the name of the people, I have signed a decree nationalizing the Universal Company of the Maritime Canal of Suez! In the name of the people! At this very hour, as I am speaking to you, government agents are taking possession of the canal and the Official Journal is publishing the law nationalizing the company..." There is an explosion. The clamor of the crowd pauses for a few seconds to take in the words that follow: "Four years ago, in this very spot, Farouk fled Egypt. Today, on this same date, our canal returns to us!" The lamentable war that follows, in which the former colonizers, England

---

11   In opposition to Nasser's non-aligned politics, the United States withdrew the financing of the Aswan High Dam without warning. Nasser learned of this through the press, in a disparaging communiqué. And so the Suez Canal would pay for the High Dam.

and France, ally with the new colonizer, Israel, to try to recuperate the canal and unseat the "Mussolini of the Nile," the "Hitler of the pyramids," concludes, despite an Egyptian military defeat, with the political victory of Nasser, who keeps the canal and gains the stature of a colossus, idolized by hundreds of millions of Arabs and by all the people of the Third World.

Suddenly his tone changes as he starts to talk about the Suez Canal

The great orator, head down, face tormented, voice hoarse, delivering his greatest speech

June 1967, the First Death of Gamal Abdel Nasser

June 5, 1967. Trauma, humiliation, disillusionment, loss of blood, loss of faith, distress, sadness, wreckage. The Middle East is annihilated, devastated. In just six hours, Israel has destroyed the entirety of the Egyptian air force on the ground. In just five days, Sinai, Gaza, the West Bank, Golan, and Jerusalem are lost. Nasser is preparing to give a televised speech. The young officer in tears who was asked to type it hands it to him. Nasser reads it and makes a single modification. He removes the words "ready to assume my share of responsibility" and replaces them with "ready to assume all responsibility." Egypt is glued to the television. He resigns. Egypt takes to the streets. Immediately, even before the speech has ended. All of Beirut, Baghdad, Damascus, and Algiers, too. "Nasser! Nasser!" Shouts, cries of despair, the crowd begs him to stay. He stays. He will die three years later, at the age of fifty-two. But really he died on that day in June 1967, as the Arab world began to slide into a bottomless pit...

A Very Black September

Sami, his mother, and his sister are now watching Gamal Abdel Nasser's burial, emotional. A moment of collective suffering throughout the entire Arab world. As soon as the news was announced, three days earlier, people everywhere took to the streets once more. On September 28, 1970, Egyptian radios and television stations interrupt their regularly scheduled programming. Verses from the Quran are broadcast and then also interrupted. Anwar Sadat informs the Egyptian people that their leader is dead. In the background are the stifled sobs of a television technician. The shock and stupor are tremendous. In the cinemas, films are interrupted to announce the news. Spectators shout their despair before evacuating the theaters in silence. A crowd of 5 million people in indescribable distress pour onto the streets of Cairo to follow the coffin. A tidal wave of sadness, sobs, scenes of despair. All of Egypt wails like an eight-year-old child—they are a sentimental people. In every Arab town the people are in the streets. Beirut ignites with machine-gun fire. Lebanese radio stations broadcast verses from the Quran, prayers are said in the mosques and relayed over loudspeakers, funeral processions pass through, stores close, the baccalaureate exams are cancelled. The press runs the headline: "The Man Whose Death will Change Everything, Everything that was Changed by his Arrival."

Women weeping in Beirut...

This time, it's really over: the world crumbles. For the West, he was a dictator who oppressed his people. Perhaps the English, the French, or the Israelis with their colonies find it morally superior to oppress people other than their own. On the day of the funeral, the "oppressed people" cram themselves all the way up electrical poles, on balconies, spilling over onto roofs, riverbanks, and bridges, with some even falling off... There isn't an empty centimeter anywhere in the city, it is full as far as the eye can see. A delegation of women with stylish hair, in sunglasses, wearing short, black, sleeveless dresses, hold a banner: "For the man who removed our chains." Hardy men hurl themselves to the ground in pain, shouting: "The one who restored our honor is dead!" A vagrant in rags and in tears yells at the top of her lungs: "The wild beast, my wild beast is dead!" Workers, peasants from the delta or Upper Egypt, dignitaries, intellectuals, artists, the bourgeois, officers—they all know that a page has just been turned. Definitively. And that the future will be dark.

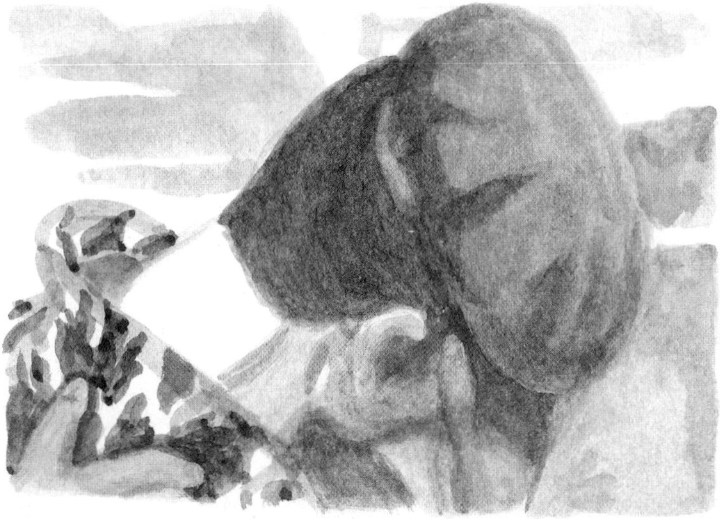

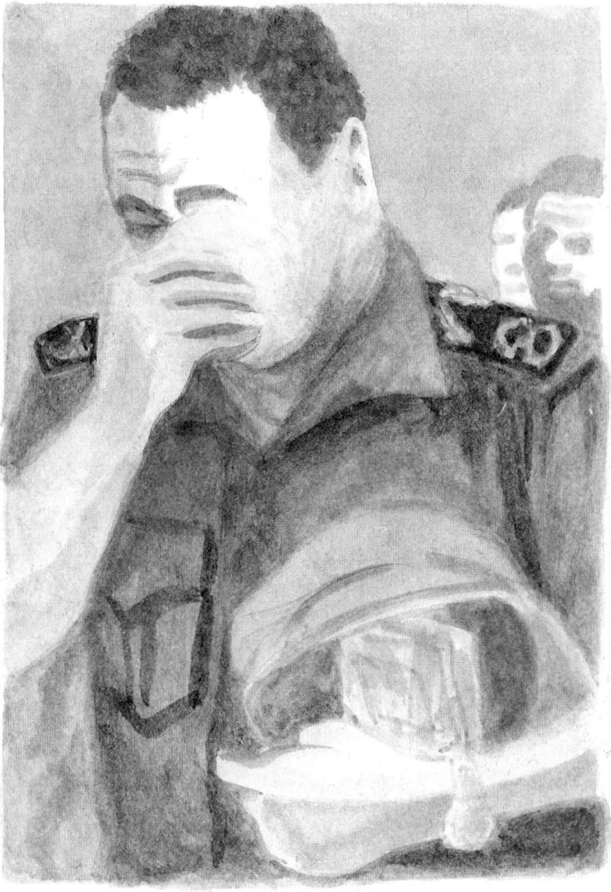
CO

...men, in Cairo

In Lebanon, a Palestinian says her final goodbye

Amid indescribable chaos, people approach the mausoleum entrance

They bring the coffin into the mausoleum where Nasser will rest. The chaos is indescribable. Everyone is crying, screaming, pushing, trying to touch the sarcophagus. Dozens of people cling to it, the crowd is compacted together as tightly as possible, ready to enter the tomb along with him. Sami, his mother, and his sister are overwhelmed with emotion. Only one meter left to go. Those who can, throw themselves at the coffin to kiss it. Suddenly a scream. It's Sami's mother, she shouts: "It's Zaki! It's Zaki! It's your father!" It takes a minute for Sami to understand... he rewinds... A young officer takes off his helmet to kiss the coffin, another literally collapses onto it, sobbing. It's his father. He replays those five seconds ten times in slow motion. The next second, the coffin disappears into the tomb. Then his mother speaks.

It's over, the coffin is placed in the tomb. The crowd clings onto it with indescribable distress

Overcome with emotion, those who can, throw themselves on the coffin to kiss it

87

This young man, collapsed in sobs over the coffin, is their father

Zaki

Like many Egyptians and Arabs, Zaki revered Nasser, and the defeat of 1967 and the authoritarian regime made no dent in that. When he died, Zaki was filled with immense sorrow, and as a low-ranking officer who was somewhat close to the president, he arranged to be among those carrying his coffin. Their mother knew that, even though she hadn't met him until four years later. In fact, it was one of the first things he had told her about himself! But obviously she had never seen the video... Did she think she could stop the story there? For Sami and Taheya, overwhelmed by emotion, it was impossible. Now that they had seen him, that young man who was so moving, so handsome, so passionate, they wanted to know everything about him. So, the story goes, Salwa marries Zaki four years later. They have three children in five years. In 1977, Zaki is sent to Beirut as part of the Arab League's quadripartite committee, which includes Egypt, tasked with enforcing the Cairo Accord in Lebanon. He remains there for the two months that the committee's mission lasts. Egypt finally washes its hands of all responsibility—as do the other two members of the committee, Kuwait and Saudi Arabia—and leave it to Syria alone to enforce the agreement, that is, to occupy Lebanon. While in Beirut, during a raid on the Shatila refugee camp, Zaki meets Fadia, a young Palestinian, with whom he becomes infatuated. When he returns to Egypt, he puts an end to this impossible romance with a heavy heart. He is a man of honor; he will not abandon his wife and children. Sami is born in 1978, the year of the Camp David Accords. Zaki, who is already not fond of Sadat, flies into a rage. He recognizes immediately that the establishment of a separate peace agreement will allow the Israelis to concentrate their forces elsewhere, that is, in Lebanon. What seems ironic, Sami muses, is that the committee that awarded the Nobel Peace Prize to Sadat and Begin was not as far-sighted as the humble little Egyptian officer. Zaki understood that the Palestinians in Lebanon were the most at risk. He explains everything to Salwa in a great melodramatic scene straight out of a Studio Misr film before returning to Beirut to rescue Fadia from her fate. After that, Salwa mostly lost the thread of events. She only knows that Zaki managed to get Fadia out of the camp before the tragedy. Unable to bring her back to Egypt, and since Fadia had lost her entire family in the massacre, they moved to a village in South Lebanon where he became a peasant. This is the village you will bring the two Egyptians to the next day.

At the White House, right after the signing of the loathsome accords

She invites you into her home...

Fadia and Her Sons

The hillside village of Odaisseh overlooks Galilee. Sami asks where his father's house is. People point to the road without comment. At the place they are directed to, they find a heap of rubble. Children playing nearby point you to a carcass of cinder blocks across the street. That heap of rubble was their house until July 2006.[12] They reconstructed it, next door. An old woman comes out to greet you. It's Fadia. Zaki is no longer there. He's gone. He went mad. Their three sons died in 2006 and Zaki went mad. She doesn't know where he is, perhaps he's dead, she hasn't had any news. She managed not to go mad herself because she had to take care of the little ones. Who else would do it? Their mother, the wife of her eldest son, works day and night to provide for them. Maybe someone named Jamal, who lives in the Shatila camp in Beirut, can help them. Maybe he knows where Zaki is. What do you want with him anyway? Up until that point, she had spoken in a monotone voice, almost absent, detached. When Sami introduces himself, a rush of emotion consumes her and she bursts into tears. Sami does, too. A moment goes by. You find yourself, along with

---

12   A month-long Israeli offensive throughout all of Lebanon, with the goal of destroying Hezbollah. It resulted in more than a thousand civilian deaths, the destruction of the majority of the country's infrastructure and many homes, and ultimately, Israel's failure.

the two Egyptians, inside the house with a glass of *Tang*. Fadia tells Sami that his father was never able to sleep after he left Egypt. Sami is touched by her kindness. She shows you a photo of her sons. As you are leaving, she begs you to find Zaki. "I don't care that he hasn't come back, but Nada left with him. She's my only daughter, I haven't seen her in ten years. I want to see her again before I die. Until then, I will continue to have my coffee each morning overlooking Occupied Palestine."

...and offers you a glass of Tang

You don't hear much more from Sami. You know only that he went to Shatila to find Jamal. Then you receive a text message: "I found my father. I found my sister. Too much suffering in this country, I'm going back to Egypt." The messages you send back to Sami asking what happened remain unanswered. You promise yourself that one day, you too will go to Shatila.

At each fishmongers in the souk, a portrait of the revered imam

In the Tyre Souk

Is there anything more enjoyable in the world than strolling through the small Tyre souk behind the port! A peaceful entanglement of gently sloping alleys with a very singular charm: not a single tourist. There are several large, very old houses in shambles; they have not been repaired since the various Israeli bombings because often they are the property of families that have emigrated to Australia or South America. What is most striking is the profusion of portraits of Musa al-Sadr on each stall, in each alley. Decades after his disappearance, the legendary imam lives on in Tyre, and throughout the South. His smile and enigmatic gaze have always disconcerted you... What is the mystery behind the sudden shattering of his destiny?

Ali's taxi will bring you into the heart of the South

You find a taxi near the port. You will continue your pilgrimage through South Lebanon. You want to revisit Beaufort Castle and Khiam detention center, or what remains of them. Beaufort, destroyed by the Israelis, served as their headquarters upon their retreat from Lebanon in 2000. Khiam, also destroyed by the Israelis during the "war" of 2006. You daydream about the threatened monuments and sites in Syria and Iraq, and you and Ali, your taxi driver, talk about the magnificent holy places of Shii Islam, already destroyed countless times throughout history.

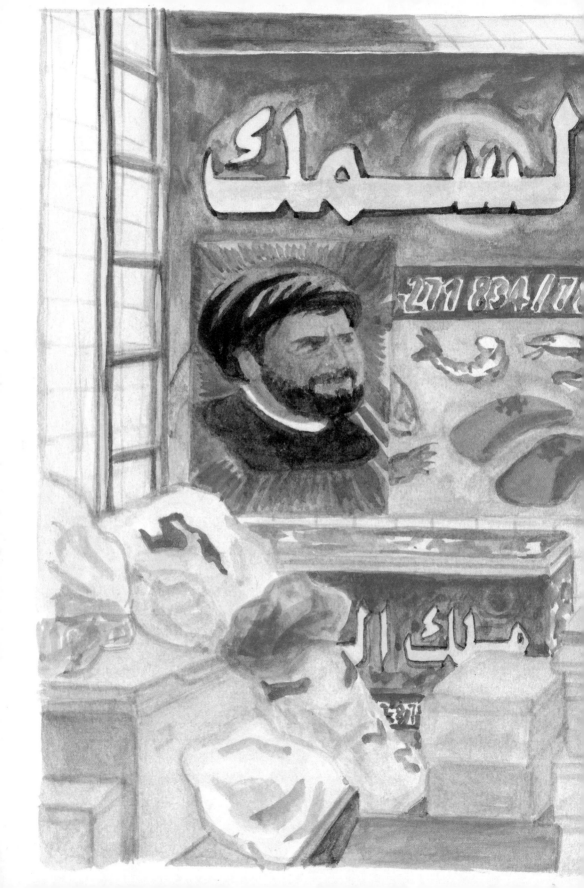

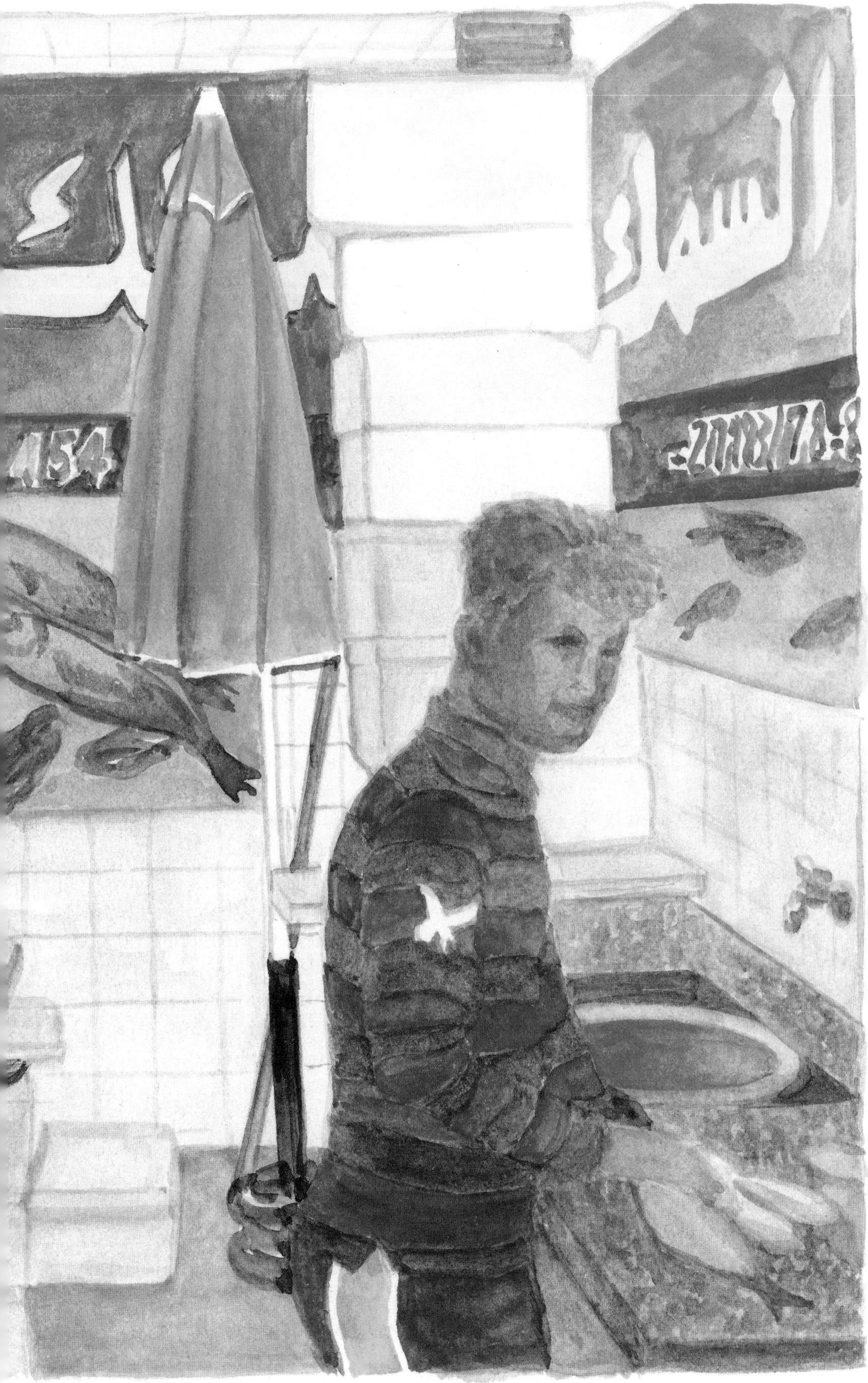

Imam Ali Mosque

From Najaf to Kufa; Mausoleums in Mesopotamia

In the heart of Iraq, Najaf is the birthplace of numerous religious, intellectual, and scientific movements, and houses one of the largest Shii seminaries in the world, a major center for theological studies, and several Sufi schools and congregations. That's where, for more than ten years, Imam Khomeini led the primary opposition movement to the regime of the Shah of Iran. Imam Ali's tomb is located in the middle of the city, at the very place where Adam and Noah were buried, according to Shii tradition. It has been continually destroyed over the centuries, especially in the nineteenth century by the Saudis, and during the First Gulf War, and then the second. Since then, it has been the stage for numerous assassinations, attacks, and battles. Every year it attracts millions of pilgrims, considered the fourth holiest site in Shii Islam after Mecca, Medina, and Jerusalem. It has an impressive golden façade, as well as two large minarets and a central dome also covered in gold.

Once inside, it is hard to know where to look: the doors incrusted with precious metals and fine engravings, the walls studded with multi-faceted mirrors, the numerous calligraphic verses from the Quran, the glistening chandeliers, the precious objects... Everything comes together to inspire spirituality and reflect the beauty of the beyond. The ambiance is surreal, outside of place and time. Far from the tumult of the city, you can't hear a thing but the hushed sounds of whispered prayers. As you advance farther, the crowd thickens. Sounds of sobs break the monotony of the murmurs. Now you can see the golden walls of the imam's tomb that everyone tries to touch, kiss, or at the very least brush with the tips of their fingers.

A dense crowd of pilgrims, sobbing and sighing, throng around
Ali's tomb in an attempt to touch it

Wadi al-Salaam. The cemetery stretches as far as the eye can see

A few dozen meters from Ali's tomb is Wadi al-Salaam, the largest cemetery in the world, stretching over several square kilometers with more than 10 million graves in which 35 million people are buried, including several prophets and great mystics, and even the Mahdi himself, the famous "concealed" twelfth imam awaited by the Shia. Today, the registers, scrupulously maintained by hundreds of gravediggers, grow longer each day in an incessant funereal ballet with the addition of dozens of young soldiers or militiamen who die in clashes with ISIS.

*The area for new arrivals, young soldiers or militiamen who have
died in clashes with Daesh, expands at a dizzying speed*

Not far from Najaf, the Great Mosque of Kufa was constructed in the
same place where the fall of Adam occurred and where Noah's Ark was built.
Numerous prophets came to pray here, including Abraham, Muhammad,
and the angel Gabriel. Most importantly, this is the place where Ali was
assassinated in 661 while he was praying. According to some accounts, as
he was dying, he asked his loved ones to carry only the back of his coffin,
as the front would be guided by the angel Gabriel toward his sepulcher. Of
course, Gabriel stopped where the current tomb in Najaf was constructed.

Karbala

Karbala, at last! A city located where the famous battle took place between Najaf and Baghdad, it is the fifth holiest place of Islam and attracts millions of Shii pilgrims each year, especially during Ashura. The city was constructed around the shrine of Imam Husayn, grandson of the Prophet and son of Ali. The shrine itself was constructed around the tomb that houses his body. In a grave at the foot of Husayn's tomb rest his seventy-two companions who died during the battle—the martyrs of Karbala. Like the Imam Ali Mosque in Najaf, it has been destroyed several times over the course of history and, during the nineteenth century, suffered the savagery of the Wahhabis, who demolished even the tomb of Muhammad's grandson!

O Husayn, O martyr...

Although Husayn's body was buried in Karbala, his head is located at the Umayyad Mosque in Damascus, where it was brought to Caliph Yazid after the battle. According to other sources, it ended up in Cairo, where it was brought after passing through Ashkelon in Palestine, for reasons that remain obscure. In any event, the Al-Hussein Mosque in Cairo is one of the most visited in the city, and the mausoleum inside it is a place of worship without parallel. There is also a museum in Aleppo, which houses the boulder upon which Husayn's head is said to have rested, and onto which a drop of his blood is said to have spilled.

Above: Al–Hussein Mosque and mausoleum
Below: Al–Abbas Shrine and mausoleum

In Karbala, there is another tomb visited each year by millions of Shia: that of Abbas, son of Ali and half-brother of Husayn, buried in the exact spot where he fell from his horse after an arrow pierced his eye. Its design, like those of the Imam Ali Mosque in Najaf and the Al-Husayn Mosque in Karbala, is inspired by Persian-style architecture and, like them, it has also been subjected to destruction and pillaging throughout the centuries.

Loyal Abbas...

The mausoleum of Zaynab, the daughter of Imam Ali, sister of Husayn, and granddaughter of the Prophet, is another important Shii pilgrimage site. The Sayyidah Zaynab Mosque is located in the south of Damascus. However, according to some, Zaynab, a survivor of Karbala, died in Cairo, where she was buried in a mosque that also welcomes the sighs, tears, and lamentations of her worshipers.

One of the mausoleums of Al-Baqi Cemetery in Medina before its destruction

Mecca and Medina, or Disaster and Delirium

The worst destruction of the holy and historic sites of Islam has not taken place in a country at war—neither in Iraq, nor in Syria—but in Saudi Arabia where 95 percent of the country's religious sites and thousand-year-old buildings, including some of the most important sites of Islam, have been dismantled, razed, and erased by... the Saudis themselves! Historic mosques, sacred mausoleums, celebrated tombs, homes of the Prophet, his family, and the first caliphs, have been the targets of radical destruction since 1925, when Abdulaziz Ibn Saud seized Hejaz. Visiting tombs or historic sites is considered idolatry by the Wahhabis and does not at all conform to their stringent doctrine. Wahhabism is the bedrock of political power for the royal family of Saudi Arabia. Therefore, since 1925, they have been razing it all, and they are not done razing yet—far from it.

Dismantled Ottoman porticos

Since 2014 there has been an official project, publicized by the Saudi Ministry of Islamic Affairs, to destroy the tomb of Muhammad himself and transfer his remains to an anonymous grave. This deranged plan was only stopped *in extremis* thanks to the outcry of the rest of the Muslim world, principally Turkey, Egypt, Iran, and Indonesia. However, the famous Ottoman porticos that surrounded the Kaaba in Mecca for almost five centuries could not be saved and disappeared in 2014, despite the same protests and vehement condemnations from the most prominent Muslim countries who railed against these barbaric acts of cultural massacre. The bulldozers did their work in the dark of night.

A short list of the destruction helps to give a sense of the breadth of the disaster and delirium: the house in which Muhammad was born in 570 in Mecca, razed; the house of Khadijah, his first wife, where he had the first revelations, razed; Muhammad's house in Medina, where he lived after the Hijrah, razed; the house of Abu Bakr al-Siddiq, Muhammad's companion, one of the very first believers and the first caliph of Islam, razed (now there's a Hilton in its place); the first Islamic school where Muhammad taught his religion, the house of Ali where the grandsons of the Prophet, Hassan and Husayn, were born, the mosque of Fatima al-Zahra, his daughter, razed, razed, and razed... The tomb of Khadijah in Mecca, razed; the tomb of Abu Talib, uncle of Muhammad and father of Ali, in Mecca, razed; the tomb of Muhammad's mother, razed, doused with gasoline and burned; the Tomb of Eve in Jeddah, razed; the tomb of Muhammad's father in Medina, razed...

The bulldozers did their work during the night

The only photo that has ever been taken of Muhammad's tomb, in the nineteenth century

A View of the Al-Baqi Cemetery...

The Al-Baqi Cemetery in Medina, the location of which was chosen
by Muhammad himself so that his family and close companions could be
buried there, and where he regularly stopped to pray, was razed entirely in
1926 by the King, Abdulaziz ibn Saud. Here are just a few of the people
who were buried there: Halimah, the foster mother of Muhammad;
Ibrahim, son of Muhammad; all of Muhammad's wives except for Khadijah;
Muhammad's three daughters, Ruqayya, Umm Kulthum, and Zainab. There

...before its destruction

was also Khadijah, mother of the caliph and imam Ali ibn Abi Talib; Imam Hasan, son of Fatima al-Zahra and Ali, Muhammad's grandson; the fourth, fifth, and sixth imams; all the direct descendants of Muhammad; Uthman, Muhammad's companion and third caliph...

Today, the Al-Baqi Cemetery is a vast deserted terrain where each razed tomb or mausoleum is represented by a single pebble.

Khadijah's tomb in Mecca before its destruction

The Al–Baqi Cemetery today

You took this photo of a mural in South Lebanon, on the border with Israel

Dome of the Rock

You're approaching Beaufort, Khiam, you're delving further into the region that resisted the most, that suffered the most... After leaving Tyre, you speak with Ali, your driver, about the destroyed or threatened mosques, the mosques in Saudi Arabia and Iraq... But a very specific sanctuary punctuates your journey, reproduced on signs, posters, banners, flags, painted on walls, or made into miniatures, often looming behind the portraits of martyrs... The mosque—which is not a mosque—is certainly the most depicted and the most celebrated in the world, no doubt also the most coveted, probably the most threatened. Of course, it is none other than the Dome of the Rock.

O Jerusalem... We're coming!

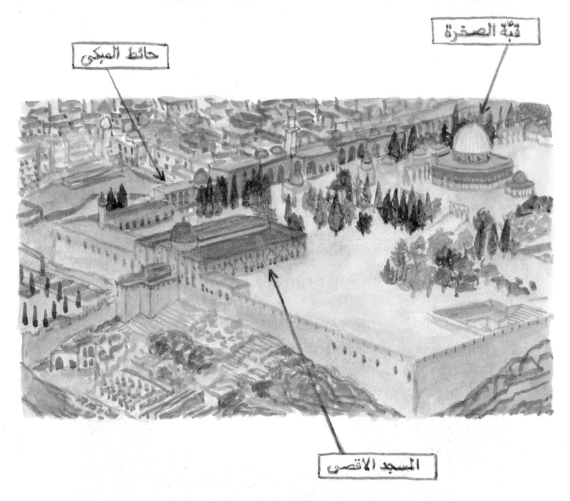

قبّة الصخرة

حائط المبكى

المسجد الأقصى

Aerial view of the Esplanade of the Mosques and the Western Wall

The Dome of the Rock has no minaret or minbar. It is hexagonal and located, like the Al-Aqsa Mosque, on the Esplanade of the Mosques in the heart of Jerusalem. In its center is the rock where Muhammad is said to have arrived from Mecca with the angel Gabriel and on his horse Buraq, during his night journey. It is also the place from where he temporarily ascended, that same night, to heaven. To the seven heavens, rather, where at each level he met one or two of the most eminent saints and prophets, from Moses to Jesus, to St. John the Baptist, Joseph, Adam, and Abraham. He had a conversation with each of them. Moses advised him to ask God for a favor: to reduce the number of daily prayers from fifty to five. According to another version of the story, Muhammad arrived at what would become Al-Aqsa. There are numerous variations of this night journey, but its very existence makes Jerusalem the third holiest place of Islam. According to the biblical tradition, this is also the place where Abraham came to sacrifice his son Isaac. It is also where Solomon constructed his temple, with the help of his friend King Hiram of Tyre, who gave him the cedar wood and the skilled men to carve it, in exchange for reserves of wheat, olive oil, and twenty cities in Galilee. When the second successor of the Prophet, Caliph Umar, captured Jerusalem in 638, there was no bloodshed and the Christians were assured that their lives and their possessions, as well as their religious practices, would be respected.

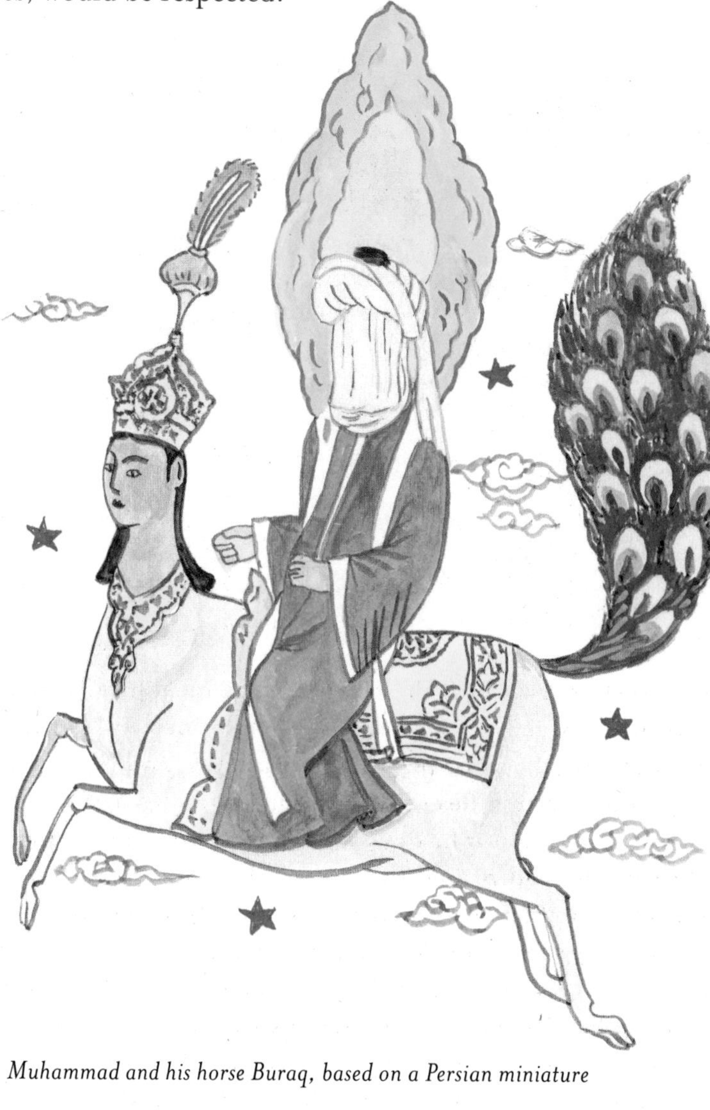

Muhammad and his horse Buraq, based on a Persian miniature

When the Greek patriarch of the city comes to meet him, Umar asks to
be brought to the holy sites of Christianity. While they are in the Church
of the Holy Sepulchre, the hour of the prayer arrives, and he asks where he
can lay his rug to prostrate himself. The patriarch invites him to stay where
he is, but Umar answers that if he does so, Muslims will want to appropriate
the church because he had prayed there. He takes his rug to kneel outside
instead. His prediction had been correct: a mosque bearing his name would
be erected at that very location. When Saladin recaptures Jerusalem from
the Crusaders several centuries later, he will also be magnanimous. With no
massacre or pillaging. His emirs and his troops are given clear orders: do not
touch any Christian, whether Frankish or Oriental. Nor their possessions,
nor their holy sites. He even authorizes the Crusaders who fled to return

on a pilgrimage and resettles Jewish families, who had been forced out by the Christians, back into the sacred city, returning their synagogues to them and the Holy Sepulchre to the Christians.

The Crusaders, however, are not as gracious. When they take back Jerusalem, they celebrate their triumph with the slaughter and barbaric sacking of the city. The Mosque of Omar is ransacked, the Tomb of Patriarchs is destroyed, the Muslim population is massacred, the Jews are gathered in their synagogues and burned alive. Those savages from the West don't spare the Oriental Christians either. The different rites which, according to an old tradition, used to share the Holy Sepulchre, have been ruthlessly expelled from it. The brutality of Western invaders still continues today.

صلاح الدين

Saladin

His generosity toward his vanquished enemies, his forgiveness of the worst traitors, his magnanimous spirit, his selflessness, his largesse, and his weakness toward his adversaries would earn him great reproach in his own camp. But these are precisely the virtues that made him into a legend. Certainly, for posterity, these qualities are just as important as his conquests.

120

A photograph you took of Beaufort Castle in 2008, with the Hezbollah flag and Hassan Nasrallah's portrait at its peak

Beaufort Castle and its Unobstructed View of Galilee

You continue down the roads of the south. Gentle curves, biblical olive trees, ancestral walls where Barbary figs grow, elegant minarets and jade or sea-green cupolas, beautiful bell towers, thousand-year-old date palms, welcoming vales, peaceful hills, the serpentine route—all in perfect harmony. Even the unfinished cinderblock frameworks, poorly and hurriedly constructed, entirely suit this ideal landscape.

You arrive at Beaufort! The rocky outcrop where the castle is located was a strategic position during the biblical and Roman periods. Since then, it has changed hands constantly over the centuries, from Saladin to the Lebanese State, by way of the Franks, the sultan of Egypt, the emirs of Transjordan and the maliks of Damascus, the governors of Acre, the counts of Saida, the Knights Templar, the Mongols, the Druze, the Ottomans, the Palestinian resistance, the Israeli army...

But it is only in recent history that it has become for the Lebanese, and especially those in the South, an object of incomparable national pride: a symbol of victory against Israel. Following the Israeli retreat, many Arabs are quick to see Hassan Nasrallah as a new Saladin, even if (almost) no one expects the liberation of Jerusalem to happen anytime soon.

From the café terrace, an unobstructed view of the wall

After Beaufort, a long, winding road leads to the most mind-blowing section of the border. If you are not Lebanese, you have to have a letter of safe conduct issued by the Saida barracks to enter this high-risk area. Not long ago, the spectacle offered by this zone with its explosive reputation was quite unexpected: Bawabat Fatima, a square in the village of Kfar Kila, offered an unobstructed view over all of Galilee, especially from the café terrace located fewer than ten meters from the barbed wire, behind which you could see the Israeli soldiers make their rounds as you sipped your lemonade. The café and its surroundings were covered in Hezbollah flags and banners, photos of martyrs or of Nasrallah, triumphal arches... The Israelis, exasperated by this taunting display, constructed a wall hundreds of meters long. Today, the wall is entirely covered in images of martyrs, logos, slogans, graffiti.

A slogan: our strength is in our unity

To see the Israeli soldiers, you have to climb to the café's roof, where the owner has set up another seating area. Or else you can go a few hundred meters to the left or right of the wall and find the flimsy barbed-wire barrier demarcating one of the most dangerous borders in the world. The souvenir shop attached to the café is very well stocked. They sell mugs, stickers, lighters, T-shirts, postcards, and keychains bearing the effigy of Hassan Nasrallah or in Hezbollah's colors, as well as CDs, cassettes, and DVDs of the Sayyid's speeches. The two welcoming young men who manage the store know all of the best lines and turns of phrase in his latest speech, which was particularly brutal toward Saudi Arabia, and take pleasure in reciting them to you.

...O Jerusalem, we're coming!... Hezbollah is always victorious...

...the passion of the martyr...

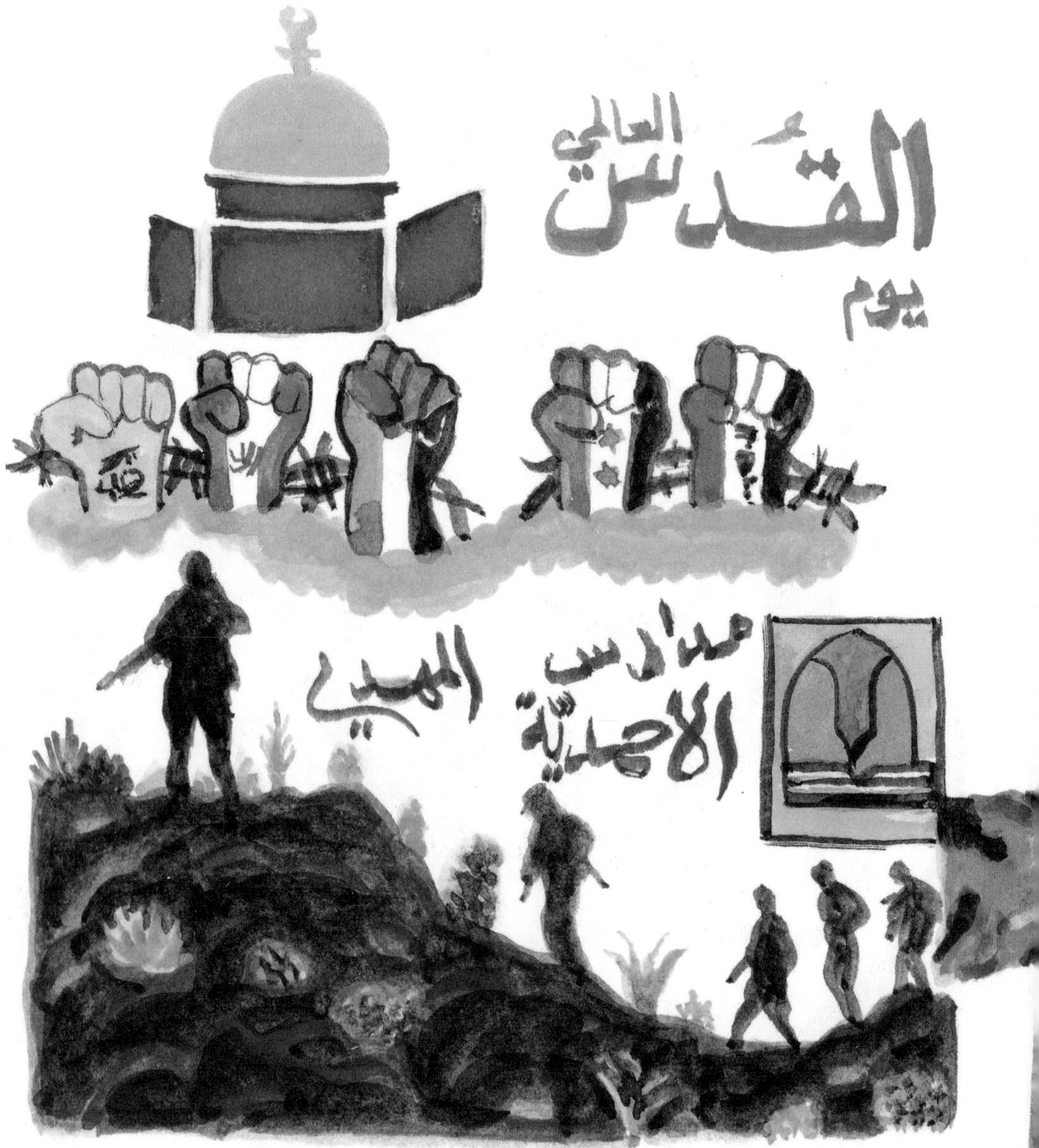

القدس
العالمي
يوم
مدارس
المهدي
الاسلامية

... Jerusalem Day...

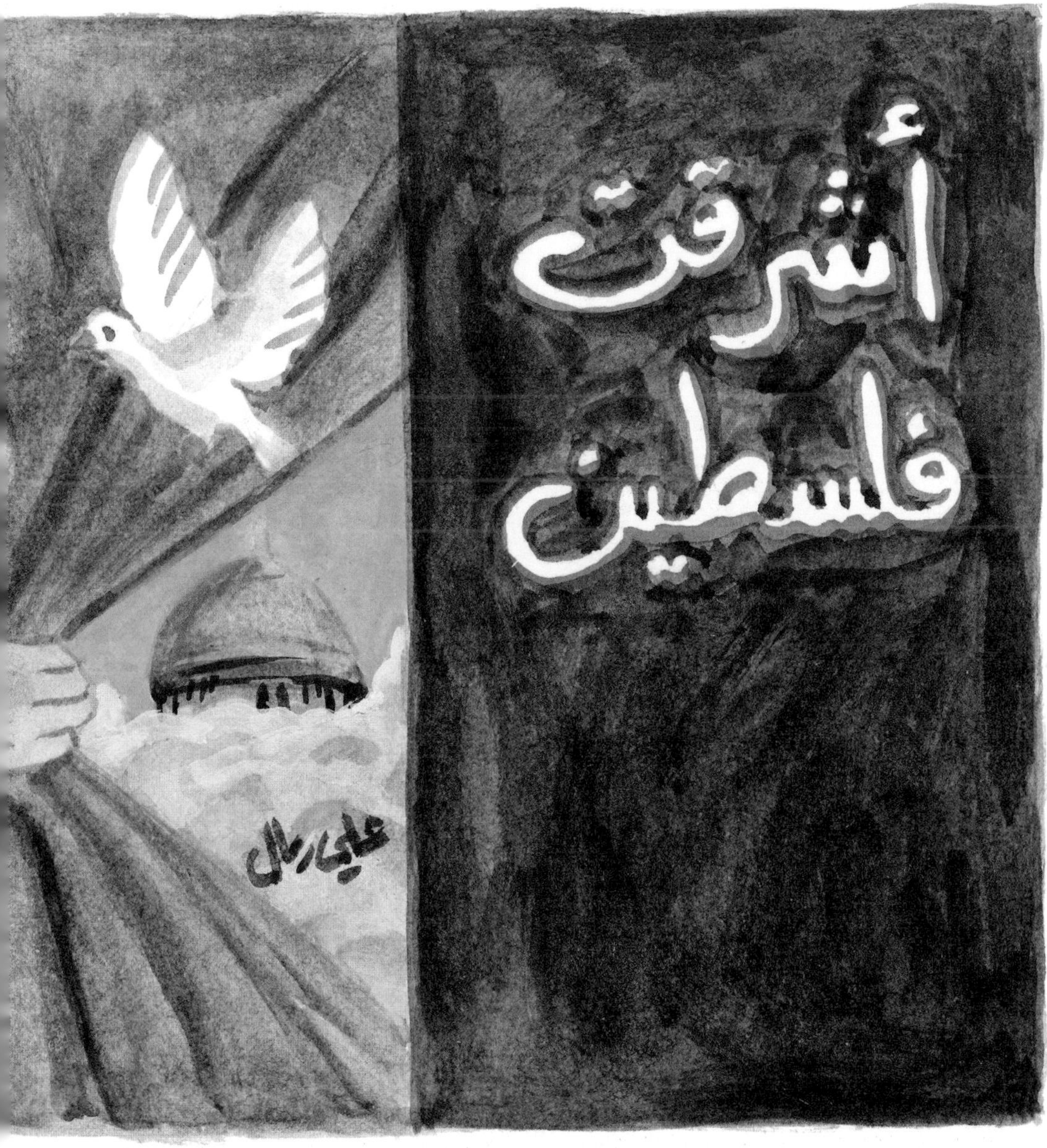
أشرقت
فلسطين

...Palestine rises...

المقاومة
بالمرصاد

...the resistance lies in wait...

Following page, top: In the village of Odaisseh, a bit farther on, there's an excellent viewing point over Galilee. They've even installed benches for people to take in the view.
Below: Young people smoking a hookah whistle at the Israeli soldiers below them, while the United Nations Interim Force in Lebanon (UNIFIL), leaning on the same balustrade, in the shadow of Hezbollah and Amal flags, and a portrait of Nasrallah, keep watch.

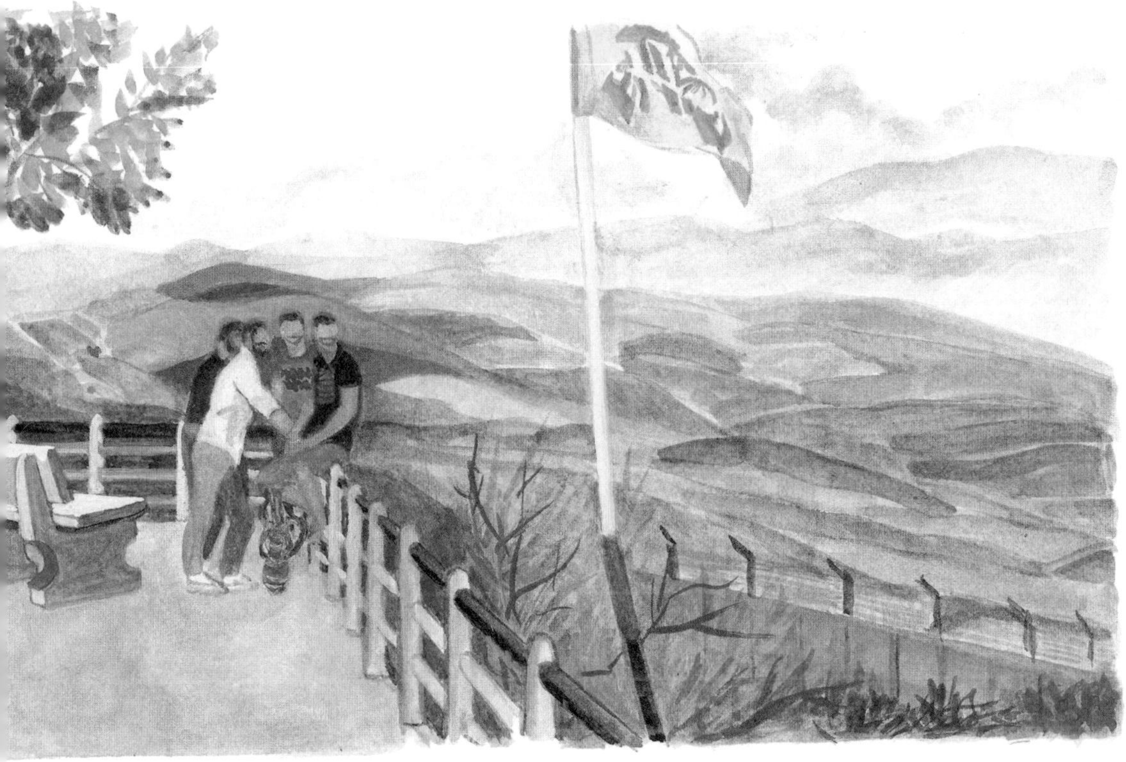

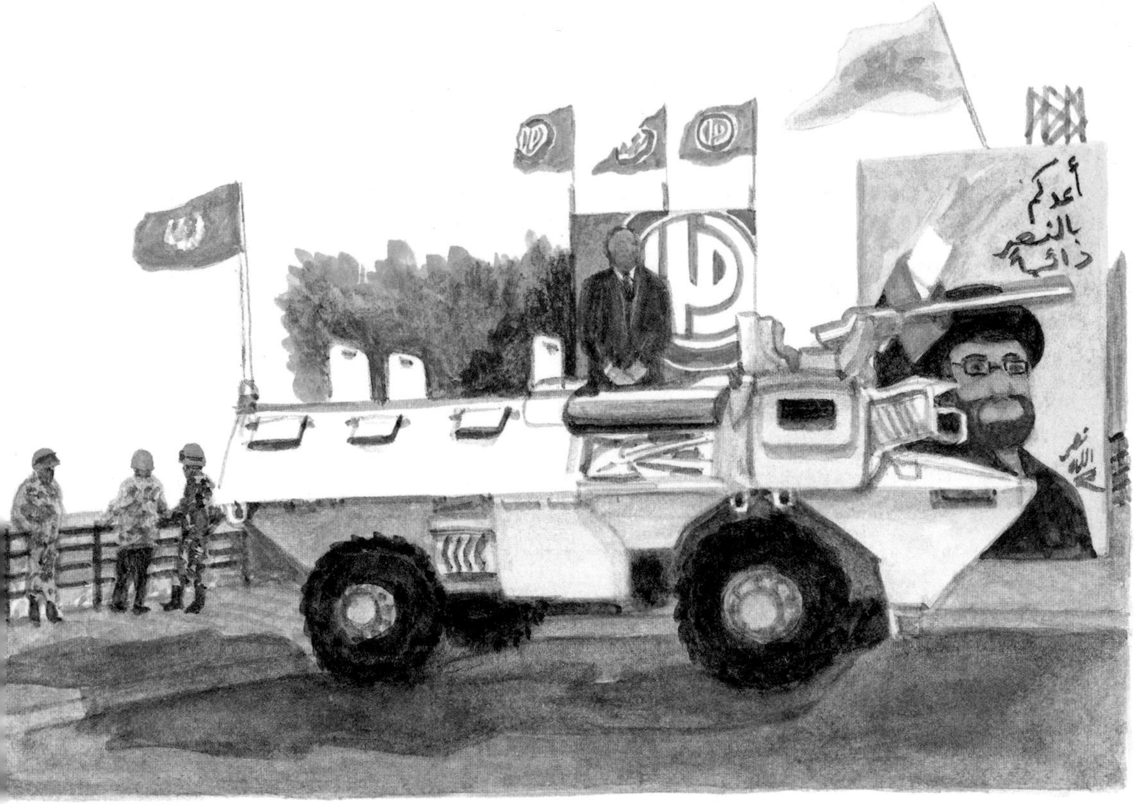
أعدكم
بالنصر
دائماً
نصر الله

The Sheikh in Hiding

The most powerful and popular man in Lebanon, for both Muslims and Christians, is not a fundamentalist, a fanatic, an extremist, or a terrorist, contrary to what Westerners might believe, but a hero of the resistance against the Israeli occupations and attacks that South Lebanon has been subjected to for more than forty years, well before even the existence of Hezbollah. Nasrallah, who strongly condemns ISIS, declaring their acts vile and inhumane, insisting that their attacks in Europe do more harm to the Prophet and Muslims than those books, films, and caricatures that insult the Prophet, also emphasizes the right of an occupied people to attack their occupier.

Hezbollah combines guerrilla tactics with the methods of regular armies, blending discipline and imagination. When the Hezbollah forced Israel to evacuate Lebanon in 2000 and fought back against Israeli assaults in 2006, Nasrallah was idolized. Up until then, no Arab army, not even the Palestinian resistance, had ever defeated the all-powerful Israeli army, destroying in just one day around forty tanks said to be invincible, the famous Merkavas that had infiltrated Lebanese soil.

Nasrallah, the eldest of nine children, is born into a Shii family in a poor neighborhood of the northern suburbs of Beirut. His father is a fruit and vegetable seller. He is only fifteen years old when he leaves to study Islam in Najaf, after joining the Amal movement founded by Musa al-Sadr, whose mysterious disappearance, a few years later, profoundly shocked him. Hezbollah was founded in 1982, as a direct result of Israel's invasion of Lebanon. After Israel's assassination of the party's Secretary General, Abbas al-Musawi, along with his wife and son, Nasrallah takes over Hezbollah; he is thirty-two years old.

Forced into hiding to escape the assassination promised by Tel Aviv, today he gives speeches broadcast by videoconference to gigantic, packed halls. His particular intelligence is recognized by his friends and enemies alike, and he is a masterful orator as well, with an innate understanding of the art of captivating his audience and a wicked sense of humor. For him, language is as important as any weapon. An educator, he methodically demonstrates the legitimacy of his theories. Unlike the Islamic extremists, he is tolerant and a realist.

In 1997, when he learns of the death of his eldest son, Hadi, just eighteen years old, in a battle against the Israeli army, he masks his sadness and gives his speech as planned, without batting an eye. He would confess, years later, that he cried away from the cameras, alone in his room, and that he missed his son tremendously. Incorruptible, he stands out from other Arab leaders. When someone who said to him, "You are Israel's biggest threat. Without you, their soldiers would have stayed in Lebanon for a hundred years," he replied: "A hundred years is nothing for them. They waited three thousand years to return to Palestine."

Following the Beirut port explosion on August 4, 2020, the pedestal Hassan Nasrallah stood on for decades is smashed into a thousand pieces. He is largely to blame for the country's catastrophe. His conduct in the days after tarnishes him even further. He is cursed from then on like any other corrupt politician of the country. A gallows is erected in the street where protestors hang his effigy.

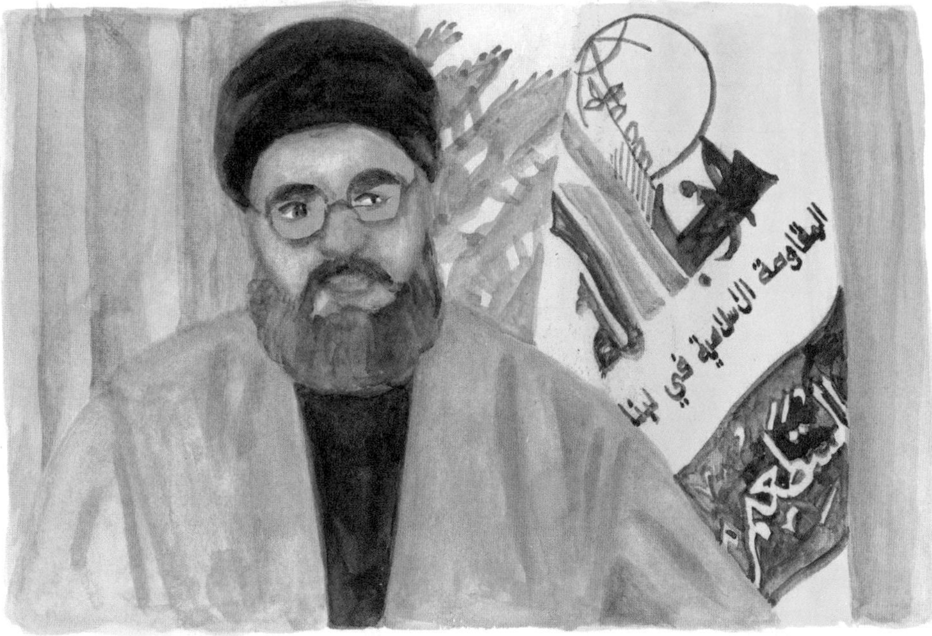
المقاومة الاسلامية في لبنان

Nasrallah's appearances are always the same: in the rectangular screen, with the flags of Lebanon and Hezbollah behind him. Few other images of this man exist

The words of one of Nasrallah's speeches, addressed to Hezbollah combatants in 2006, were used by a Christian Lebanese singer, famous for her passionate activism on behalf of Palestine, in a very beautiful song, "Ahibaii." Forty years after Fairuz, who sang for the Palestinian cause in 1960, and Marcel Khalife, who drew inspiration from the moving poems of Mahmoud Darwish, Julia Boutros takes up the torch.

Above: The cover from Julia Boutros's first album, The Sun of Justice has been Eclipsed.

Hezbollah's logo

Undoubtedly one of the men who receives the most death threats on the planet, Nasrallah benefits from an extraordinary system of protection. A politician friend who was granted the privilege of an interview explained to you how it works. Three men came to pick him up at an agreed-upon location, in the southern suburbs of Beirut. He had to leave behind his men, his weapons, his car, his telephone, and follow them alone. They asked him to climb into a car with opaque windows, in which the driver was separated from the other passengers by a black curtain. He was driven to an underground parking garage where three other men were waiting for him with another car. The same scenario played out in a third parking garage, where another team was waiting for him. Once at the fourth parking garage, they led him to an elevator. When the elevator doors opened on the fourth floor, the Sayyid was in front of him and welcomed him with a warm smile into a tiny lounge with only three armchairs and a coffee table with a small tray of sweets. The procedure is the same for a former president of the republic as for Hezbollah's second-in-command.

The day of liberation...

Khiam Detention Center

On the day of the Israeli retreat, the most extraordinary celebration was for the liberation of Khiam. Khiam, one of the most violent and inhumane detention and torture centers, is controlled by the Israelis, but run by the South Lebanon Army (SLA). Men and women, fighters for the Communist Party or for Hezbollah, Christians and Muslims, the elderly and children, were detained there without trial and subjected to torture and abuse. Sometimes the fathers, mothers, sons, or daughters of members of the resistance were held there for months on end. Many of these prisoners lost their lives.

On May 23, 2000, the 144 detained there do not understand what is happening. Hundreds of villagers and Hezbollah fighters rush from the surrounding areas, toward the prison, screaming and brandishing large iron bars. Inside, the detainees have had an inkling since that morning that something was happening, but they don't know what. They are consumed by anxiety.

...the South resounds with millions of ululations

A former prisoner, a Christian who joined Hezbollah, which had become the sole party of the resistance over the years, recounts: "Starting in the morning, the sound of Israeli tanks roared endlessly. The guards were agitated, the tension showed on their faces. We were completely isolated from the outside, but we knew more or less that the Israelis were evacuating. We could hardly believe it, after more than twenty years... Cries ring out outside, the uproar grows even louder. We're terrified: 'They'll send us to Palestine!' 'They'll execute half of us and send off the others!' Outside, gunfire reverberates amid the screams. We panic. 'They're going to kill us all! The mass execution has begun!' The shouts draw closer—there are ululations and prayers, women and children. Suddenly the doors are forced open from the outside with metal bars. 'You are free!' 'Allah Akbar!' 'You are free!' I fell to my knees. I thought I was hallucinating. A little while later, I was the first prisoner captured on camera. My parents, who were watching the liberation of Khiam on television because their village was still occupied, didn't recognize me. Maybe because my beard and hair were so long, but I think it was actually because I cried: 'Allah Akbar!'"

The entrance to the prison transformed into a museum

The Most Famous Prisoner

Khiam detention center is transformed into a museum to honor the resistance. This is an intolerable affront to Israel, which denied the prison's existence for a long time. In 2006, one of the primary objectives of the Israeli Air Force is to destroy Khiam. The memory of this camp—including portraits of the prisoners, objects they secretly made during their imprisonment displayed in the museum, messages engraved on the walls—is completely demolished. Nothing remains but a heap of rubble.

A poster made in support of Souha Bechara during her imprisonment

Souha Bechara, a Christian and a Communist, is the most famous former prisoner of Khiam. She spent ten years there for her assassination attempt, when she was twenty-one, of General Antoine Lahad, leader of the SLA. She was subject to torture and isolation. One might imagine that the prisoners' most precious wish would be for the destruction of their prison. In fact, it is quite the opposite. Its destruction was a new level of cruelty: by smashing the camp to smithereens, the former prisoners were robbed a second time of the years they did not get to live. "If they had destroyed my house, that would have been less awful for me," says a former detainee. So Souha decided to reconstruct its memory through words. Here are a few excerpts from her book:

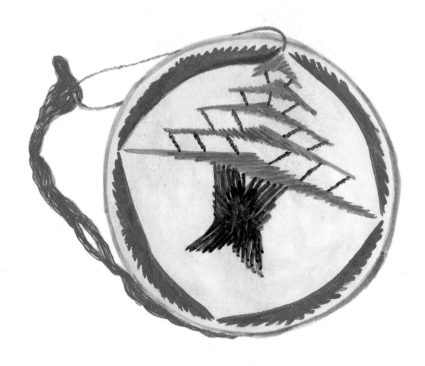

*The prisoners secretly made trinkets and other small objects with
the most rudimentary and ingenious means*

...entire years can go by without seeing a face. Certain faces will remain
forever unknown. We also begin to recognize footsteps and associate them
with the timbre of a voice and the first name used by the guards, we imagine
a look, a smile, the color of their skin...

...there she is, passing in front of my cell door, five years after we
discovered each other's presence in the camp, five years during which
we tried, constantly, to communicate. One day, I had engraved on an
orange peel "here we resist" and left it for her in the bathroom. In return,
she engraved a heart and a love note on a piece of soap. I never saw the
soap, she never saw the orange peel...

Each portion of cheese is wrapped in a thin piece of aluminum foil

...Kifah will discover the first camp pencil... Kifah is playing with the golden paper wrapping of the piece of cheese. Distractedly, she's grazing the cardboard cheese box with the folded bit of paper, and she realizes it has left little marks. She looks more closely at the fine markings, like pencil scratches. She makes the same movement, trying her best, and manages to write letters...

Olive pits made into a small bracelet

...they brought her into her cell a few moments ago at the end of a surprise torture session, after the guards found slogans engraved on the bathroom wall.

Prisoners like slogans... The newcomers tend to engrave giant slogans. Bold phrases written in visible places. Over time, they get into the habit of writing them at the foot of walls, as discreetly as possible, in places where no one can read them, and they're forgotten.

Kifah, that day, frenetically engraves on the bathroom wall "Israel is an absolute evil," and then returns to her cell with the feeling of having accomplished an historic mission.

Private messages on secret talismans:
"How to forget you, my mother, I ask for your blessing"

...Today, I can't even cry... I couldn't even cry when I saw you there in front of me. They allowed you to visit me after seven years. But the way you entered the visiting room was peculiar, to say the least: you came in on your hands and knees, you stood up, and you cried, "My daughter!" You had sworn that you would enter the camp on your hands and knees if they ever allowed you to visit me one day.

HOW CAN WE STAND BY
AND ALLOW THIS TO GO ON?

ROBERT FISK REPORTS ON ISRAEL'S SLAUGHTER OF 54 CIVILIANS MOST OF THEM CHILDREN

The front page of The Independent

The July War

After Beaufort, Kfar Kila and Khiam, you continue along the route. Hills and vales one after another. Soon, you don't notice them anymore, lost in your thoughts, your head full of the cruel memory of the images that circulated around the planet in July 2006 to general worldwide indifference. You are on the road to Qana.

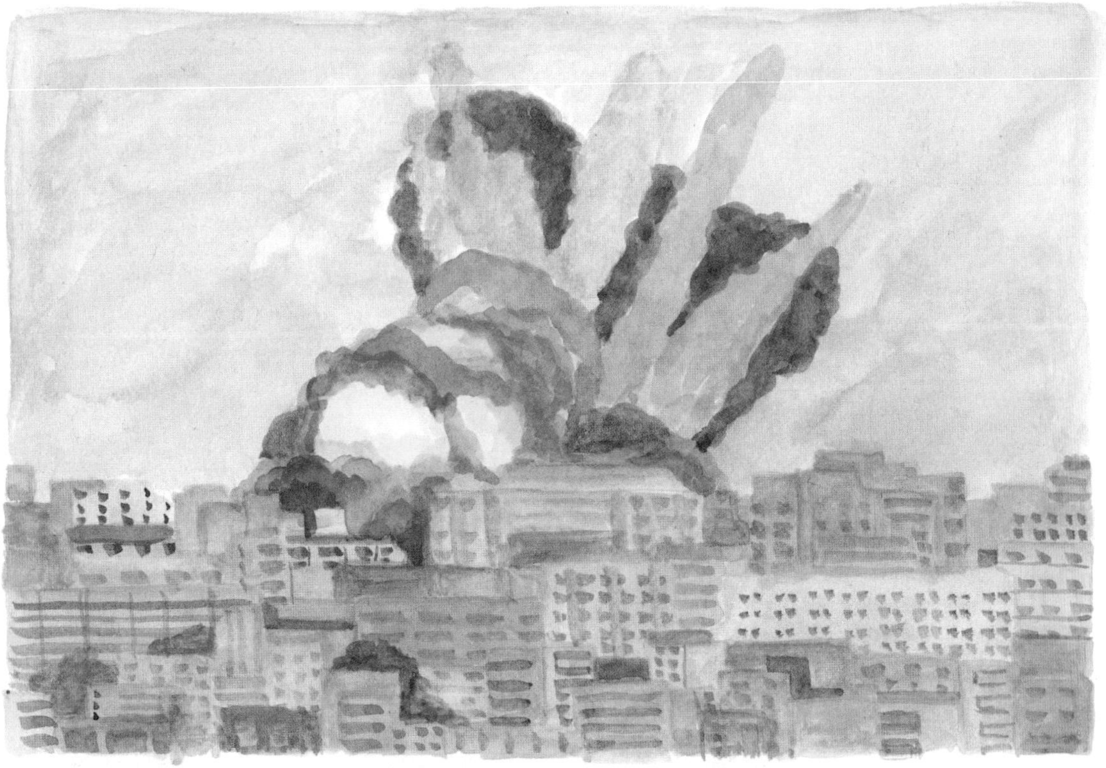

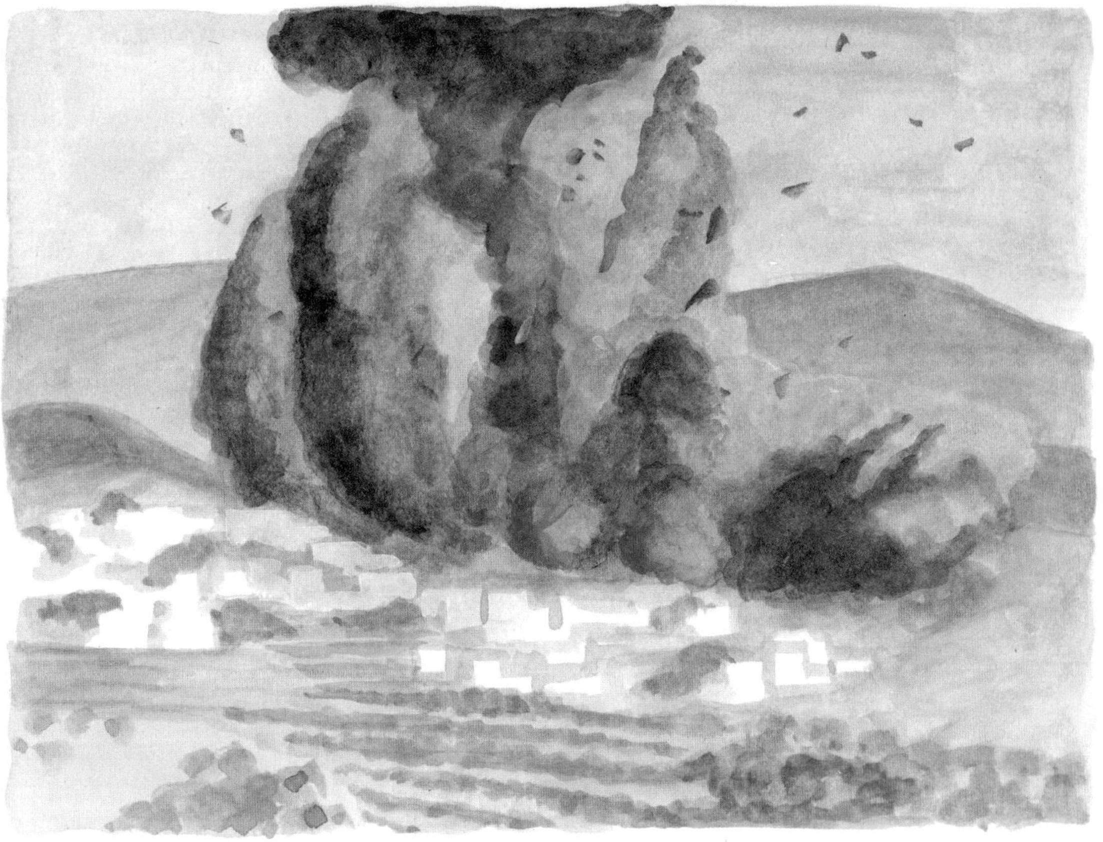

A child cries...

Next page, above: During the collective funeral rites in Ghazieh. On a banner:
"This is the democracy of America and Israel: massacres and destruction."

Below: The funeral procession will be bombarded, too, hence the
caricature published in a Lebanese newspaper:
"with Israel's condolences."

غارة خلال تشييع شهداء الغارة

التعازي الإسرائيلية

أطفال قانا
مذبحة قانا ـ ٢
والدعم الأمريكي
لـ «إسرائيل»

"Second massacre of Qana, with American support of Israel"

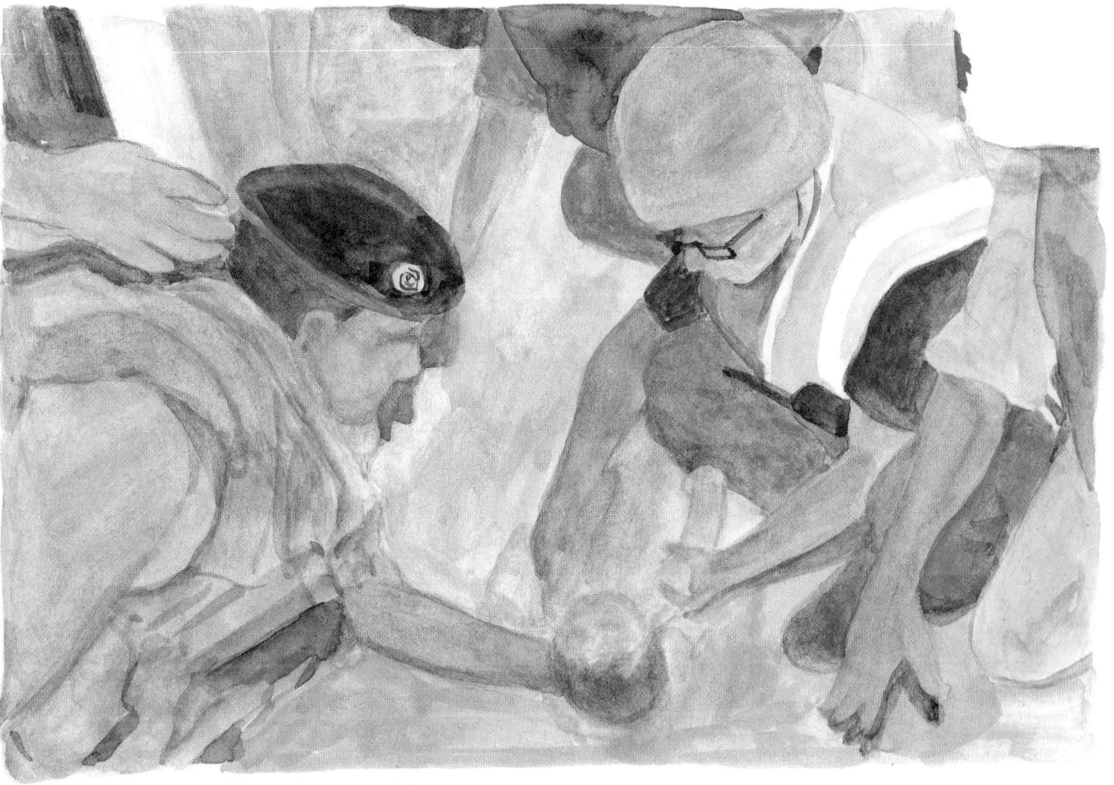
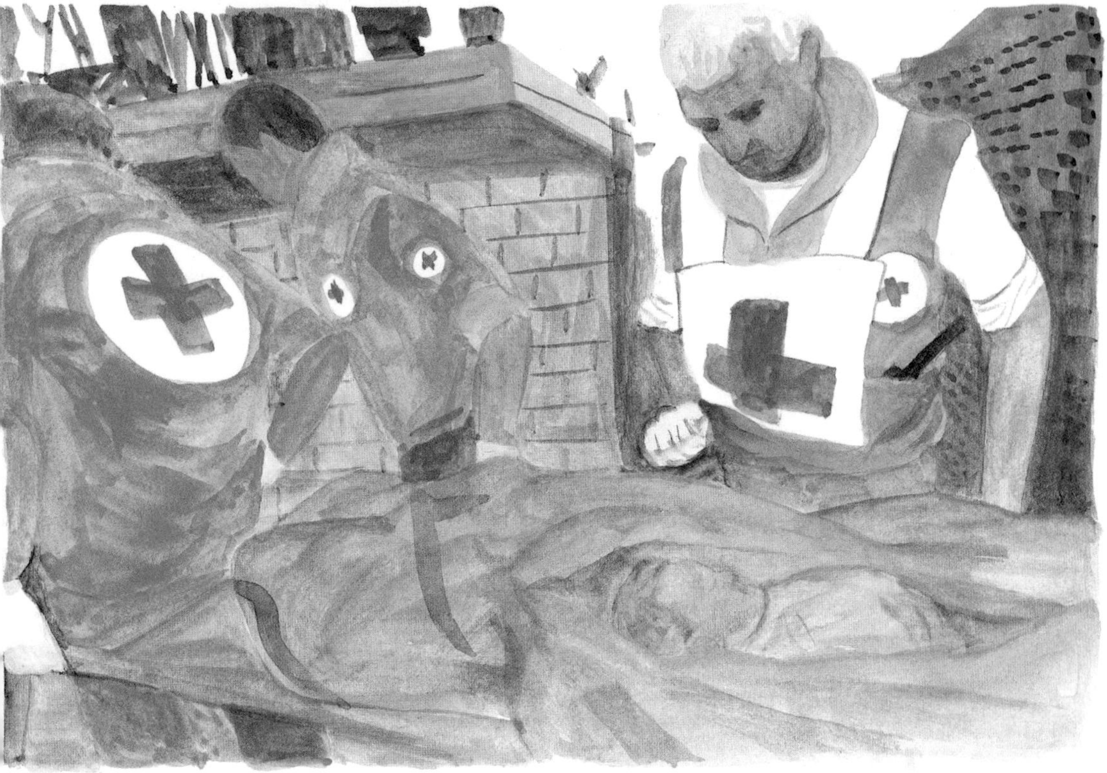

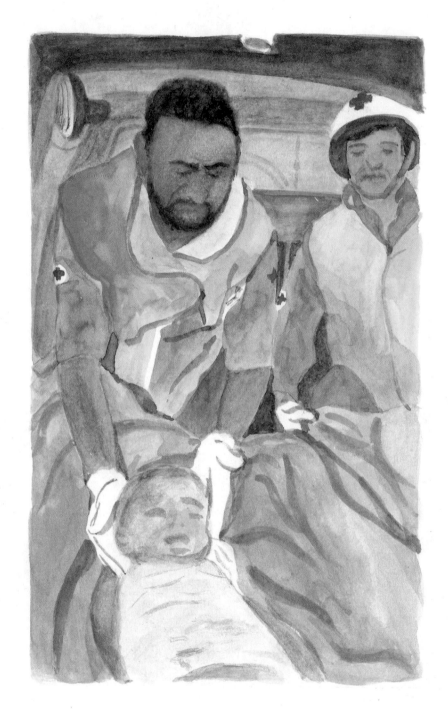

A paramedic cries

"A Red Cross ambulance is bombed; two paramedics are among the victims"

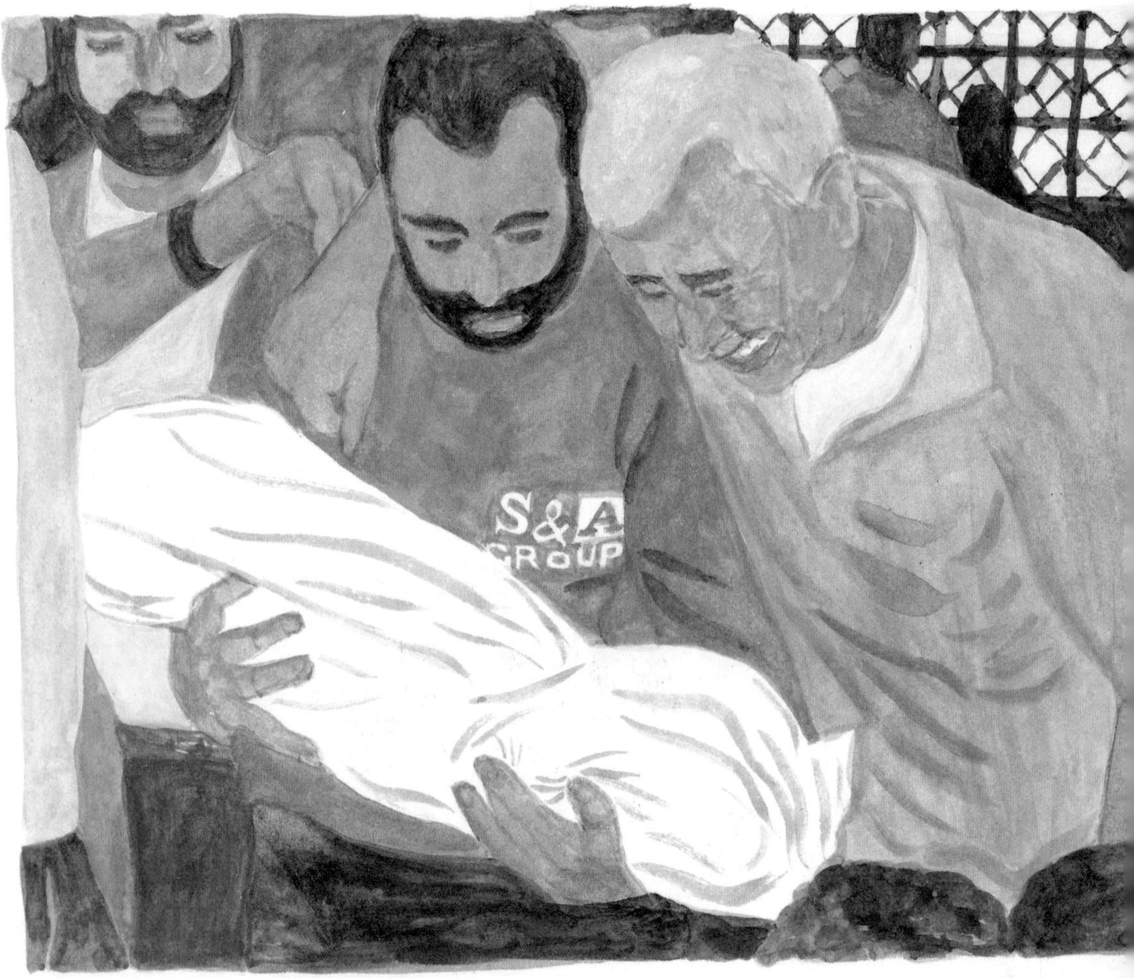
S&A
GROUP

هي البسمة يا نور قلبي
ما كانت تفارقك

"Your smile, light of my heart, never left your face"

In every house, framed portraits of martyrs, often depicted in a paradisiacal landscape

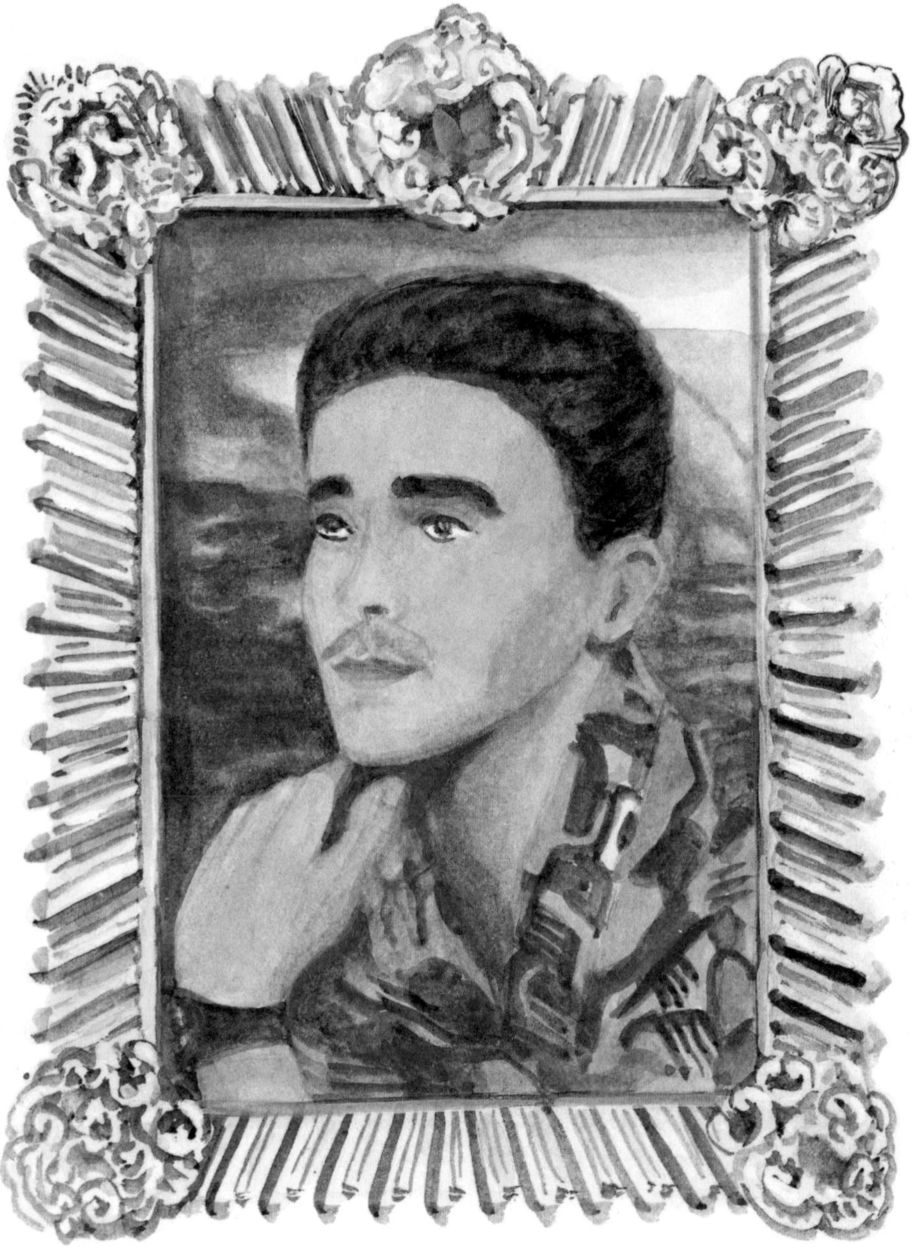

The victims of 2006...

...like those of the first Qana massacre, in 1996...

...are shining stars forevermore...

...in the firmament of martyrs...

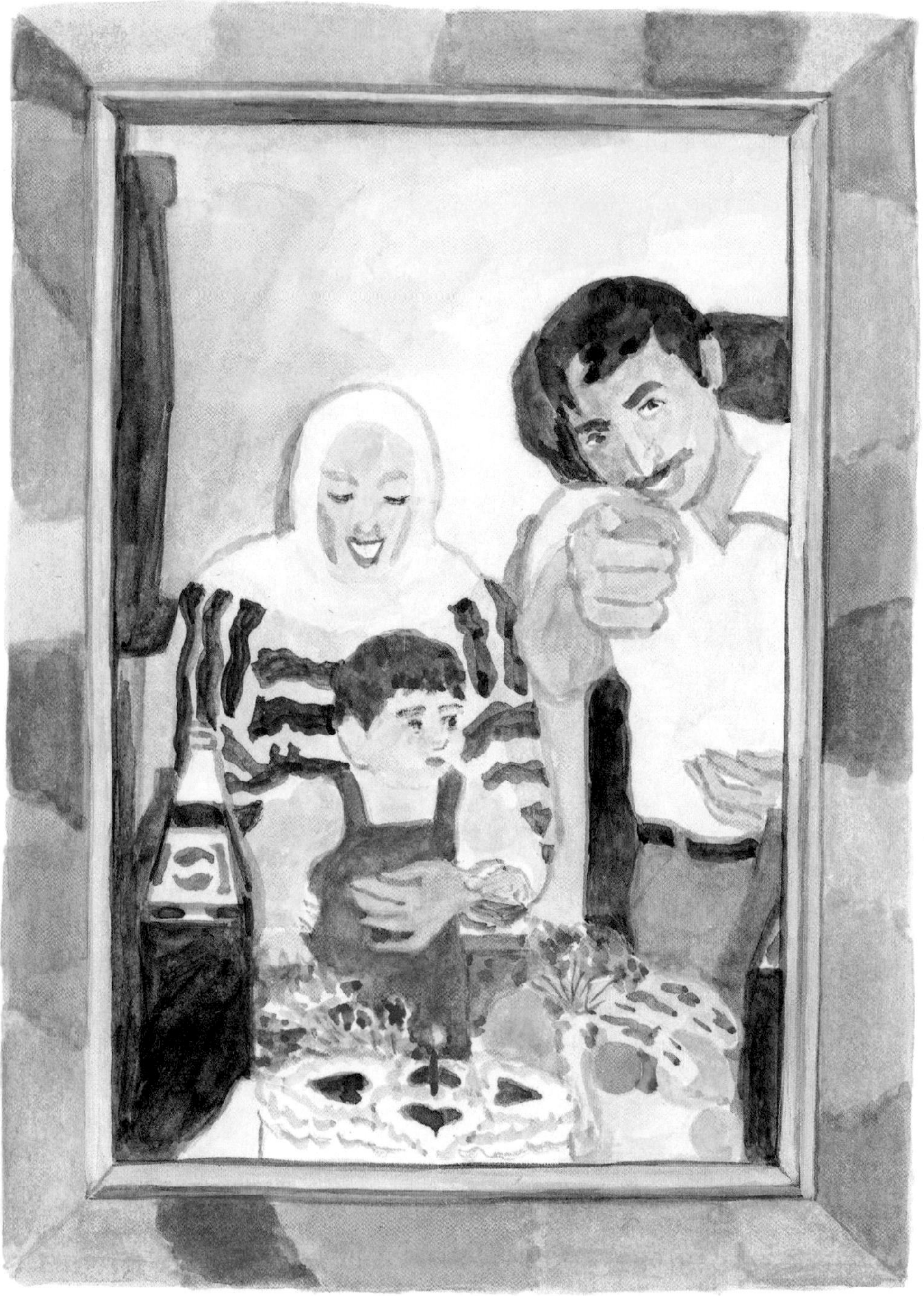

2006

The UNIFIL flag, omnipresent throughout the South

You've reached Naqoura. The location of the headquarters of the United Nations Interim Force in Lebanon, UNIFIL. It's very distressing. The lovely South is no more, the folkloric atmosphere of Bawabat Fatima is gone. On the coast, after you pass the last road sign pointing the way to Palestine, you will see no more civilian cars, no more farmers, no more banana trees, or terraces with gardens, no more flags, no more martyrs, nothing but an empty road, endless high concrete walls topped with barbed wire, watchtowers, UNIFIL positions, tanks and vehicles of all kinds marked UN... It's so frightening that, suddenly, you think: "If we keeping heading south, we're going to set off another war!" Ali makes a U-turn in the middle of the road and you head back toward Tyre.

A photograph you took in 2016 of the final road sign pointing the way to Palestine

The Dictator and the Civilized West

On the way back to the hotel, you go for a swim a little ways down from the cemetery. Within just a few strokes of the shoreline, you bathe above a Roman road, columns, and capitals lying under the sea! In the evening, you have a drink at a bar not far from the port. A man who looks like Omar Sharif mopes in style, sipping his umpteenth whiskey. You have a conversation with the bartender about the July War. The man soon joins in. Or rather, begins a monologue. It's like a scene out of a classic movie.

Allow me to tell you about another tragedy that took place in the Arab world in the year 2006! I'm still in shock. All of the Middle East is still in shock! It's not in the same category as those bombings and those children massacred in Lebanon, but it's another revolting demonstration of the perpetual disdain, the constant arrogance, and the unrivaled barbarity that the marvelous West, land of the free, imposes on any Arab who does not serve its interests… I'm talking about the trial and execution of Saddam Hussein, closely monitored by the Americans. How could that puppet court, that travesty of a trial, that judicial masquerade, that hasty death sentence and that infamous hanging on Eid have been possible?[13] When there is no trial, that's called an assassination. The day of Eid! The intent was humiliation, as always! Since the Crusades, has good fortune ever arrived in our part of the world from the West? The problem with democratic countries is that they forget all about their values when it comes to us.

A man who looks like Omar Sharif, lounging at the bar with a drink and a cigarette

13   Eid al-Adha commemorates the sacrifice of Abraham, who agreed to immolate his son when God asked but who, stopped by God right before he was about to commit the act, sacrificed a lamb instead. Today, in remembrance of that devotion, Muslim families sacrifice an animal.

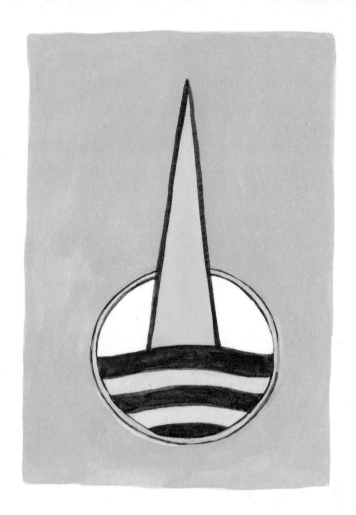

IRAQ PETROLEUM COMPANY
LIMITED

America, through some pretty extraordinary propaganda, presented him as Hitler combined with Stalin! Whether we like it or not, that man did a lot for our country. I'm Iraqi, I know what I'm talking about. Do you know that the Iraq Petroleum Company, a consortium that runs a monopoly on the extraction and sale of Iraqi oil, though its name would suggest otherwise, was predominantly owned by foreigners? It's 47 percent English, 24 percent French, 24 percent American, and only 5 percent Iraqi! When Saddam dared to nationalize the company, the Westerners didn't like it very much, of course, so they called him a despot!

الرئيس صدام حسين في منطقة الجيزة بالقاهرة ١٩٦٠

A rare photo of Saddam Hussein in Giza, outside of Cairo, in 1960

They only like us when we're subservient. But that heralded an era of unprecedented prosperity for Iraq. Saddam modernized agriculture, initiated large-scale projects, promoted the emancipation of women, and above all, he decreed school mandatory and launched a plan of attack against illiteracy, since he himself had had to fight against his family to learn to read and write. The number of children enrolled in school jumped 300 percent and women were able to complete higher education.

IRAQ PETROLEUM COMPANY
LIMITED

He wasn't exactly my favorite person, mind you! Of course, he was a despot. He killed his opponents in a sinister way, in front of cameras, to make an example out of them! He made sure the dismal ceremony of the 1979 purge was widely broadcast... It was the beginning of a criminal path that would never come to an end... There was the massacre of the Kurds. It was atrocious, but it didn't bother the "free world"; it wasn't given more than a few sentences in the Western press, since Saddam was serving the interests of the West against Iran at the time.

"Saddam Hussein, Chairman of the Revolutionary Command Council, President of Iraq"

Despite the lack of democracy and the police state, we lived, in Baghdad. We worked, we went to school and to the market, we listened to music. Today, the country is destroyed and people are dying. In the First Gulf War, more than 100,000 Iraqis died, soldiers and civilians, compared to 500 people on the coalition side. Western politics sowed death and savage destruction, forcing an exodus of thousand-year-old communities, the guardians of the most ancient human civilizations. Where are they, those bloodthirsty killers? I might have been opposed to Saddam, but I am even more opposed to the West and its shitty policies!

*During his trial, he led the dance.. He contested the tribunal, mocked the judges,
insulted the Americans, called Bush a criminal...*

After his death and the humiliating images of his capture, Saddam was
more popular than ever! They turned him into the greatest Arab martyr.
His prestige and the people's love for him only grew. To his credit, he
held firm and did not tremble when they put the noose around his neck...

In 1920, when the Iraqis rebelled against the occupation of their
country by the English, the revolt was violently repressed. About 7,000–
10,000 were killed on the Iraqi side, compared to 400 English and
Indian soldiers. The Royal Air Force fleet bombarded tribes on horseback
on the order of Winston Churchill, who was then Secretary of State for
the Colonies. Bullshit politics, I tell you! This is civilized Europe, giving
lessons in morality to the entire world! Lessons in morality lessons on
the one hand, and weapons sales to the obscurantist kingdom of Saudi
Arabia on the other! If I have problems with Saddam, let me handle them
on my own. It's not up to those barbaric Americans, or the English, or the
French, to come and solve my problems with Saddam. Their arrogance
knows no bounds.

A wake held by Saddam's supporters at his tomb

The Death of King Ghazi

On April 4, 1939 at nine o'clock in the morning, a distressing announcement is made by Nuri al-Said, prime minister of Iraq and Britain's man: King Ghazi has just died at twenty-seven years old, after the car he was driving crashed into an electricity pylon. Widespread anger erupts; there are suspicions that the English were involved in the beloved king's death.

Ghazi, the only son of the legendary Emir Faisal, first king of Iraq, was born in Mecca and was educated in London and at the military school in Baghdad. A skilled horse rider and a brave pilot, he succeeds to the throne upon the death of his father. Married to the daughter of his uncle, the king of Hejaz, he has one child, Faisal, who is three at the time of the accident and would become the last king of Iraq. The political situation Ghazi inherits when he ascends the throne is simple: the British control the country, and no decision could come from the palace without their approval. But Ghazi sees things differently, he has other aspirations: to fight against all foreign influence, be a pan-Arab leader, and help the countries of the region liberate themselves from Western hegemony and unify. He openly opposes the British. His popularity continues to grow. Especially after he installs a special radio in the Palace of Flowers (Qasr al-Zouhour), the king's residence, for the express purpose of broadcasting his speeches and reflections. On the airwaves, the king scorns the English and the French for continuing to impose their mandate on Syria, Lebanon, and Transjordan, and vigorously denounces the British for handing Palestine over to the Zionists, by virtue of the European peoples' right to control others. Three years before his death, Foreign Office officials were already planning Ghazi's deposition.

The announcement of the Iraqi king's death is met with great emotion in the Arab countries, especially in Syria, Lebanon, and Palestine, where protesters take to the streets accusing the English of murdering Ghazi. The funeral prayer is given at Al-Aqsa Mosque, while in Iraq the people's wrath is boiling over. In Mosul, the crowd attacks the British consulate and the British consul is killed. The people are not convinced by the Commission of Inquiry's report, which acknowledges that the king's valet

King Ghazi I, the second king of Iraq

and the technician responsible for his personal radio were with him in the car when the collision took place, but that they have since vanished into thin air. The funeral takes place the next morning, in an explosive atmosphere. They do not wait for the arrival of King Abdullah of Transjordan, Ghazi's uncle, who had expressly requested it. The British chargé d'affaires gives a frightening description of the funeral: "The crowd's distress is so intense that when the procession passes, people burst into sobs, beat their chests, tear out their hair. The men cry along with the women and children. Everyone repeats the story of British involvement over and over. The strangest part is seeing the police and soldiers crying like children. Countless times, we felt in imminent danger, it seemed as if crowd would break through the protective human shield and reach us…"

Faisal II ascends to the throne at three years old. He will be brutally assassinated at twenty-three.

The Slain Colonel

The Omar Sharif lookalike is staying at the same hotel as you. "No use telling you what I think of Gaddafi's death," he says over breakfast. You confirm, there's no need for him to say it, you are in total agreement with him. "What a scandal, there are no more limits, no restraint," he says, "the Westerners really do whatever they want, without limits; we are all rats to them. At least Gaddafi had class! From the family of horrible dictators, atrocious tyrants, monstrous despots, abominable oppressors, I present to you: the guide! But he had class, the colonel! Imagine demanding that the UN General Assembly fit the abolishment of Switzerland into their agenda? Declaring that Switzerland was not a state but a global mafia that had to be divided between France, Germany, and Italy? What class! What elegance!

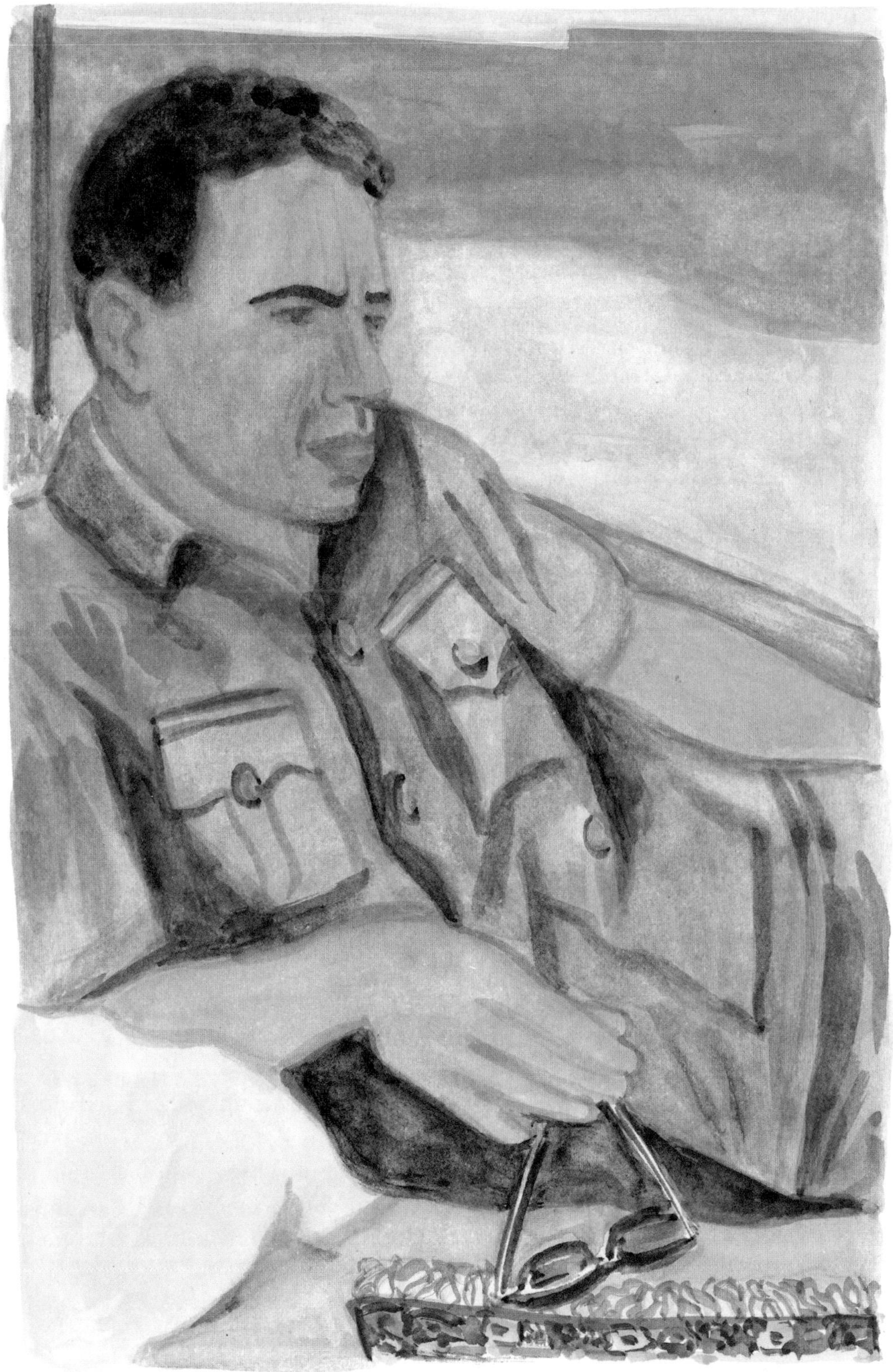

What is the UN, anyway? An organization that produces salvos of resolutions legitimizing the brutal aggression of the West against Iraq after the occupation of Kuwait, in the name of liberty, democracy, human rights, and international law. But not a single UN resolution in favor of the Israeli retreat from Palestine and Lebanon has been enforced in decades! What a joke! Saddam's popularity increased by a thousand percent when he proposed that all the problems of occupation in the Middle East be handled in the same way, and linked the Iraqi retreat from Kuwait to the Israeli retreat from Palestine and from Lebanon. He became a thousand percent more popular, but only among Arabs. The Americans and the Israelis did not appreciate this proposal. But anyway, Gaddafi, he was an elegant man!

Then he speaks about blatant Western disinformation, how they presented Gaddafi as a bloodthirsty dictator who massacred his people. "Dictator, yes, bloodthirsty, no," he says, "in any case not during the Arab Spring when, contrary to what they said about him, he did not bomb the population... But of course his prisons had a sinister reputation, especially the Abu Salim prison with its famous massacre..."

Then he tells you about Nasser's relationship with Gaddafi. "He tired him out! He tired him out, the little colonel," he says. "At the beginning Nasser liked him, but very soon Gaddafi's fervent admiration and perpetual agitation exhausted him. He found Gaddafi's unpredictable reactions and extreme decisions worrying. At the Rabat summit in 1969, I was part of the Iraqi delegation. A heated discussion between Nasser and Boumediene went sour. Nasser brought it to a close: 'You know who you are and you know who I am,' he said to Boumediene, 'how dare you speak to me like this?' He got up and walked toward the exit, followed by members of the Egyptian delegation. As he was walking out the door, he heard hurried, feverish steps behind him; he turned around and, flabbergasted, saw the young Gaddafi, twenty-seven years old, snap to attention and ask, with his hand on the colt in his belt: 'Want me to shoot him?'"

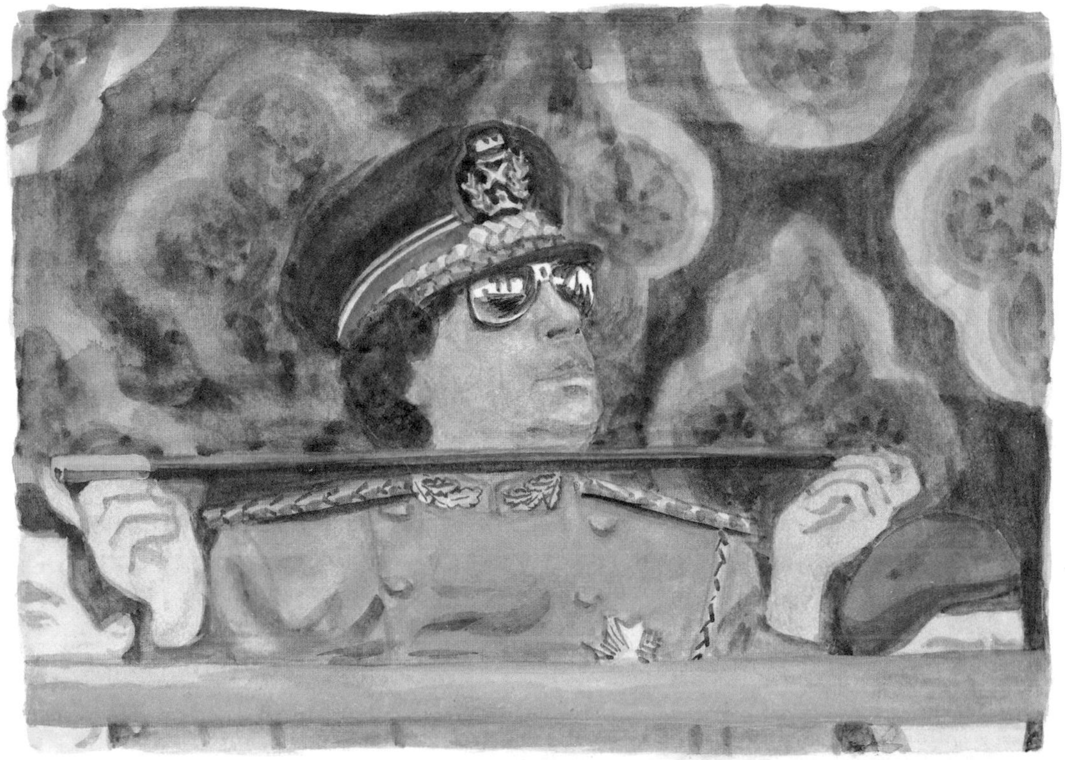

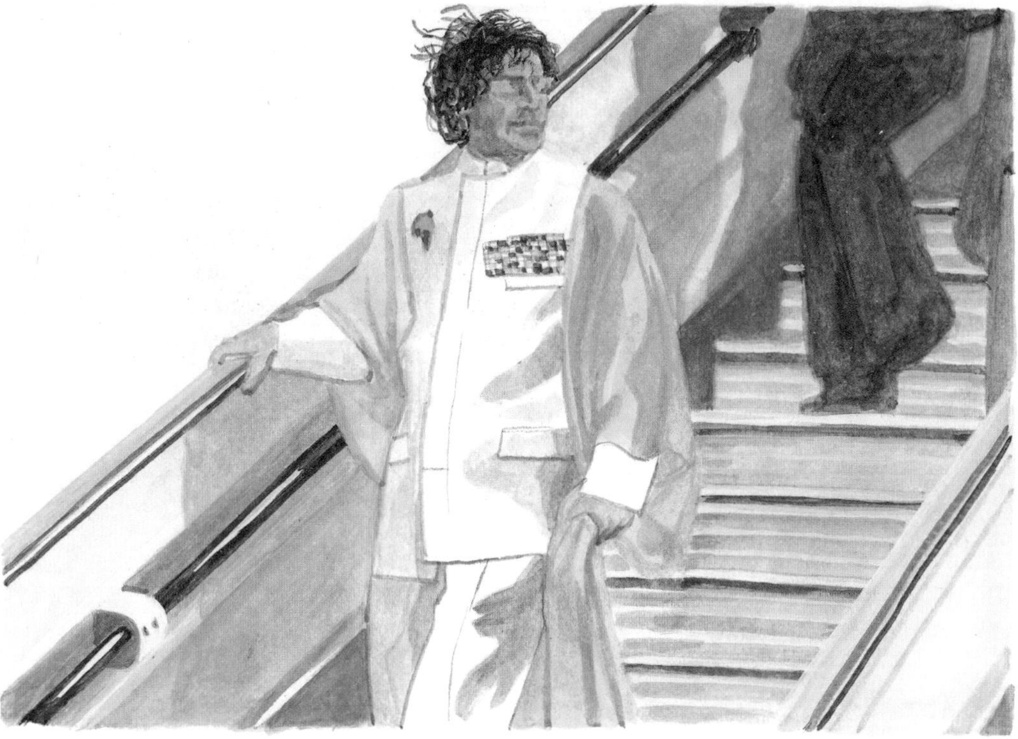

Excessive, seductive, extravagant, unpredictable, rebellious, uncontroll-able, anti-colonialist, pan-African, emotional, impertinent, irreverent, elegant. He had it all, the supreme Guide... except for one black spot. A very, very black spot: the mystery regarding what Colonel Gaddafi did with Imam Musa al-Sadr in that macabre month of August 1978 was never solved. Musa al-Sadr, the vanished imam... Musa al-Sadr, whose face and spirit still live on in the heart of the South and the rest of Lebanon, forty years later... But more on him later. For now, you need to get back on the road, they're waiting for you in Beirut for lunch.

PART TWO

RETURN TO BEIRUT

Rendezvous in Shatila

A few days later, you make your way to Shatila. You're meeting Jamal at "Rond-Point Shatila," behind the army check-point. You called him, without really knowing why. Your wandering through South Lebanon, and now in Beirut, is aimless, meaningless, you follow an invisible thread without resisting and without knowing where it will lead you; you are diverted from your natural trajectory by an irresistible attraction... submissive, surrendered, captivated, you go wherever the heady scent of sulfur takes you. The meeting point is between two cemeteries dedicated to Palestinian martyrs and soldiers. In the shade of parasol pines, in red earth full of dusty undergrowth, they are far less cheerful than the Tyre cemetery. Here, you immediately feel all the tragedy and horror of the Lebanese Civil War.

Jamal is a tall guy, skinny and gaunt. He is handsome, except for one detail. His teeth are indescribable. Actually, describing them is easy: half of them are missing, and the remaining half are rotten. That doesn't stop him from welcoming you with a large, radiant smile, sparkling eyes, and a cigarette. He takes you inside the camp, a few hundred meters away.

Today the word camp is used to describe a shantytown of tiny narrow and ruined alleys with cinderblock structures several stories high, completely unregulated and run down, with an unimaginable chaos of electric wires. It's hard to believe that it doesn't all come crumbling down with a single sneeze. "It's because everything is interlocked," Jamal tells me, "so it holds very well. That said, there are problems from time to time. Last year, the second floor of my house suddenly became the ground floor during a storm." Everywhere there are posters and frescos of martyrs, of Arafat, of the Dome of the Rock, and the cities of Palestine. They considerably brighten up the camp which, otherwise, would be uniformly gray.

The door of the Red Crescent, undoubtedly the most vibrant door in the camp

Decorations for Ramadan brighten up the miserable alleys

When you reach a poorly hung but very attractive painting of a young martyr, you ask Jamal if you can take a photo of it. When you entered the camp, he recommended that you not take any photos without asking for permission. As not all the inhabitants of the camp are on the same side, he wants to avoid any issues that might arise if you were to take a photo that offended a rival faction or a hostile neighbor. Jamal gives you the green light to take a photo of the martyr, but you've barely lifted your camera toward the banner when you hear from behind you a thunderous "STOP!" and the noisy strides of someone running toward you while yelling. Oh, here comes trouble...

You lower your camera and turn around. A young man, about twenty years old, strides toward you. But he passes you by and rushes toward the painting of the martyr, climbs briskly onto a kind of motorcycle parked underneath it; standing on its seat, he tries to straighten out the banner you wanted to photograph. "Thank you," you say, while the young man jumps to the ground with a large smile. Then you take the photograph and continue on your way. "That was his brother," Jamal tells you once you're a few meters away.

The entrance to the mausoleum

The Fascination of the Fedayeen

"If you're interested in martyrs," Jamal says, "I'll show you the mausoleum of the camp heroes. It's right before my house." A few alleys away, on the ground floor of a building that is almost as bleak as the others, a metal door that looks like all the rest has a marble plaque above it announcing: "The mausoleums of the martyrs killed while defending the Shatila camp, 1985–1987." Jamal goes to fetch the key from the grocer's across the street. He opens the door onto a large cold room that reminds you of a morgue. Paver tiles on the floor and walls, aluminum windows, and all along the walls and at the center of the room, one meter high, are large coffers also constructed from paver tiles. It's like an indoor mass grave. Lists of names are engraved in marble on an entire wall, while the portraits of men and women, mounted within a frieze in Palestine's colors, cover the top of the walls. Jamal points out a few in particular, of parents and friends. These are the combatants who died in the camp in 1985, 1986, and 1987, during the famous "War of the Camps," during which Palestinians fought the Shii militia. They were buried there because it was impossible at the time, due to a barrage of uninterrupted gunfire, to take them to the cemetery. Jamal fought in those battles, came out alive and swore to never again wield a weapon, sickened by the number of former friends he'd had to kill. "My best friends were Shia," he says, "who can understand the Lebanese Civil War?"

Like an indoor mass grave… The combatants of the "War of the Camps" are buried here, not the victims of the 1982 massacre, who have another mausoleum outside of the camp

The time of the fedayeen is long past... Shadia Abu Ghazaleh, who died in 1968 in an explosion at her home in Naplouse while preparing a bomb

"I have three kinds of friends," Jamal says as we exit the astonishing indoor cemetery, "those who are dead, those who have left, and those who went mad... The time of the fedayeen is over..."

The fedayeen were such a symbol of prestige and style ... After 1967, the legendary status of the fedayeen kept growing. Not only among the Palestinians themselves, those in Palestine and those in the Jordanian, Lebanese and Syrian camps, but also throughout the world.

Training of the fedayeen in Jordan... in Lebanon... the Battle of Karameh...
the discovery of Yasser Arafat, alias Abu Ammar

The fedayeen are immensely prestigious, among both their friends and their enemies

A poster celebrating the fifth anniversary of Fatah,
the Palestinian National Liberation

Movement, founded by Arafat in 1965
After the 1967 defeat, the fedayeen of the Popular Front for the Liberation of Palestine (PFLP)
would usher in the era of plane hijackings. Leila Khaled is their most famous member

For the Fedayeen

A few days ago, plunging as you often do into your parents' massive library in Beirut, with hills, slopes, mountains of books piled up in front of long shelves that are themselves heavily overloaded with older books, by chance you stumbled upon a tiny forgotten volume that looked tired, lost. A book from 1969, *Pour les fidayine*, written by Jacques Vergès and published by Éditions de Minuit.

Here is what Jérôme Lindon wrote in his preface to the book:

They themselves had that advantage procured, in Western countries, through a long history of study and honing techniques. As a result, they were able to acquire land, houses, posts, and finally—through deadly battles—gain control over a country that no one would have thought to say, at the beginning of the century, was not an Arab land...

... And there you have it, today it's a Jewish state, with a Jewish army, a Jewish diplomacy, a Jewish government. The Arabs who remained have become second-class citizens. From childhood, they know that they will never attain a place of honor or responsibility: those positions are reserved for the newcomers for the sole reason that they are Jewish...

..."We are condemned to be vanquishers," the Israelis say. Vanquishers, that's what they've been for more than twenty years. A situation that brings countless advantages but at least one limitation: it prohibits them from simultaneously claiming to be victims. The survivors of Auschwitz who founded the State of Israel switched camps after that without noticing...

...The problem is no longer whether Israel paid or did not pay a fair price for the lands it possesses, it's that the Palestinians feel dispossessed of their national sovereignty and that they demand it all the more forcefully because they have nothing more, other than life, to lose...

...Nothing, you understand. On that front, they don't run any risk. There is not even a risk of big collective penalties: they have no borders, no state. Why would they obey, for example, the rules of air traffic control invented by the aircraft owners for their own profit?

...Designated as the defense attorney of the commandos who attacked the planes of the Israeli airline El Al in Athens on December 26, 1968 and in Zurich on February 18, 1969, Jacques Mansour Vergès, registered at the bar of Algiers, found himself twice, due to bias, denied the right to practice law by the authorities. Those circumstances gave rise to this book.[14]

---

14   Jérôme Lindon, in Jacques Mansour Vergès, *Pour les fidayine* (Paris: Les Éditions de Minuit, 1969). Jérôme Lindon is the publisher and director of Éditions de Minuit.

The Icon with the Kalashnikov

Leila Khaled was born in Haifa in 1944. Her family flees to Tyre in 1948. After boarding with evangelical Americans in Saida and obtaining her baccalaureate in 1962, she begins studying at the American University of Beirut but then leaves to teach in Kuwait. Later she leaves her teaching job to undergo training in Jordan. In August 1969, two months after Golda Meir declares that the Palestinian people do not exist, Leila Khaled and Salim Issaoui hijacked TWA flight 840 from Los Angeles to Tel Aviv. They board in Rome during a layover, take control of the plane not long after takeoff, and force it to land in Damascus. They pass symbolically over Haifa, Leila and Salim's hometown. In Damascus, they disembark the 116 passengers and blow up the plane. By the next day, the photo of Leila with her Kalashnikov has made its way around the world, a world that knows from then on that the Palestinian people exist. Overnight, Leila becomes the most wanted woman on the planet.

After undergoing plastic surgery to modify her face, she tries, the very next year, on September 6, 1970, to hijack an El Al plane flying from Amsterdam to New York. This time she is accompanied by an American of Nicaraguan origin, who is a supporter of the Palestinian cause. When the plane is over the British coast, they stand up, take out their weapons, head for the cockpit and demand to be let in. The pilot does a maneuver to throw them off balance. Her companion is killed by a security guard and, having given up on pulling the pin out of a grenade, Leila is seized by the other passengers. The pilot reroutes to Heathrow, where Leila is arrested by the British police. This operation is part of a series of four simultaneous hijackings carried out by the PFLP. The other three operations succeed, ending up on the runway at Dawson's Field in the Jordanian desert. This is the catalyst event for Black September. The British government will eventually release Leila in exchange for the 310 hostages from the other hijackings.

This photo made its way around the world
On her finger, Leila wears a piece of jewelry made from a grenade ring and a lead bullet

Leila upon her exit from the London prison
She was exchanged for 310 hostages from three hijackings carried out by the PFLP
that landed on the runway of Dawson's Field in Jordan

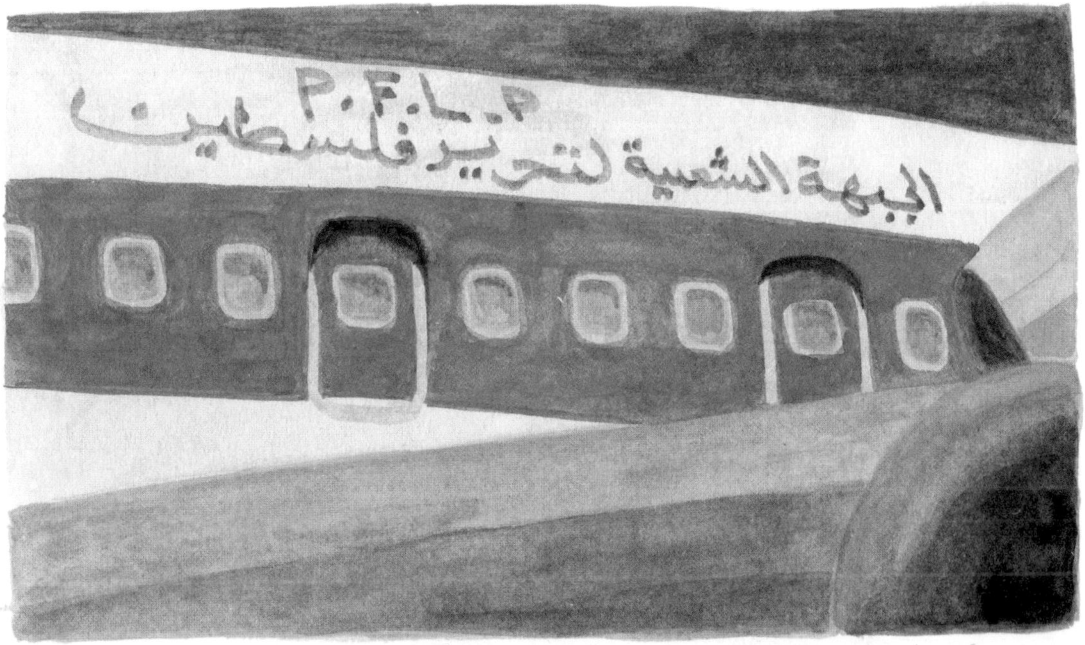
P.F.L.P.
الجبهة الشعبية لتحرير فلسطين

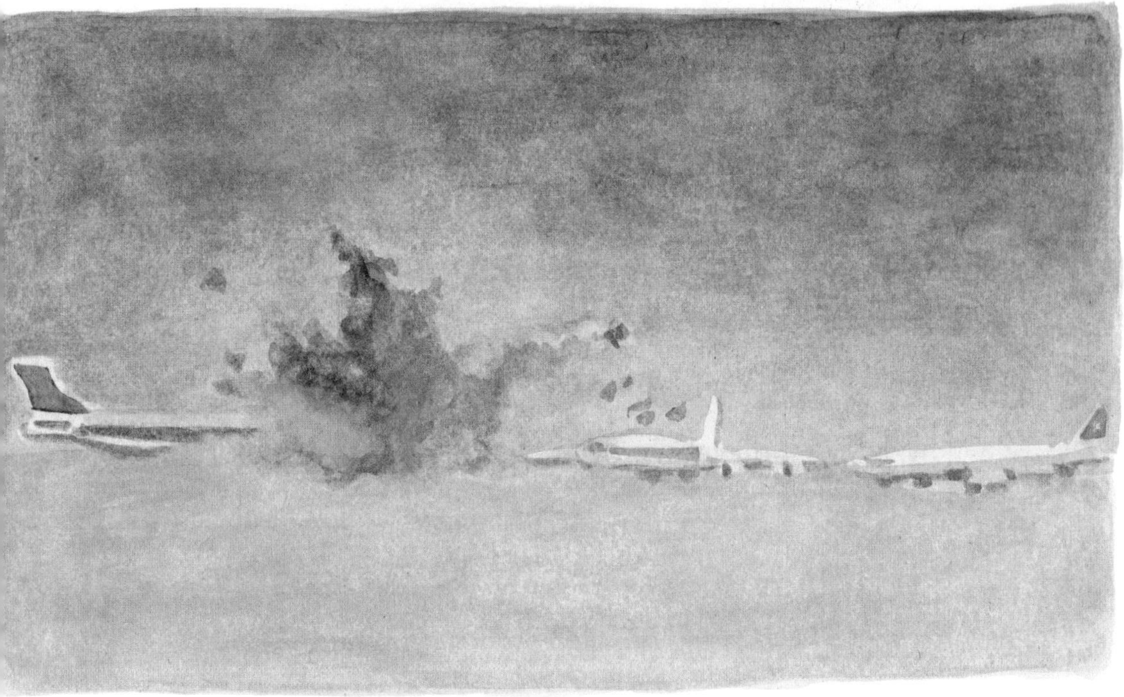

Dalal al-Mughrabi and the Deir Yassin Commando Unit

Born in the refugee camp in Shatila to a family originally from Jaffa, Dalal decides, while studying to become a nurse, to join Fatah instead. In 1977, she undergoes an intensive three-month training, and resolves to take action by pointing her gun "in a single direction, toward Israel." She is part of an operation that will make her a legend. Operation Martyr Kamal Adwan, named after the famous Palestinian leader assassinated by Mossad in Beirut in 1973, is led by the Deir Yassin Commando Unit, named after the massacre that began the Palestinian exodus. The operation is organized by Abu Jihad himself. It takes place during the negotiations between Sadat and Israel over the peace accords that outrage the Palestinian people, and hopes to derail them. Dalal directs the commando unit, composed of a dozen men. She is just twenty years old.

For each member of the group, there is a poster commemorating the event:
"Operation Martyr Kamal Adwan / Deir Yassin Commando Unit
Mohamed Saleh al Shamr
fallen in Palestine"

"Operation Martyr Kamal Adwan / Deir Yassin Commando Unit
Mohamed Raji Cheraane
fallen in Palestine"

The small team leaves by boat from the port of Tyre and travels along the
Israeli coast at a distance, then heads to the beach by raft, disembarking a
few kilometers north of Tel Aviv and then taking the road south.

"Operation Martyr Kamal Adwan / Deir Yassin Commando Unit
Mohamed Fadl Abdel Rahim
fallen in Palestine"

At the end of the road, death awaits: the deaths of dozens of Israelis, and the deaths of Dalal and ten of her companions. Although the operation is a fiasco in terms of its objectives, it is considered the most serious fedayeen attack on Israeli soil.

"Operation Martyr Kamal Adwan / Deir Yassin Commando Unit
Mohamed Mahmoud Abdel Rahim
fallen in Palestine"

A daughter of the nation...

The last time she went to see her mother, she brought her a photo of herself to be framed, but didn't mention her plans. Her father isn't home, so she writes him a goodbye note.

Papa,
It is so difficult to write about you, to you. You taught me humanity, the gift of self and sacrifice for our land. You were a model of these things. I won't write to you anymore. As for my mother, I won't say anything about her because I am distraught and my morale will falter.

I went by the house on Thursday morning to see you but I had bad luck, you weren't there. I didn't say goodbye to you and didn't see you, Papa, but know this: even if I disappear, know that I am always by your side and that I will always live among you.

Don't shed too many tears, because from now on, I am a daughter of the nation.

The famous Djamila Bouhired during her trip to Egypt,
surrounded by Mohamed Abdel Wahab and Abdel Halim Hafez

The Heroes of the FLN

A decade before the fedayeen, other members of the resistance fought for their colonized country. Their movement is what inspired Fatah. They are the National Liberation Front (FLN) of Algeria.

Malika Gaid is a nurse at the Guenzet hospital when she begins to help the revolution by supplying the mujahideen with medicine that she steals from the French administration's health services. At the request of Colonel Amirouche, she leaves her native region and is integrated into the National Liberation Army, in the renowned Wilaya III, which he commands. She dies at the age of twenty-four, weapon in hand, in a cave hospital during a violent French military operation directed by the paratrooper Colonel Marcel Bigeard.

Ourida Meddad and Hassiba ben Bouali...

Ourida Meddad is nineteen when she is captured and tortured in the summer of 1957 in the Sarrouy school in Algiers, which had been transformed by the French army into an interrogation and torture center. The man known for his particularly inhumane torture methods is a certain Lieutenant Schmitt, who would go on to become the Chief of Staff of the French Army, notably during the First Gulf War. The only way Ourida finds to escape the atrocious suffering she endures is suicide. When her torturers aren't paying attention, she throws herself out the window of the torture chamber and her naked body shatters in the school courtyard.

Hassiba Ben Bouali is recruited with other young students into the "bomb network." She is in charge of stocking the laboratory, transporting bombs, and even planting them. When the network is discovered, she goes back into hiding. She is found on October 8, 1957, with Ali la Pointe and Petit Omar in the Kasbah. When they refuse to surrender, the French paratroopers, who surround the house where they're hiding out, blow it up. The three meet their deaths. Hassiba is nineteen years old.

Larbi Ben M'hidi upon his arrest

Now for the tragic end of Larbi Ben M'hidi, leader of the FLN: he is arrested during the Battle of Algiers in February 1957 and, after refusing to speak under torture, is summarily executed without a trial—in a hanging disguised as a suicide. It's not until 2001 that the truth is revealed by General Aussaresses, who admits to having murdered him in the abandoned farm of an extremist colonist. A judge had written the report on the alleged suicide even before it took place. Six of Aussaresses's men prepared the execution. A paratrooper prepares to cover Larbi Ben M'hidi's eyes but he asks that his eyes remain open. His demand is refused, and he is hanged blindfolded. He remains silent until the end.

The cousin of Colonel Amirouche, photographed as he identifies the body

"Amirouche the Terrible," "the Wolf of Akfadou," as the French called him, the unassailable and legendary colonel of Wilaya III, is surrounded, hiding with his men in the caves of cliffs. They are a group of only forty Algerians, but it is impossible for the French to get near them. For reinforcements, they call on the Legion, the second squadron of the first Spahi regiment, and an infantry regiment. They bomb the caves by air and by land using Panhards. After a violent and unequal battle against 2,500 French soldiers, thirty-five Algerians are killed. Amirouche's corpse is among them. A helicopter fetches his body to present it to the press and to the people. They bring in his cousin to confirm his identity in front of the cameras.

Taleb Abderrahmane, the chemist of the Kasbah...

The army embalms his body. Numerous officers and soldiers are photographed with his corpse. The army prints thousands of leaflets which are spread by planes over all the wilayas: "The leader of Wilaya III, Amirouche, is dead. Abandon those who would lead you to an absurd and useless death! Join us! You will find peace once more!"

Taleb Abderrahmane, who is enrolled in the faculty of sciences for a chemistry degree, manages to get in contact with those running Wilaya III, and shares with them his plan to supply the maquis with explosives. He sets up a preliminary makeshift installation in the Kasbah, soon followed by a second. After the deadly attack on Rue de Thebes in the Kasbah by radical militants of French Algeria, he decides that his bombs will henceforth also be destined for the European city of Algiers.

Malika, the nurse of Guenzet

Arrested in June 1957, he is tortured for over a month. His calvary begins in Boufarik, on the sinister Perrin farm, and continues in El Biar, an area known for its sophisticated and merciless torture. His lawyers are the most astonished of all: the young resistance fighter confesses nothing—except for his sole and entire responsibility in all the bombings committed in Algiers, knowing that this single confession will condemn him to death.

He is sentenced to the guillotine. Charge: manufacturing explosives. Taleb Abderrahmane is beheaded on April 24, 1958, at dawn, at the age of twenty-eight. To the sheikh appointed to read him Al-Fatiha before his execution, he says: "Grab a weapon and join the maquis!"

At the end of an alley, a rusted plaque...

The Museum of Memories

Jamal closes the metal door of the astonishing indoor mausoleum, returns the key to the grocer, and the two of you continue on your journey through the labyrinth of pot-holed streets. A bit farther along, a sign with an arrow points out the "Memories Museum" at the end of a tiny cul-de-sac. A few meters on, before you reach the end of the cul-de-sac is a closed metal door. "It's always closed," says Jamal, and he calls Doctor Mohamed el Khatib, the museum owner, who arrives five minutes later with a friend to open the museum for you. Using a flashlight, you enter into a large dark room with walls covered in damp. While the friend tries to cobble together a few wires and switches to generate an electric current, the doctor begins the tour with his flashlight. When the objects are finally illuminated, what a surprise!

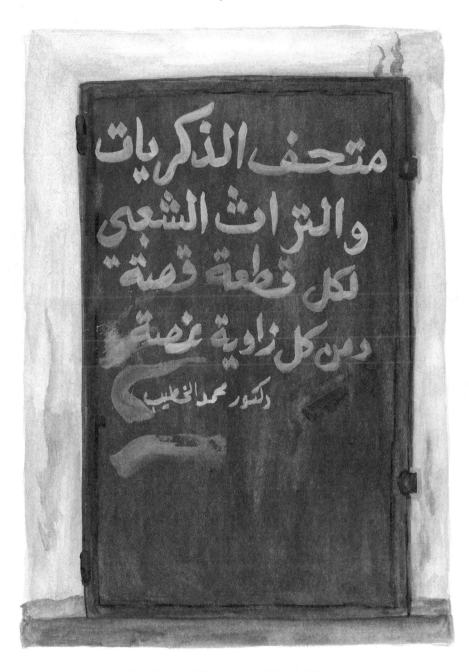

The Museum of Memories and Cultural Heritage
To each object, a unique story,
and from each village, calamity
Doctor Mohamed el Khatib

On the model ship, the piece of paper reads:

The Boat of Return.
Made by Yacoub Roubin Iskandarani, the sailor, in 1935 in Jaffa.
His son, the engineer Rafik Yacoub Iskandarani, gave his name to the boat and watched over it
as one of his children before kindly offering it to the Museum of Memories in January 2005.

There are heaps of old things, made from leather, clay, or wood. There
are lanterns, plates, carafes, agricultural and workshop tools, utensils, and
trinkets of all kinds. It looks like the back room of an antique store... You
were expecting something more captivating.

You are slightly disappointed. You thought you would find weapons of
all kinds, Fatah or PLF posters, clandestine newspapers, photos of the
fedayeen or of battles and massacres, flags, logos, keffiyehs, combat
uniforms... but the doctor's explanations deeply move you.

His son donated this portrait of an oud player to the Museum of Memories

These objects were brought by the camp residents or by their parents when they fled Palestine and were entrusted to him to preserve their memory. Objects with no historic, ethnic, aesthetic, or economic value, but which are all that remains for them of their country. Some donated their objects, others only left them there temporarily. The tour continues by flashlight; the friend can't manage to get the lights on. The doctor makes you a coffee and comments on each piece. Almost none hold any interest apart from simply being there, in this camp. Only a few exude an aura of great tragedy.

Cardboard models of the houses of two brothers, on which are written:

*Model of the house of the late Hajj Hamdé Ben Ahmad Abou Hachmeh,
in the city of Haifa, mount..., Tabor Street, Occupied Palestine.*

*Model of the house of the late Hajj Mahmoud Ben Ahmad Abou Hachmeh, in the city
of Haifa, mount..., Tabor Street, Occupied Palestine.*

*If you lift the roofs of the model homes, you can see the rooms in which the two brothers
and their families lived.*

One of the few objects in the museum that has no relation to Palestine...

A photograph you took of the walls of Shatila in October 2015

The Legend of Abu Ammar

It's striking, the number of photos, posters, banners, and murals in the camp depicting Arafat, so many years after his death. "Here," says Jamal, "we think he lives among us. He is not dead." With immense pride, he tells you that he crossed paths with Arafat twice in 1981, when he was thirteen years old and on guard duty with his Kalashnikov in front of places where Abu Ammar visited.[15] One day, the most blessed day of all for Jamal, Arafat placed his hand on the young boy's tousled hair and said: "There it is, the green grass of Palestine."

---

15   Abu Ammar was Yasser Arafat's nom de guerre.

Yasser Arafat is elected president of the General Union of Palestinian Students
(second from the right)

Now for the legend of Yasser Arafat, who was venerated as much as he was detested, including by the Palestinians themselves. This is the saga of the man who turned a center for international terrorism into a political organization with formal status within the United Nations. This is the myth of a man who surrounded himself with the greatest Arab intellectuals as well as the worst mercenaries, accomplishing the rare feat of seducing the former and dominating the latter. We don't really know if he was born in Cairo or Jerusalem, on August 4 or 24, 1929. He is four years old when his mother dies and he goes to live with his uncle in Jerusalem. Back in Cairo, as a university student, he is disgusted by the 1948 Arab–Israeli War and participates in operations against the English. Elected president of the General Union of Palestinian Students in 1952, he then relinquishes this post after obtaining his engineering degree, passing it on to Salah Khalaf, aka Abu Iyad, who would become his closest friend.

Salah Khalaf, alias Abu Iyad, and Khalil al-Wazir, alias Abu Jihad, his closest companions,
whom he met in Cairo, would both be assassinated

Around the same time, he meets his other best friend, Khalil al-Wazir, aka Abu Jihad, who is studying in Alexandria. All three begin to organize training for young Palestinians, but after facing hostility from Nasser's regime, they leave for Kuwait, where they establish Fatah. In 1967, the Naksa. The tragedy ends with the invasion of Sinai, Golan, Gaza, the West Bank, and, worst of all, Jerusalem, where the ancestral Maghrebian neighborhood, which is also his uncle's neighborhood where Arafat had spent his childhood, is razed to the ground starting that very month of June to create an esplanade in front of the Wailing Wall. Arafat joins the Karameh camp in Jordan, where Fatah's first operations are organized. Jamal tells you that when they, in the camp, heard on the radio about the very first operation, his grandfather said, with tears in his eyes: "It won't be long now before we return to Palestine." Then comes the Battle of Karameh, the battle that would solidify the prestige of the fedayeen and the mythical status of Abu Ammar. He fights in battles; he is adored. He appears out in the open, with a keffiyeh on his head, a gun in his hands, and wearing Ray-Bans. Then comes Black September. In Jordan, the king wants to get rid of those Palestinian organizations that have come to represent a state within a state: On September 1, Hussein escapes an attack; on the 6th, three passenger planes are hijacked and rerouted to Amman; on the 12th, the PFLP blows up the empty planes in front of the international press. Hussein has had enough. He bombs the camps for ten days straight, then razes them.

al-'Asifah, the military branch of Fatah

His first appearance during the Battle of Karameh...

The UN Speech in 1974
"I come bearing an olive branch in one hand,
and a freedom fighter's gun in the other
Do not let the olive branch fall from my hand"

Aboard the Atlantis, leaving Beirut...

There are thousands of deaths. Arafat and the fedayeen retreated to Lebanon where their massive settlement leads directly to the war five years later. Faced with the weakness of the Lebanese army and government, Arafat becomes one of the most influential and powerful men in the country. People speak of the "État-Arafat" and Fatahland. This is unacceptable for the Christian leaders, who oppose him with weapons. In 1982, Israel pursues one of its most persistent dreams: the invasion of Lebanon. This time, the Israeli army pushes all the way to Beirut, through indescribable violence. Amid apocalyptic bombardments, the blockade of West Beirut lasts three months. Then the Palestinians surrender, and the soldiers and Arafat depart from the Port of Beirut. The Lebanese prime minister bids him an official goodbye and insists that the president of the republic appoint a Christian minister to join the Muslim leaders that will accompany Arafat to the port. The president replies that it's not necessary to have an extra minister when the prime minister is present. "This is not a protocol situation," he answers,

*Surreal scenes from the crossing, during which Abu Ammar gives
interviews while sitting in a deckchair*

"but a historical situation. It must not be said that Arafat left Lebanon
without a goodbye from a Christian representative." And so it is done.
Climbing aboard the *Atlantis*, in response to the international press who ask
him where he's going, Abu Ammar declares: "I am going to Palestine." At
the time, the entire world finds it pitiful. The Palestinians remaining on
the quay—women, children, and the elderly—will be the first to see, through
their tears, incredulous, Arafat's arm brandished in a V for victory. The
soldiers are defeated, scattered, disarmed, their governance divided... Then
come the Sabra and Shatila massacres. The hard blows will just keep coming
after that. In 1988, his oldest companion, Abu Jihad, is assassinated. After
he proclaims the independence of the state of Palestine to an emotional
audience in Algiers and openly renounces acts of terrorism, Arafat is invited
to speak at the UN. The United States refuses him entry into their territory.
The UN changes locations to Geneva so that he can speak. In 1991, his other
lifelong companion, Abu Iyad, is assassinated.

Watching television in his office with Mahmoud Abbas, upon the death of Yitzhak Rabin...
The darkened face... the disillusionment...

"I Invite You to My Funeral"

Then come the Oslo Accords and finally, a miracle: Arafat's return to Palestine. Everyone in the camps in Lebanon was euphoric, Jamal tells you: "The old man went back, so maybe we'll go back soon." Then everything crumbles. Rabin is assassinated. As soon as the announcement is made, Leila Shahid visits him, locked in his office alone. She finds him with a dark expression on his face. "The situation is difficult," she says. "Much more difficult than you think.—You mean to say that this calls the entire process into question?—There is no more process.—But why?!—Because he was the only one who was sincere."

A disastrous and dictatorial management also aggravates the situation. The resistance fighter is not equipped to manage daily affairs. But the fighter is still there. Under pressure, threats, and intimidation, in 2000 at Camp David, he does not cede on the right to return, or on Jerusalem. To a furious Clinton, who assures him that if he returns from Camp David without an agreement, there will be war and his life will be in jeopardy, he responds: "I invite you to my funeral." Indeed. In 2001, Sharon surrounds Arafat in his office with an Israeli army; thus begins the final voyage. In the firing line of the Israeli tanks beneath his windows, Arafat cannot attend the Arab League Summit in Beirut. Nor can he attend, as he has done every year since his return, the Christmas Mass in the Church of the Nativity in Bethlehem. The Israeli tanks destroy all the buildings surrounding his, while people throughout the world watch on their televisions. The journalists who manage to gain access to him film him by candlelight because there is no more electricity. Then, finally, he falls ill and is transported to Paris, where he dies. The theory of poisoning has still to this day not been ruled out by the various inquests. For the Palestinians, including his appointed doctor, there is no doubt about it. In France, following official protocol, a full and prestigious ceremony is held to bring him to the plane. His return to Palestine is met with jubilation. The Israeli authorities refuse for his final resting place to be Jerusalem.

The buildings that surround his office in Ramallah are blown to smithereens in front of the televisions of the entire world, while tanks threaten outside his windows

In the Church of the Nativity, a keffiyeh covers his empty chair

You were in New York that day and you photographed the piles of newspapers announcing the news on the sidewalks of Times Square. "The monster is dead," "the devil," "Satan," "the horrible." "Good riddance!" These headlines frightened you, saddened you, until you reminded yourself that to be so hated by the Americans was in fact a real achievement! You contemplate his incredible trajectory... His charisma, his audacity, his intelligence, his talent, his courage, and style. But for you, he committed a monumental error. Colossal. The deadly sin of breaking the small country that had welcomed him. And this crime he committed against Lebanon did not even help him in his fight.

Everything they own fits on a single shelf
In the golden frame, a photo of Jamal's mother, taken in Palestine

"I Knew Palestine"

You finally arrive at Jamal's house. His wife, Mona, is beautiful, compelling, and determined. She's in a T-shirt from the 1980s and ripped plastic slippers, like Jamal. Three handsome smiling teenagers come to greet you. Mona explains to you proudly that her eldest son is completing his degree in psychology at the university. He is the first member of his family to leave the camp. One of Jamal's neighbors is there too. He is disabled but seems too young to have been a soldier. "He was born during the War of the Camps," Jamal says. "He was in his mother's arms when they were struck by shellfire. He was four months old; his mother died, and he never walked." You ask Jamal what age he was when he arrived at the camp. "I was born here!" You're shocked, and barely manage to hide your astonishment. Stupidly, you thought Jamal was old enough to have been born in Palestine! "You know," Mona tells you, as if reading your thoughts, "there are even sixty-eight-year-olds who were born here. They arrived in 1948, in their mother's stomachs. Soon, in this camp, no one will be able to say: 'I knew Palestine' anymore." You chat about lighter topics, too. Mona and Jamal are witty and cheerful, with a dark sense of humor. Jamal shows you the handicrafts made by the camp scouts, whom he is in charge of. You have a hard time believing that this is the same man who confessed to being a fierce soldier just five minutes ago...

The camp coat of arms, designed by Jamal and drawn by one of his artist friends

A photo you took in 2016. Sitting between Jamal and Mona is their son Nidal; in front, a neighbor and their two daughters, Hanan and Farah. In the background, a photo of Jamal's brother, who was killed in Tal al-Zaatar

"The scouts work with several humanitarian and cultural associations, Lebanese and Western," says Mona. "We're lucky... Swedes, Italians, Americans, Norwegians, Germans, Australians... some are Jewish... We've hosted two Jews here, in this house, in the middle of the camp! An American university student and an Irish humanitarian aid worker who, like many other Jews in the world, fight for the Palestinian cause and don't support Israel's crimes committed in their name. Before Zionism, Jewish people lived very well in the Middle East while those in Europe were being massacred. The only Jews we have a problem with are the ones who came from Europe and live in Palestine in our homes!" "Two years ago," Jamal says, "I asked a guy, an Italian who worked in an NGO in Lebanon and had become our friend, to go see what happened to my parents' house in Jaffa when he would go to Palestine.

A souvenir bought in a camp store

He went, rang the bell, someone answered the door, he said he was a friend of the former inhabitants who were now living in a camp in Lebanon and asked if he could visit the house. They slammed the door in his face without a word. What I don't understand," Jamal laughs, "is how they manage to live with themselves. I would not want to be in their place," he concluded, a thin ironic smile framing his cigarette.

The entrances to the two cemeteries are directly opposite each other,
just behind the Rond-Point Shatila

Jamal finally tells you about the day Sami came to see him when he was searching for his father. Sami asked Jamal whether his father was in the camp, if Jamal knew where he could find him. "Ah!" Jamal had said to him, "Of course! Your father and my father are very close. Like two peas in a pod, inseparable," he had said with a big jovial laugh. "Come, I'll bring you to see them." They left the camp and headed for the Rond-Point Shatila. When they reached the cemetery, Jamal entered nonchalantly. "My father is buried here," he said pointing to a corner of the cemetery, "and yours, here. You see, they're very close..."

Martyrs of Palestine cemetery

Martyrs Cemetery

"He died of severe pneumonia," Jamal tells you, "eight years ago. It had been two months since he'd come back and settled in the camp. He was sleeping in the scouts' quarters." Jamal confirms that he had in fact gone mad, truly mad. "A man so enamored with justice, liberty, and honor can only go insane in our corner of the world, don't you agree?"

You ask Jamal to take you to the cemetery so you can take some photos. It's the only cemetery in Lebanon where Muslims and Christians are buried together. It's a cemetery for Palestinians and for supporters of the Palestinian cause, a cemetery of martyrs. There are Lebanese, Syrians, Kurds, Armenians... There is even a Frenchman! You read the names and dates. What's striking is the age of the deceased. People don't live to be very old around here. Those are many graves for people who died in their twenties. There are also years that were more unfortunate than others... Your stomach is in knots.

A gravestone in memory of the camp martyrs

Jamal makes jokes, winding his body between the tombs. "Here," he says, pointing to one that's slightly more imposing than the others, "this is Muhammad Amin al-Husseini. Yes, yes, it's him," he says, seeing your startled expression, "that's right, the Grand Mufti of Jerusalem... Even though he's dead, he still elicits embarrassment for the influence, alleged or imagined, he had on Hitler..." He continues, with a soft, sarcastic smile: "We didn't know, us Palestinians, that we had played such an important role in the history of Europe!"

The tomb of the Grand Mufti of Jerusalem, who died in 1974 in Beirut

There are many graves for those who died in 1982...
This is the only cemetery in Lebanon where Christians and Muslims
are buried side by side

Following page: Above: a sister and a brother, martyrs, who died at seventeen and sixteen years old.
Below: a martyr who died during an attack on the Palestine Research Center

✝

قال يسوع
من آمن بي ولو مات فحيا
الشهيدة هلا شكري عيد
١٩٥٧ـ١٩٧٤
وبالروح
الشهيد تزيكار شكري عيد
١٩٦٠ـ١٩٧٦

حُسين حسن الحُسيني

✝

الشهيدة
حنه شاهين جريس

ولدت في قرية فولا في فلسطين
بتاريخ ١٩٤٧/٨/٨
استشهدت في حادث تفجير مركز الإرسال الفلسطيني
بتاريخ ١٩٨٣/٢/٤

الجندي البطل
حسن أبو إبراهيم اللاجئ
فلسطيني
الشهيد وقام على الثورة
الخالدة

You suddenly stop in front of a tomb, taken aback, and you glance
questioningly at Jamal. "Yes, that's really him," Jamal says, "he's buried
here..." Ghassan Kanafani, the writer, one of the most important
figures of the Palestinian cause, one of the most renowned intellectuals of
Beirut, one of the greatest Arab authors... assassinated by Mossad in Beirut
on July 8, 1972.

On his gravestone: "The great writer, martyr Ghassan Kanafani,
a member of the political office of the PFLP,
born in Acre, Palestine, in 1936, died a martyr on July 8, 1972"

Ghassan Kanafani

Born in Acre, he attends a French Catholic school in Jaffa. In 1948, the exodus. In a letter to his son, decades later, he would recall the intense shame he felt, even though he was just twelve years old, seeing the men of his family surrender their weapons and become refugees. The Deir Yassin massacre takes place on his birthday. He would never celebrate his birthday again after that. His family lives in exile in Damascus, and he finishes high school with a certificate from UNRWA.[16] His first job is as a teacher in a refugee camp. There he begins writing books for children, to help them contextualize their situation. At the same time, he continues studying Arabic literature at the University of Damascus, where he meets George Habash. After he is expelled from the university for his affiliation with the ANM, he leaves Damascus to teach in Kuwait.

---

16   The Arab Nationalist Movement (ANM) was founded at the American University of Beirut in the late 1940s. It was known for its revolutionary, pan-Arab philosophy and was composed of an intellectual elite opposed to colonization, Western imperialism, and Israel. The PFLP was born out of the ANM.

He devours Russian literature. He becomes the editor of *Al Rai* (The Opinion), a newspaper affiliated with the ANM, then leaves Kuwait to settle in Beirut, capital of the free press and free thinking. There he edits *Al Hurriya* (Freedom), the central organ of the ANM, and not long after becomes the editor-in-chief of *Al Muharrir* (The Liberator), a Nasserist newspaper where he launches the supplement *Filastin* (Palestine), then takes over *Al Anwar* (The Illumination), another Nasserist newspaper, which he subsequently leaves to run the weekly magazine *Al Hadaf* (The Target), organ of the PFLP, after affiliating himself with the organization. His political writings have a large impact on Arab thought of the time. But it is literature, he says, that shapes his political, militant, and journalistic ideology. Novels, poems, plays, stories, essays. His assassination will put an end to all that: at thirty-six years old, when he turns the key in the ignition of his Austin 1100 as he is leaving his house to go to his office, a several-kilo plastic bomb detonates. He is blown to smithereens along with his seventeen-year-old niece, Lamees, who has just arrived from Kuwait with her mother and is eager to discover Beirut, a city she's never been to before. A Lebanese newspaper writes in his obituary that he is a commando who has never fired a gun—his weapon was a ballpoint pen.

George Habash was born in Lydda, Palestine,
to an Orthodox Christian family forced into exile in 1948.
After studying medicine at the American University of Beirut, he founds ANM.
After some time in Jordan, where he opens a clinic in the Palestinian camps, and in
Syria, where he spends time in prison, he moves back to Beirut where, after the defeat
of 1967, he founds the PFLP, whose ideology is based on Marxism–Leninism and
Arab nationalism. He joins the PLO, although he is politically more extreme
than the much more moderate Yasser Arafat

Al Muharrir, Al Hurriya, Al Anwar...
A few titles of newspapers that published Ghassan Kanafani's explosive articles

Ghassan with Lamees as a child

After Lamees was born, Ghassan would write and illustrate a book for his beloved niece for each of her birthdays. With his delicate hands, he lovingly cut and pasted the drawings he had sketched onto beautiful paper. After the explosion blast, all that remained of Ghassan and Lamees's love were these small, charming books.

A few pages from "The Little Lantern"...

بعد كل هذه السنوات يبدو لي التي عرفت، الحبر؟،
من أنا وايه طريقي .. ولذلك فانني لن استطيع
ان اكتب لك شعرا؟ وثني لست شاعرا؟ .. ولا مقالا؟
لانني لست كاتب مقال .. وكي احافظ على وعدي
لك، هديتي البلد قررت اه اكتب لك قصة،
مهمتي اه اكتب قصة .. وسوف اكتب لك
واحدة اسمع القنديل الصغير، تكبر معك كلما
كبرت ...

...a story that Ghassan wrote...

244

...and illustrated for his beloved niece

"And here is his niece's grave," Jamal says, "she was sitting next to him in the car. Pieces of their bodies were found meters from the pulverized car frame by his young son, his wife, his sister…"

"Lamees Najim, a seventeen-year-old girl, was on her way to do
some shopping at souk el Tawilé with her uncle Ghassan when her limbs
were scattered along with his"

Abu Hassan, the Red Prince

"Follow me," Jamal says, a dead twig gathered from a grave between his teeth. "I'll show you the cemetery's star, its most flamboyant resident!" Shuffling gracefully in his slippers, he stops in front of a series of five identical tombs and points at the one in the middle. You read, or rather you exclaim: "Ali Hassan Salameh!" Jamal had not been exaggerating about this person's prestige! "Abu Hassan," a mythical figure of the Lebanese Civil War, one of the most legendary and captivating Palestinians, the famous Red Prince (a nickname given to him by the Israelis), assassinated by Mossad in the middle of Beirut in 1979.

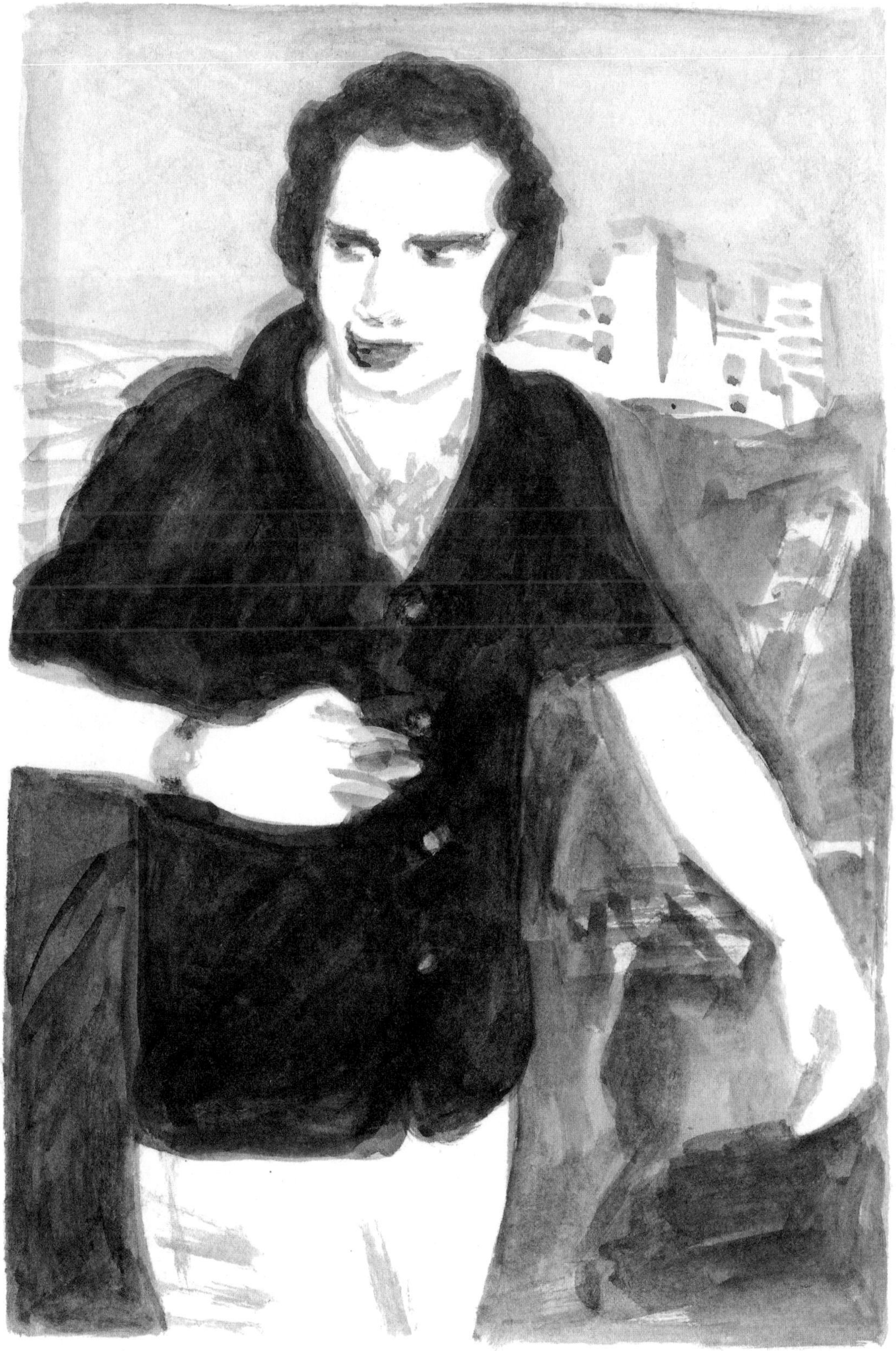

With his mother

Abu Hassan is one of the lieutenants closest to Arafat, who loves him like a son. He is the alleged mastermind of the Munich hostage-taking, and head of the Black September organization, and therefore at the top of the list of Palestinians to be eliminated by Mossad. Born to a wealthy family near Jaffa, he studies in Germany, trains in Cairo and Moscow, joins Fatah in Jordan, and spends his honeymoon in Hawaii and Disney World. A playboy who enjoys nights out in Beirut, he marries the beautiful Georgina Rizk, Miss Lebanon who became Miss Universe. He has just said goodbye to her when, taking rue Verdun, his Chevrolet and that of his bodyguards drives by a parked Volkswagen that explodes as they pass.

The beautiful Georgina, whom he marries in 1976

A photo of Abu Hassan and his son with Arafat

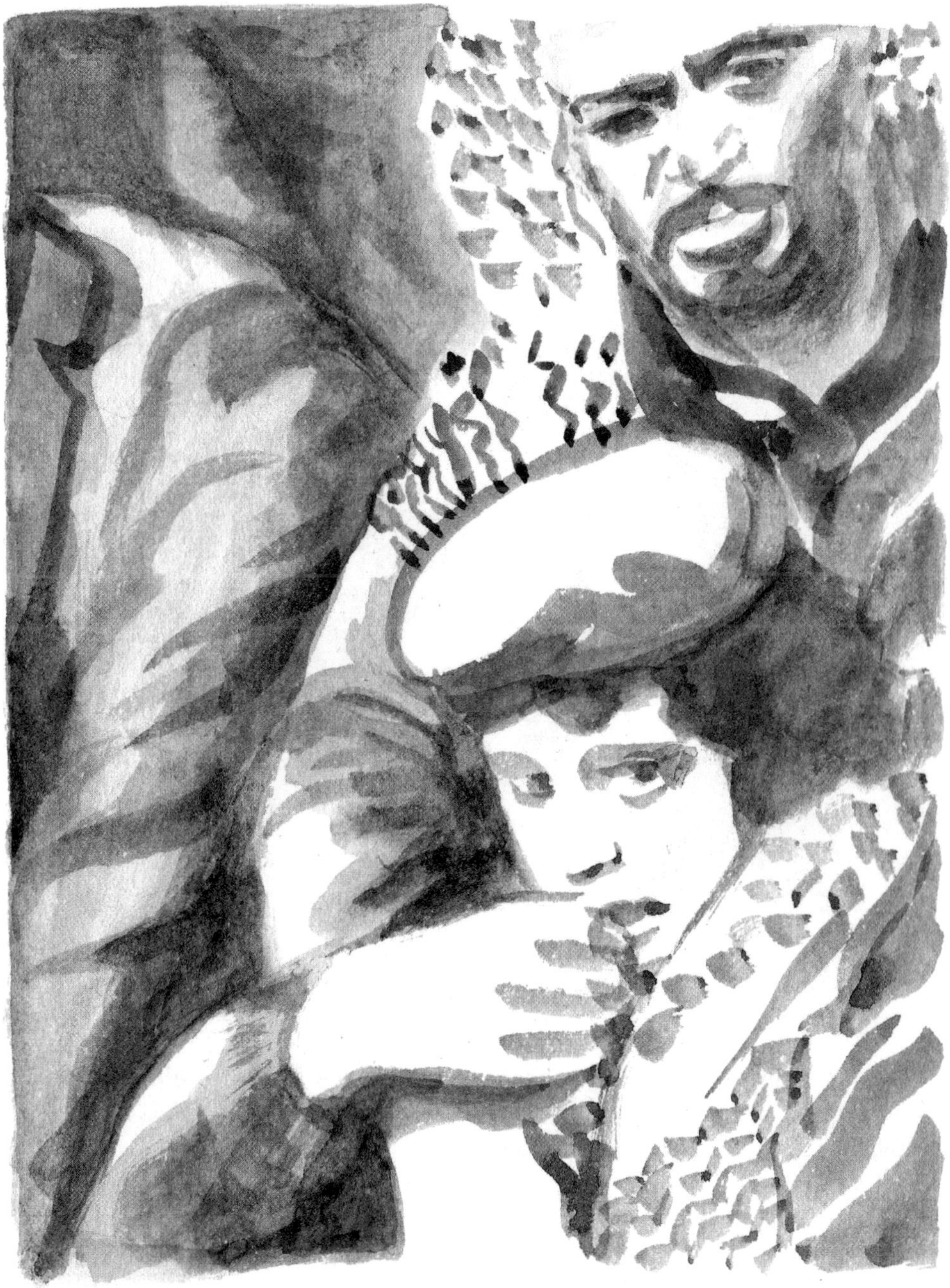

At Abu Hassan's funeral

Georgina during a press conference at Al Bustan hotel

His killing seems to have been motivated by reasons other than his involvement in the taking of hostages in Munich. As Fatah's head of intelligence and counter-espionage, he is the contact person of the PLO for the CIA, and a precious intermediary between the Palestinians and their adversaries, the Lebanese Christians.

Two priceless connections made possible by his openness, his diplomacy, and his charm. It is certainly his excellent relations with the Americans and the Phalangists that bothered the Israelis the most.

الشهيد البطل القائد

علي حسن سلامه

"أبو حسن"

A poster rendering homage to Abu Hassan

After the death of the Red Prince, the Mossad agents' operation—Wrath of God—should have been complete. Ten Palestinian figures linked to Munich had already been killed by them in various European cities and in Beirut. In reality, the people on the "Golda list" did not need to have participated in the taking of hostages in Munich, either from near or from afar, or even to have been members of Black September. Mostly it was enough for them to be a Palestinian who was a brilliant intellectual, militant or moderate. A great ambassador of the Palestinian cause, an important contact for the West, someone that would be missed... The first was Wael Zwaiter.

They Assassinate the Light

Rome, October 1972. Returning from dinner in town, Wael Zwaiter is killed in front of his building by two Israeli agents who put twelve bullets in his head and chest. The PLO will declare that he was in no way connected to either Black September or to Munich and that he was resolutely against political violence.

Twelve bullets to the head and chest

Born in Nablus, Wael Zwaiter is the son of an eminent historian and lawyer who translates authors such as Voltaire, Rousseau, and Montesquieu into Arabic. He studies philosophy and Arabic literature at the University of Baghdad. He speaks five languages and is passionate about music. Upon his arrival as a student in Rome, he enrolls in singing lessons, and his teacher remarks that he has perfect pitch. He reads the *Thousand and One Nights* to his Arab students in a bar on Via del Vantaggio near the Accademia di Belle Arti, hangs out with leftist artists and intellectuals, and counts Moravia and Pasolini among his friends. Still in debt, he takes a job as a translator for the Libyan Embassy. As soon as he has saved a bit of money, he spends it on records and books. After the war of 1967, he is so shaken that he decides it is his duty to fight for his country. He contacts the PLO and becomes their official spokesperson in Rome.

His copy of Thousand and One Nights penetrated by a bullet

By the time of his death, he had been working for years on the colossal project of translating the *Thousand and One Nights* from Arabic into Italian, which had never been done before. They find, in his jacket pocket, a copy of the second volume of the celebrated story penetrated by a bullet.

With a friend, in a trattoria where he was a regular

Wael Zwaiter's artist and intellectual friends, who wrote many articles and testimonies in the years after his death, said that by assassinating this exile from the West Bank who appreciated Mahler and Jean Genet, the Israelis were actually trying to eliminate a brilliant Palestinian who was in the middle of winning over the Western intelligentsia to the Palestinian cause.

Photo of the young student from Nablus upon his arrival in Rome

A poster commemorating the three martyrs
From the left: Kamal Adwan, Kamal Nasser, Abu Youssef al-Najjar

The Shock

On April 10, 1973, three of the highest-ranking officials in the PLO are assassinated in their homes in the heart of Beirut, in the middle of night, by an Israeli commando that arrives by sea in a Zodiac. Youssef al-Najjar, aka Abu Youssef, one of the founders of the PLO, and head of the intelligence wing and third-in-command of Fatah. Kamal Adwan, also a founder of the PLO and the chief of operations for the organization in occupied Palestine. Finally, Kamal Nasser, spokesperson of the PLO and a member of the executive committee, as well as a poet and journalist. The three men are surprised in their sleep, in their homes, among their families, in their pajamas. None of the three have time to draw their weapons before they are gunned down. Lebanon is in shock. April 12, the day of the funeral, is a memorable day in the history of Beirut. Some 250,000 people take to the streets, bursting with grief and anger. At the funeral for the three Palestinians at Nejmeh Square, amid the spectacle of long, chrome-trimmed American cars, the Lebanese leaders and senior politicians are all out in

The funeral... on the front page of a newspaper:
"They were a quarter of a million people"

force, including their fiercest opponents, their most persistent enemies. Notably Sheikh Pierre Gemayel, leader of the Phalangists, who, despite the risks he incurred by entering the hostile crowd, and despite the pleas of his security officers, insists on being there to calm down the situation. Warned ahead of time by Abu Hassan, Arafat welcomes this initiative and provides security for Sheikh Pierre, who arrives at Nejmeh Square with his armed escort at the same time as Kamal Jumblatt, the ruthless opponent. The simmering crowd then begins to shout both of their names as they enter the mosque together. The final image of Lebanon standing at the edge of the abyss, desperately trying not to fall in.

The body of Kamal Nasser, the poet…
In Palestine, 8,000 people walked 8 kilometers on foot after the Israelis banned the use of their cars, in order to offer their condolences to Kamal Nasser's mother.

Abu Jihad

Khalid al-Wazir, alias Abu Jihad. Salah Khalaf, alias Abu Iyad. The historic founders of Fatah, together with Yasser Arafat. His two lifelong, closest companions. They are both second-in-command of the PLO at the time of their death. They are both assassinated in Tunis, a few years apart.

A refugee at thirteen years old in a camp in Gaza and then a student in the UNRWA, Abu Jihad participates in attacks against Israel from a very young age. He is briefly a member of the Muslim Brotherhood, serves prison time in Egypt, meets Arafat, begins an engineering degree in Alexandria, undergoes military training in Cairo, serves prison time once again, leaves to teach in Saudi Arabia, moves to Kuwait, founds Fatah using the FLN as his model, then moves to Beirut to publish the organization's newspaper. Any person, any group that wants to launch a newspaper in the Middle East, no matter what their political persuasion, does so in Lebanon, the only country in the region with a free press. Then he moves to Algeria on an invitation from Ahmed Ben Bella, travels to China, presents Fatah to Zhou Enlai, and meets Che Guevara in Algiers. Tasked by Arafat with creating al-'Asifah, the military branch of Fatah, he recruits and trains combatants in Jordan and Syria. He makes a name for himself during the Battle of Karameh, then during Black September. Eventually he withdraws with the other leaders of the PLO to Beirut. From Lebanon he organizes operations in Occupied Palestine, including the mission led by Dalal al-Mughrabi and her companions.

When Israel invades Lebanon in 1982, he is in favor of the retreat of the PLO from Beirut, unlike most of the other Palestinian leaders, in order to spare the city. Nevertheless, he organizes the defense of the capital and, after their defeat, climbs aboard the same boat as Arafat, the *Atlantis*. From Tunis, he sets about establishing a solid base for Fatah inside the Occupied territories themselves He becomes the exiled mastermind of the First Intifada, with an impressive knowledge of the terrain, of each village, each school, each family in the West Bank and Gaza. He is assassinated in 1988 in front of his wife and children by seventy-five bullets shot at point-blank range by a Mossad commando unit that arrives by sea.

Above: Abu Jihad and Abu Ammar
Below: The First Intifada

265

Poster in homage to Abu Jihad, the "symbol," the "hero"

Other intifadas will follow...
The ballet of the rock-throwers will be performed again and again...

Arafat has already lost so many close brothers-in-arms. Never has fury or his pain exploded as it does upon the death of Abu Jihad. The refugee child, the teen resistance fighter, the devoted soldier, the loyal patriot, the upstanding supporter, the tireless militant, the audacious leader, the friend, the brother, the lifelong companion. The funeral takes place in the Yarmouk refugee camp in Damascus, where his parents live. A human tidal wave sweeps through the camp for the final goodbye, as well as through the streets of Palestine and West Beirut. Arafat leads the procession; the speech he gives over his friend's body is incredibly desperate, vehement, poignant. Every phrase explodes with sadness and rage, his emotions are an erupting volcano that drowns out the only moment he finally pronounces the name of the scourge: them, the terrorist assassins—the Zionists.

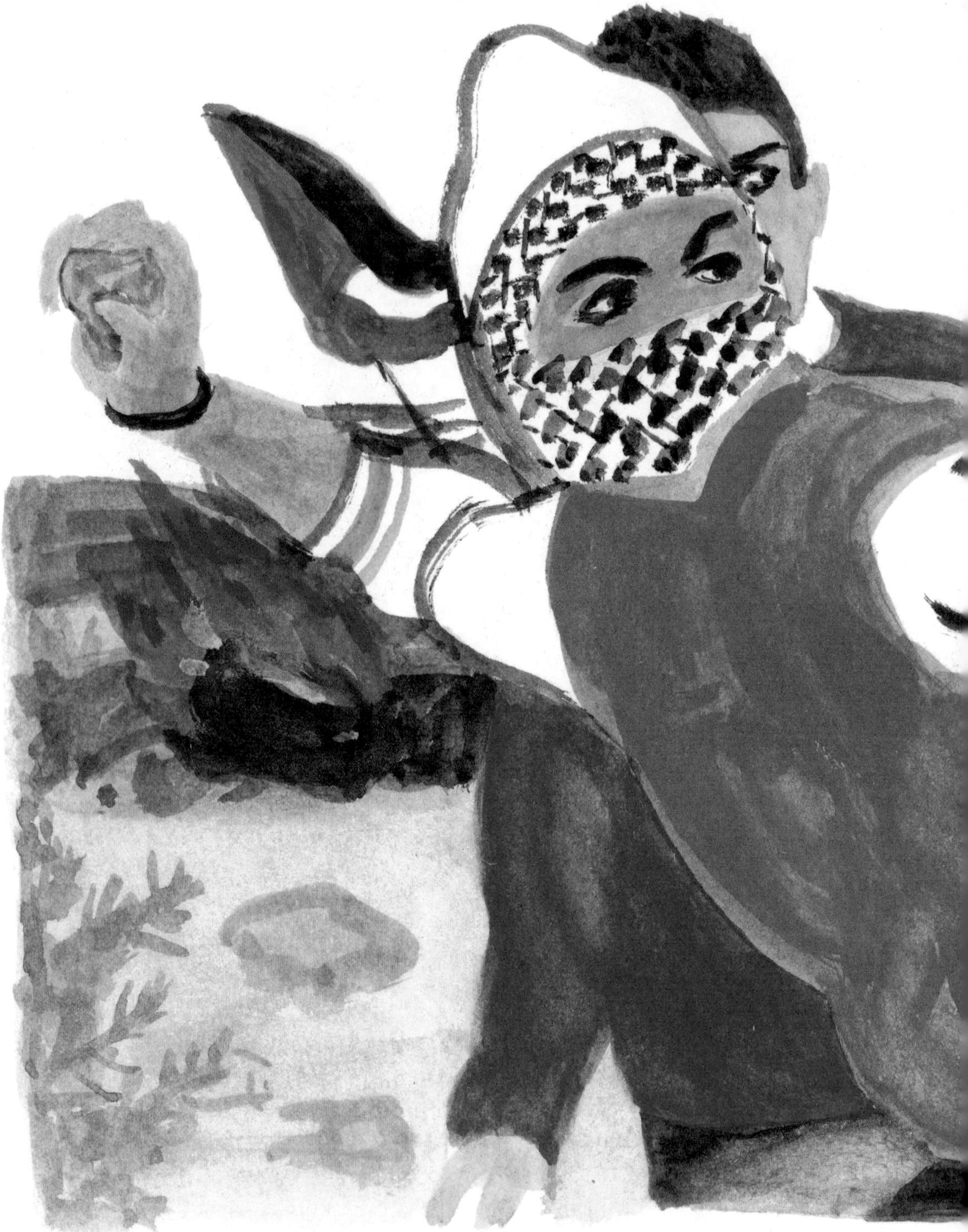

David versus Goliath...

...the pebble versus the canon.

Hamas logo

A Ton of Explosives Dropped by an F16

In the twenty-first century, Palestinian leaders are still being assassinated by Israel in large numbers. Especially the leaders of Hamas, an organization whose emergence was originally facilitated and even largely encouraged by Israel to undermine the influence of the PLO and Yasser Arafat.

Salah Shehadeh, leader of the Izz ad-Din al-Qassam Brigades

Salah Shehadeh, leader of the Izz ad-Din al-Qassam Brigades, the military branch of Hamas, is killed in 2002 in the Gaza Strip. A one-ton bomb is dropped by an F16 over his house, causing the deaths of many other victims. Fifteen deaths in total, including seven children, a hundred wounded, nine destroyed homes and twenty more damaged.

Ismail Abu Shanab, the moderate

Ismail Abu Shanab, one of Hamas's founders, its third-in-command, and the representative of its more moderate side, is killed by several missiles fired at his car from an Apache helicopter. Born in a refugee camp in Gaza, he studies engineering in Cairo and then in the United States before returning to Gaza, where he becomes the link between Hamas and the PLO and the spokesperson for Hamas, especially for the Western media. He participates in peace talks as a representative of Hamas, is a supporter of a two-state solution and is against suicide attacks, although he maintains that "this primitive weapon, which is all we have, is still less destructive than the F16s that drop tons of explosives."

Sheikh Ahmed Yassin, the founder

Sheikh Ahmed Yassin, an elderly quadriplegic in a wheelchair, founder and spiritual leader of Hamas, is killed, along with his bodyguards, by several missiles fired from a helicopter as he is leaving the mosque after the morning prayer. All three of them are blown to smithereens; the first responders have a hard time gathering all the pieces of the bodies.

The Absolute Splendor of the Umayyad Mosque

You continue the tour of the cemetery, following behind Jamal. Something unexpected catches your eye. An elderly couple, a man and a woman, are seated on two plastic chairs among the tombs. Tea and pistachios are on a small plastic table, and two young children are playing on the ground next to them. You turn to Jamal with a puzzled look. "Their son is buried here," he says. "They've come to have tea with him."

For reasons you can't fully articulate, this scene reminds you of the extraordinary atmosphere of the Umayyad Mosque in Damascus. At least, until your last visit in 2010... That peace, that calm and serenity, and reverence of the cemetery, and here are these people going about their daily business without seeming intimidated by the solemnity of the place... Something similar pervades the courtyard, and even the great prayer hall of the mosque in Damascus. As soon as you pass through the outer door, it's shocking. The beauty, the majesty, the absolute perfection of the place washes over you in an instant. That splendor and tranquility doesn't stop children from playing with a ball or on a scooter between the fountain of ablutions and the "treasury," the octagonal dome atop eight Corinthian columns. There are entire families seated on the ground sipping cool drinks, men taking a nap in the shade, children running across the rugs and beneath the chandeliers, women seated at the foot of columns holding court... The Umayyad Mosque... Like Tyre, for you it is the center of the world, a centuries-old place of tolerance and openness, a fantastic symbol of the coexistence of different religious communities in this part of the world. In fact, the mosque was constructed around the tomb of St. John the Baptist! Seriously. The mausoleum of the man who baptized Jesus sits at the center of the great prayer hall. The mosque was built on the site of the former Basilica of John the Baptist, which was itself constructed on the vestiges of the Roman Temple of Jupiter. The Basilica, small in stature, was destroyed after its purchase by the Muslim rulers around 664. When caliph al-Walid had the mosque constructed in 705, he ordered that the tomb be preserved. Of the temple and the church there remain certain walls, propylaea, towers used as minarets. The Roman columns in the prayer hall were made from the porticos on neighboring streets. The magnificent

In the heart of Damascus...

mosaics were created by Byzantine artisans hired by the Umayyads. They represent a sort of vast paradisiacal garden fashioned in the Byzantine style but adapted to the rules of Islam through their lack of human or animal portrayals. The faithful gather around the mausoleum that houses the head of John the Baptist, for Mar Yohanna al-Maamadan is a prophet in Islam. His head is not the only one in the mosque. There is also the head of Imam Husayn, brought back at the end of a spear after the Battle of Karbala. It's located in an oratory at the exit of the prayer hall, inside the wall itself. The remains of the prophet Jonah are supposedly there too, and as if there weren't already enough great historical feats and eminent figures united in one place, there is also the Minaret of Jesus! It's one of the mosque's three minarets where, according to an ancestral Muslim belief, Jesus will appear on the Day of Judgment.

275

In the middle of the mosque, the tomb of St. John the Baptist

Outside the mosque...
Saladin's mausoleum!

Jesus has a fundamental place in the Quran. He is described as "the breath," "the spirit, "the word" of God. A handsome and extraordinary man, he is able to perform miracles—while Muhammad does not. John the Baptist, Husayn, Jonah, Jesus... that's already plenty, but it's still not all. The man resting in a mausoleum on the parvis of the mosque, just in front of the entrance, is without doubt the most glorious Arab of all time: the superb Saladin! On his mausoleum, these words: "Lord, grant him his final conquest: paradise."

The mausoleum that houses the head of Imam Husayn...

St. John the Baptist as he is depicted in the Mar Nkoula church,
at the end of your street in Beirut

Making handicrafts with Nada

Nada

You ask Jamal: "And Nada, the daughter of Zaki and Fadia, do you know what happened to her?" "She was ten when she came with her father," Jamal says sadly. "She went mad, too. When they arrived in Shatila, he brought her to the city, to the home of a couple of Egyptians he knew. Then he died and she spent seven years there, without ever really regaining her sanity. The Egyptians died one after another three years ago. She returned to Shatila. She is gentle and calm. She takes care of the children after school, in the offices of a charity organization where she decorated the walls with photos of murdered children from Gaza and Lebanon when she started there. She says that she never wants to have children because she is too afraid of having to watch them die. She says that those photos are there so that she doesn't forget that. The organization's educators very quickly took them down, but every now and then she puts them up again. She does only a single craft with the children: making funeral wreaths for burials. She says that she doesn't know what else to do, that if she were a man, she would be a gravedigger..."

You ask him if Sami saw his sister when he came to the camp in 2013. And if Nada had gone back to see her mother in Odaisseh. "She went back there with Sami," Jamal says, "but, can you believe it? Fadia had died the day before, while she was hanging out her washing..."

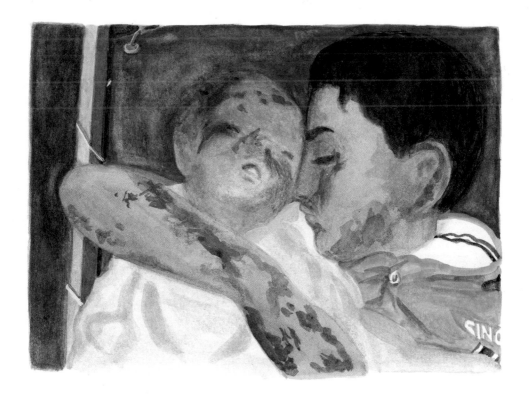

In Gaza...

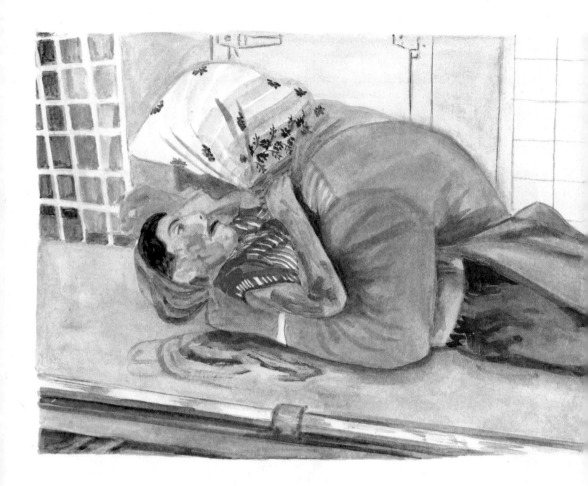

Gaza again...

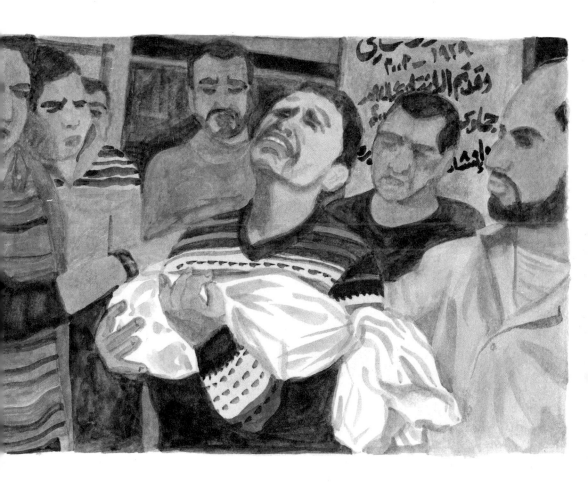

Still Gaza…

284

On the Beirut Corniche

On the Corniche

Leaving the camp, you are broken. You will go for a walk along the Corniche, the only place in Beirut that soothes you, the only place you can hope for a moment of fresh air after holding your breath all morning. You dream of a raging sea, of waves that lash the shore, crashing and splashing you... The Beirut Corniche is another center of the world for you. You walk from Manara toward the hotel district. The view of Mount Sannine comforts you. The sight of the old lighthouse amuses you... Beirut has reclaimed so much land from the sea that today it is far from the shore, surrounded by buildings! A bit farther on, the wonderful campus of the American University. It extends from the sea to the top of the hill, among the most ancient, magnificent buildings. Many Egyptian movies were filmed there in the 1960s, and countless revolutionary Arab movements were born there.

A monument in homage to Gamal Abdel Nasser on the Beirut Corniche, although this heroic man has been forgotten in his own country

Then there is the monument built in memory of Gamal Abdel Nasser. You stop to contemplate it, lost in thought... Nasser, right in the middle of the best part of the Beirut Corniche! In Cairo, there is not a single statue of Nasser. He's forgotten in Egypt, this heroic man...

Just after the giant silhouette of the Egyptian president surveying the corniche, there is the hotel district. Some, like the Vendôme, Palm Beach, and Phoenicia, have been restored. Most of the others have loomed as phantom-like carcasses since January 1976.

The Excelsior hotel has been a carcass since 1976

The Holiday Inn, the Excelsior, the Semiramis, the Pearl, and finally, the most mythic of all, the St. Georges. Right in front of the St. Georges was the Dantean explosion that took the life of Prime Minister Rafic Hariri. In Lebanon, you're never very far from one martyr or another... In this small country, the living and the martyrs coexist.

Obsessively pursuing your investigation, you decide to visit Hariri's tomb. Fittingly, it's located in what was once Martyrs' Square...

1,800 kg of explosives for Rafic Hariri... a Dantean scene...

...apocalyptic... the gates of hell were opened...

The temporary graves for Rafic Hariri and his companions...

Martyrs' Square, Beirut

Martyrs' Square, or rather what's left of it. During the reconstruction of Beirut, in the aftermath of the war, the most celebrated, most mythical, and symbolic location in Lebanon was not restored, but instead razed to the ground, wiped from the surface of the Earth in the most misguided decision imaginable. Today, it's an amorphous esplanade, half wasteland, half parking lot, comprising the ends of roads, tunnels, terraces, embankments, palisades, concrete slabs, essentially a kind of no man's land. The only surviving relics of the former site are the Cinema Opera and the adjoining building, and the martyrs' monument.

...when you photographed them in August 2005

Although the square is gone, the martyrs remain. It's the gravesite of Rafic Hariri and his seven companions who met their deaths at the same time in an attack attributed to the regime in Damascus, like the many others that will follow. A bit farther on is the headquarters of the newspaper *An-Nahar*. On its façade is a gigantic photo of Gebran Tueni, publisher and columnist of the paper, who was also assassinated not long after Hariri. At the foot of the building is a statue of Samir Kassir, eminent journalist and writer, determined columnist, also assassinated, while on the other side of the former square, the façade of the Kataeb Party headquarters depicts a photo of Pierre Gemayel, also assassinated. Yes, there is no shortage of martyrs here...

Two young women cry over the assassinated journalist,
"Martyr for the intifada and independenc"

Below: Samir Kassir's family in front of his coffin,
in the Greek Orthodox church on Nejmeh Square

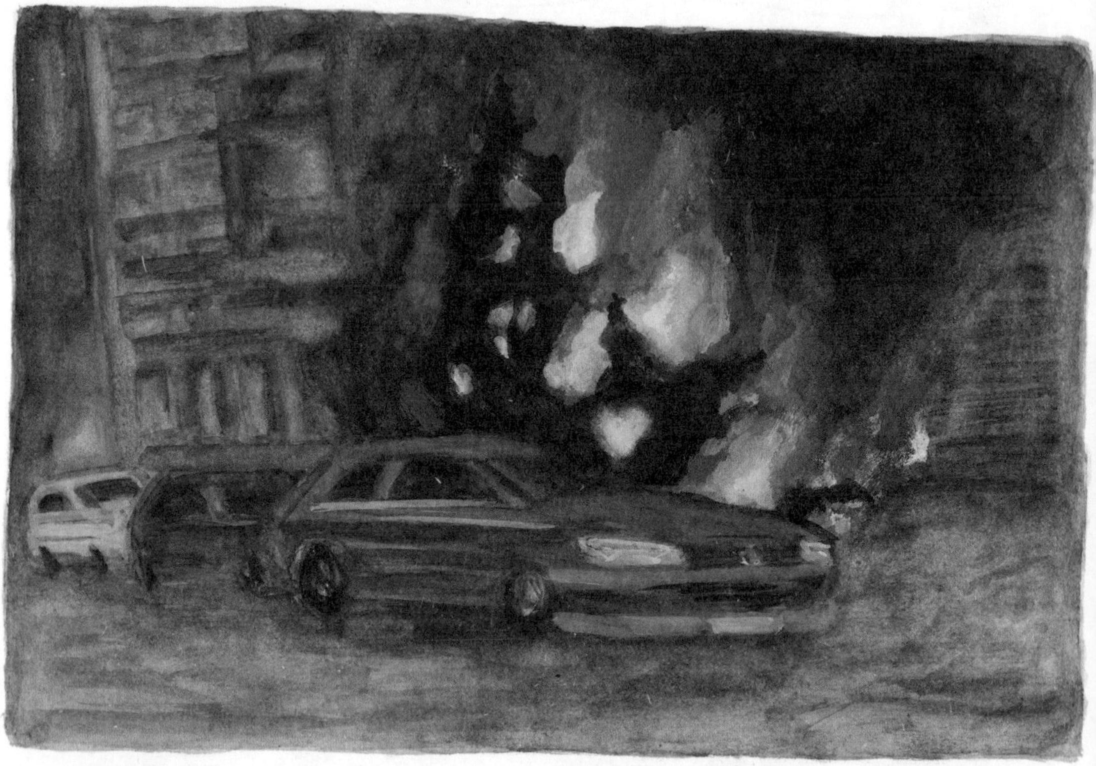

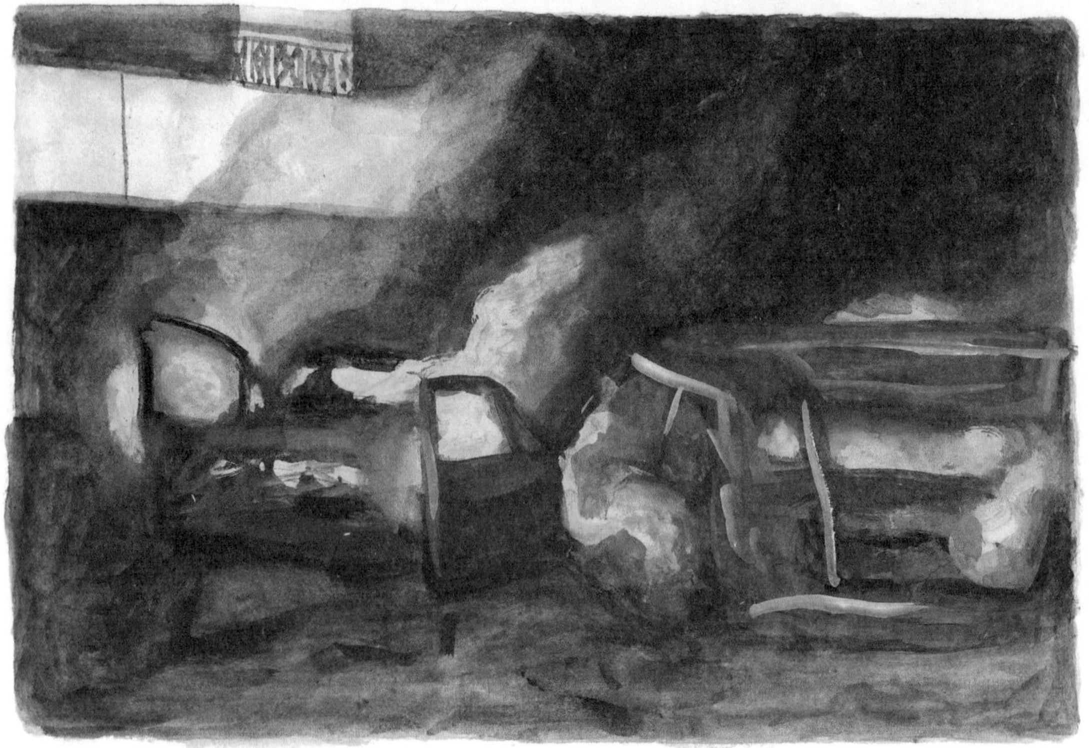

The general's two sons at his funeral...

Previous page, above: Wissam al-Hassan's car, reduced to carbonized sheet metal and still on fire, is thrown far from the site of the explosion and lands on a car parked several dozen meters away. Previous page, below: One of the many other attacks against an anti-Syrian deputy, in the heart of Beirut.

Hanged by the Ottomans...

The tragic nights that gave their name to the square unfurl in 1915 and 1916. The final hours of the Ottoman Empire will be cruelly felt in Lebanon, and the Borj serves as witness. Beirut is empty. The streets are deserted. Around the square especially, not a sound. A veil of mourning envelops the city. Silence, except for the sinister hammering of a gallows being erected. Then the passing of a horse-drawn carriage. Those condemned to death are being brought to the police barracks on one side of the square. There they are read the court-martial sentence, known in advance. The verdict is final, to be executed immediately. Accused of conspiring to separate their country from the Ottoman Empire in order to set up an Arab government, the condemned were put through a sham trial. They are given paper and asked to write down their last wishes. "Careful, no insulting Turkish honor, or we'll rip up your testaments and they'll never reach your families." They are handed large white blouses. They're brought a sheikh and a priest; the condemned are Christians and Muslims. They are made to walk to the scaffold. The night is dark but the hanging ropes are clearly visible. They die with courage and honor, before dawn. The first man with the noose around his neck doesn't wait for the executioners to do their work; he kicks the stool out from under him. This sinister scene will repeat itself three times in two years. There would be up to fourteen men hanged on the same night. Other Lebanese nationalists would also be hanged in Damascus, in Jerusalem, in Jaffa, in Aley, and elsewhere in the region.

شهداء
٦ ايّار ١٩١٦

The martyrs of May 6, 1916

Protests, Marches, Riots, and Demonstrations

Joseph, a journalist friend who has just left a meeting at *An-Nahar*, buys you a coffee on the ground floor of the newspaper's headquarters. Much older than you, he remembers the former square and tells you stories of its glory days. It was the beating heart of the city. Cafés, stores, offices, cinemas, cabarets, hotels, taxis, *bostas*, and all kinds of street peddlers… and, of course, protests, marches, riots, demonstrations… It was where you gauged the opinion of the street, the anger of the people. Beirut is known for being the city in the Arab world where it is easiest to express an opinion, no matter what that opinion might be. Revolutionaries, activists, and intellectuals of all stripes have flocked here from all over the Middle East. Silenced or incarcerated in their own countries, they thrive in Lebanon. Not to mention the important dissenters born here. The Borj was the setting of a countless number of marches for various reasons. In the second half of the twentieth century, hostility to America was a recurrent theme, with a special place reserved for Henry Kissinger.

In 1965, on the occasion of President Bourguiba's official visit to Lebanon, his portrait is plastered all over the city's streets, proud to welcome such a distinguished hero of decolonization. But Bourguiba had made statements in favor of the division of Palestine just a few days prior, on a trip to Jericho. In Lebanon, this kind of poor judgment is not tolerated. His photos are ripped down from Martyrs' Square in anger.

Bourguiba's portraits are torn down in anger.

Joseph likes to say that Beirut is a whore with a heart of gold.
Some more of his favorite phrases: "À Beyrouth, chaque idée habite
une maison." and "Beyrouth est en Orient le dernier sanctuaire
où l'homme peut toujours s'habiller de lumière."
Lines taken from a beautiful poem by Nadia Tueni

In 1971, Americans protest the visit of their Secretary of State

1971, in Martyrs' Square, Armenians commemorate the genocide of their community

"The Armenian people express their gratitude to the Lebanese people for their welcome"
"We pay homage to the Armenian and Arab martyrs who were victims of Turkish imperialism"

Protest against the visit of the Sixth Fleet in Beirut in 1968

Protest in support of the fedayeen and against the policies of King Hussein in 1972,
"Yes to the Palestinian cause, no to Hussein's plans"

One of many protests condemning the assassination of the three Palestinian leaders,
Kamal Edwane, Kamal Nasser, and Abu Youssef, in 1973.
On a banner: "America, enemy of the people"

Protest against the disappearance of Imam Musa al–Sadr in Libya

Anwar Sadat and the Odious Agreement

The Egyptian president Anwar Sadat will pay with his life for his policies on Israel. It isn't enough for him to say that he supports a two-state solution in Palestine, or to have introduced Sharia law into the constitution only a year after Nasser's death, and to have supported the return of the Islamists. Sadat went to Tel Aviv and Jerusalem in 1977 while the West Bank, Gaza, Golan, and Jerusalem were still occupied. Live on the air, a correspondent for a big French radio station compared the moment when Sadat set foot on the ground in Tel Aviv to the moment when Armstrong first stepped on the moon. The Egyptian Minister of Foreign Affairs had resigned two days earlier, followed an hour later by his replacement. In all the Arab capitals, hostile protests take place in front of the Egyptian embassies. In Beirut, loudspeakers broadcast Nasser's speeches. Syria decrees a twenty-four-hour mourning period. Sadat gives a speech in front of the Knesset and says a prayer in Al-Aqsa in the shadows of Israeli bayonets! He jokes around with Moshe Dayan, he pats Sharon on the back, even kisses the hand of Golda Meir! There's a photo of him with Begin, the two of them laughing with their heads thrown back. Some 120 million Arabs watch their television screens, flabbergasted. Indignation, rage, despondency, sadness. These are the first four words of an article in a major Lebanese daily newspaper. "It was a slap in the face to millions of Arabs," says Joseph, who vividly remembers the fever-pitch of Beirut during those years. "He destroyed Nasser's honor, cheapened his memory. But worst of all, worst of all, he sold off the fate of the Palestinian and Lebanese people. No, not sold. Gave, offered, here, take this gift. Thrown to the wolves. Less than five months later, Israel invades South Lebanon for the first time. That doesn't stop Sadat from going to Camp David after his trip to Jerusalem. He signs the peace treaties. He concedes everything without receiving anything in return. Now that they are rid of their most powerful enemy in the South, the Israelis are able to concentrate on the North. They invade Lebanon, subject Beirut to a three-month siege and a terrifying bombing. By air, land, and sea, thousands of tons of bombs... relentless. No one knows what 'tons of bombs' really means unless they've been under that much fire," Joseph says emotionally. "The horror... sometimes for more than fifteen hours straight. With no supplies, no water, no electricity, no medication. Then the Israelis invade Beirut once the city is already on death's door. Then comes the massacre of the camps. Yes, they certainly deserve their Nobel Peace Prize, Sadat and especially Begin... In fact, Begin aptly dubbed that war 'Peace in Galilee.' Sadat didn't live to see it. He was already dead, assassinated. I remember watching his funeral on television," Joseph continues. "Three former American presidents were there, Nixon, Ford, and Carter. Unprecedented. But not a single Arab or Muslim leader attended. Nor did the Egyptian people. Sometimes, what you see on the television makes you sick."

Sadat—adored by the West despite his dictatorial and extremely repressive regime, reviled by the Arab people—a few minutes before his death...

The South at war
An Israeli invasion surrounds Tyre, Saida, and Nabatieh

The fifth day of air offensives, and attacks by sea at dawn

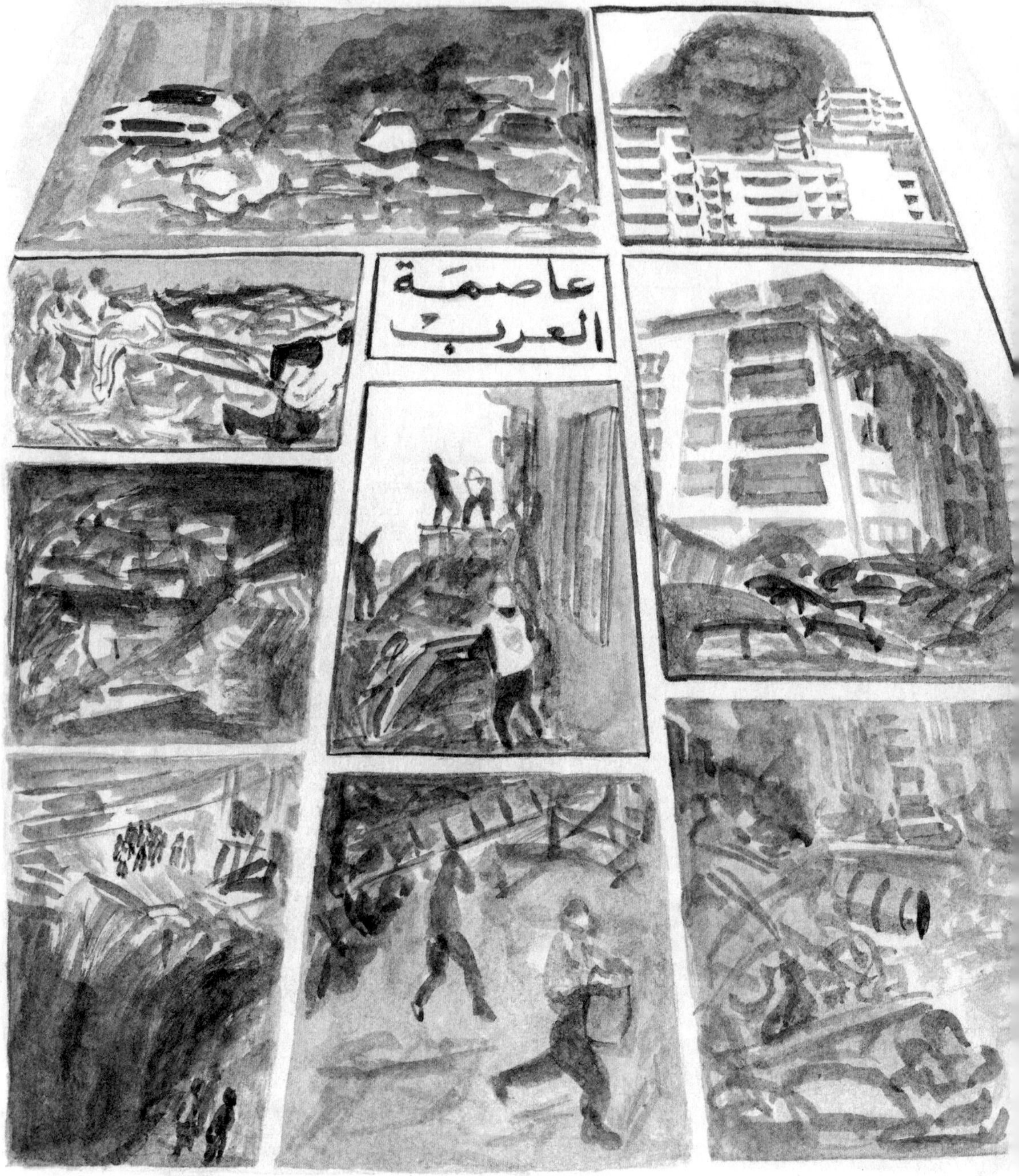
عاصمة
العرب

Capital of the Arabs ...

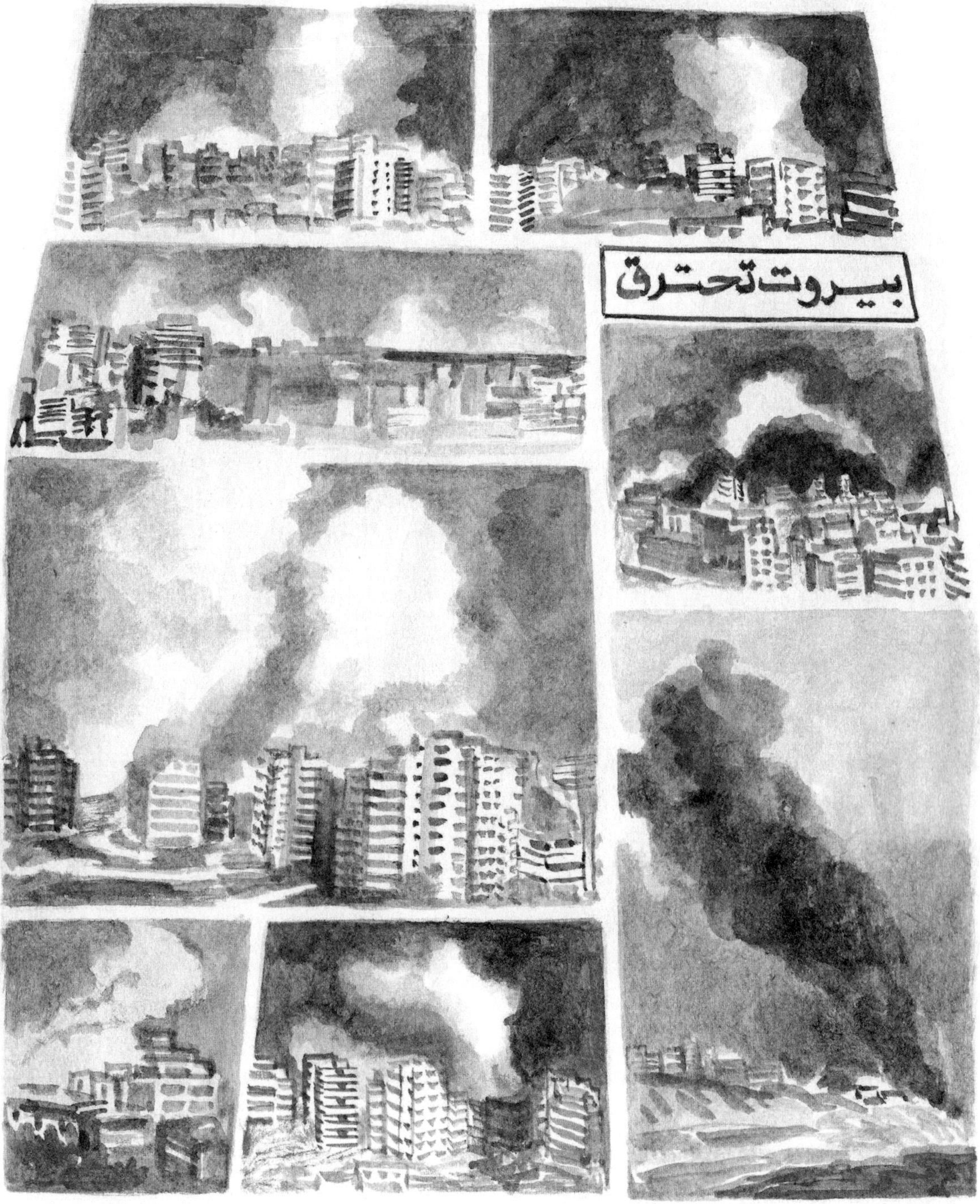
بيروت تحترق

Beirut burns...

King Abdullah, Man of the British

Thirty years earlier, another Arab leader is assassinated, in Jerusalem, on the steps of Al-Aqsa. King Abdullah of Jordan is the second son of the Grand Sharif of Mecca and King of Hejaz, Hussein bin Ali. He belongs to a prestigious family of Hashemites, descendants of the Prophet. Born in Mecca, he succeeds to the throne of Jordan by starting out as emir of Transjordan, a title given to him by the British, while they give the Iraqi throne to his brother Faisal, exiled by the French from Syria after the Hashemites led an Arab revolt against the Ottomans in 1916 alongside the British and Major T.E. Lawrence. Churchill, then Secretary of State for the Colonies, tasks Abdullah with overseeing the Emirate of Transjordan, henceforth under British mandate, for 5,000 pounds sterling per month. The British forces ensure that he remains at the head of the Emirate, but his actual power is extremely limited; the key posts of the country are controlled by the English. Abdullah has always nursed the hope of uniting Greater Syria, grouping Transjordan, Syria, Lebanon, and Palestine under the same government. But Syria, Lebanon, and Palestine are opposed to it. He sees the conflict between Zionists and Arabs in the region as a good opportunity to absorb the Arab part of Palestine into his kingdom. Spurred on by his expansionist ambitions, he nurtures secret relationships with Zionists in the hope of a territorial agreement, which unleashes the anger of Arab leaders and the people. After the 1948 Palestine war, Transjordan takes control of the West Bank and East Jerusalem, thus becoming Jordan. On July 20, 1951, King Abdullah goes to the Al-Aqsa Mosque in Jerusalem to pray. He is assassinated by a twenty-one-year-old Palestinian nationalist in front of the mosque entrance, and his grandson Hussein, who accompanied him, is wounded.

Upon his death, his son Talal ascends to the throne. He is deposed by Parliament a year later due to his fragile mental health. They say that he suffers from schizophrenia. His son Hussein inherits the throne at only sixteen years old.

King Abdullah I of Jordan unleashed the anger of the Arab people

King Hussein, America's Man

Throughout Hussein's fifty-year reign, and to this day, the Hashemite Kingdom of Jordan clings to power in the tormented region only because of the unfailing support of the British, and then of the Americans, who see the country as a shield for Israel. This has resulted in a number of assassination attempts on the "little king," which he has always come out of unscathed. But Hussein doesn't just have luck, the aid of the West, and an authoritarian regime. He also has a certain political talent, a subtle flair for making good decisions and managing to balance the resolutely pro-Western stances of his government and the pan-Arab position of his population. Among these "fortunate" decisions, there is one that would save his throne *in extremis* in September 1970, and it is a massacre—the massive bombardment of the Palestinian refugee camps in Jordan, which in the span of ten days would leave between 4,000 and 10,000 dead and 100,000 wounded. It's Black September.

King Hussein of Jordan, responsible for Black September

The Tragic End of the Last King of Iraq

His cousin, the king of Iraq, does not have the same luck. Grandson of Faisal, the first king of Iraq, and son of Ghazi, the king of Iraq who is killed in a suspicious car accident, the little prince Faisal ascends to the throne at three years old and will become, at twenty-three, the last king of Iraq, brutally murdered in an unbelievable slaughter. Upon his ascent to the throne, his uncle Abd al-llah is appointed regent and he adopts a policy of total submission to the British. Abd al-llah is a big Anglophile. He appreciates the intellectual and sophisticated friends he has made in London. His fleet of Rolls Royces is looked after by British mechanics. The palaces of the court are furnished in the British style, with dusty pink chintz lampshades and Victorian wallpaper, and a royal hunt is established. The hunting dogs, brought from England, are fed the rations of the Iraqi army rather than the vile leftovers typically given to dogs in Arab countries. The regent, thin and elegant, looks like he is from an ad for Savile Row, in his jodhpurs and jersey polo shirt under his riding jacket. This fashionable display amid the plains of Mesopotamia might help to explain his growing unpopularity. It reaches its apex with the signing of the Baghdad Pact.

King Faisal, who would serve as the model for the insufferable little prince Abdullah in Tintin, is a charming child, asthmatic and melancholic, unlike the character that he inspired. Raised in Baghdad by an English governess, he attends school in the UK: his primary education at Sandroyd, and then his secondary education at Harrow. Even after he reaches adulthood, he leaves the power in the hands of Abd al-llah and does not contest the Baghdad Pact, which is considered appalling by Arab nationalists throughout the entire Middle East. Discontent grows, and the attack on Egypt by Great Britain and France, after Nasser's extraordinary defiance of the West with the nationalization of the Suez Canal, heightens the people's revulsion for the Baghdad Pact and the government. The situation is almost the same in Jordan. The two cousins, Hussein and Faisal, who are very close because they went to school together in England, decide to unite against the nationalist wave that has been surging through the Arab world since the Suez Crisis. They found the Arab Federation of Iraq and Jordan, which would last for just five months. On July 14, 1958, the palace of the Iraqi royal family is stormed by a group of soldiers. The insurgents order the king, the regent

Abd al-llah, his wife Princess Hiyam, his mother Princess Nafisa, Princess Abdiya, other members of the family, and the servants to line up against a wall, and they gun them down in a few rounds. Abd al-llah's body is then mutilated, dragged through the streets of the city, and suspended over the door of the Ministry of Defense, where the mob burns what is left of it.

Little King Faisal and his uncle the regent Abd al-llah

The photograph of King Faisal that inspired Hergé to create the character of little prince Abdullah in Tintin: Land of Black Gold

Faisal as a melancholic teenager at his desk

A very young king

Regent Abd al-llah, thin, elegant and under the control of the British

King Faisal of Iraq and King Hussein of Jordan

The two cousins are both twenty-three when Faisal is assassinated

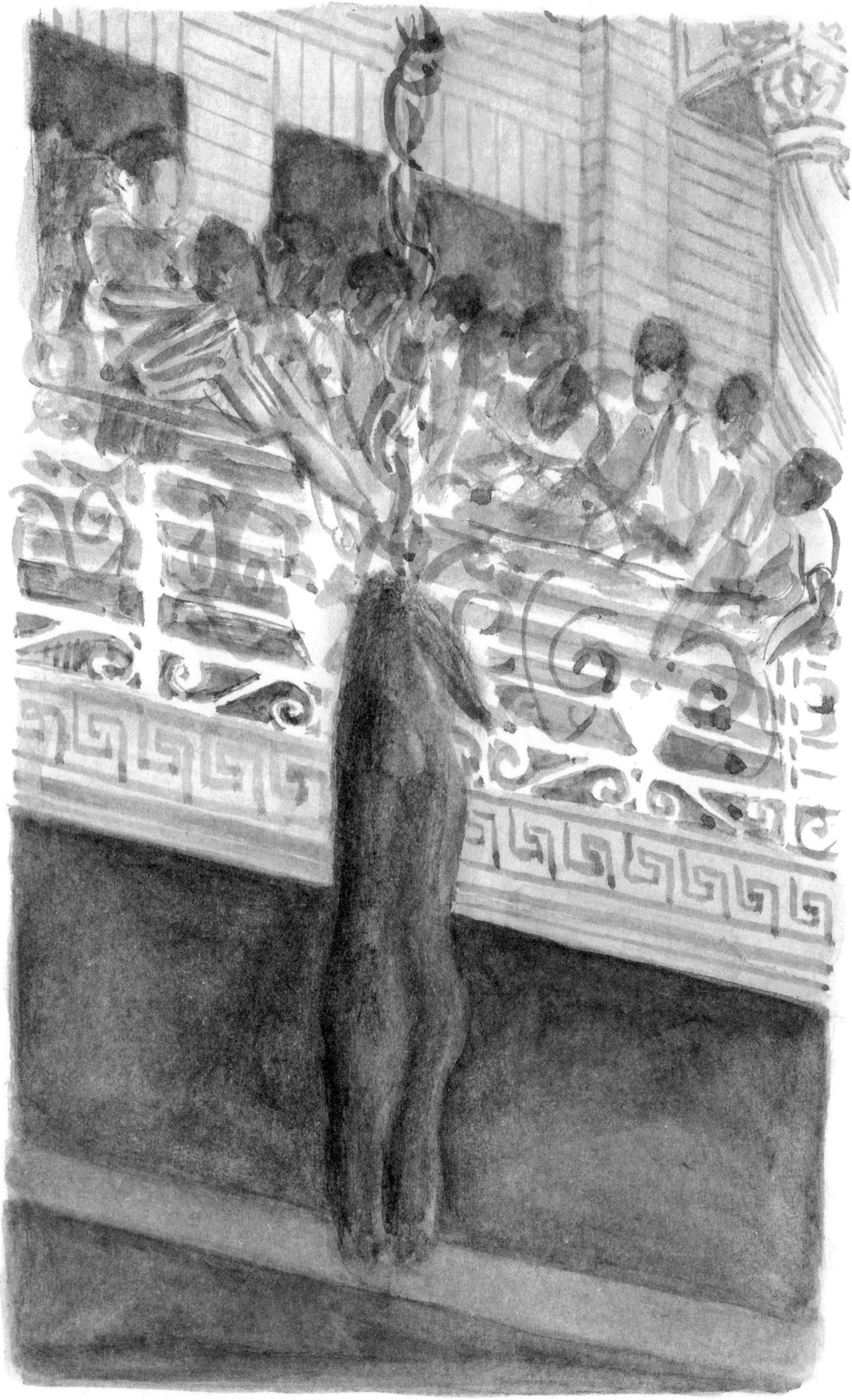

The mutilated corpse of regent Abd al-Ilah, suspended above the entrance
to the Ministry of Defense, where the crowd burns what is left of it
The body of Nuri al-Said, the despised prime minister, mutilated and burned,
dragged through the streets of the city

The king and the regent in the British atmosphere of the royal residence in Baghdad

The young king upon his ascension to the throne

King Farouk

The end of King Farouk, the last king of Egypt and the Sudan, is less violent, far from it. Not a single drop of blood would be spilled during the July Revolution. When the Free Officers seize power in Cairo and Alexandria, Gamal Abdel Nasser demands that they do not touch a hair on the head of the ousted monarch and let him board his yacht to sail to Europe, to the disappointment of many of his companions, who would have preferred that the king be executed. The fabulous yacht, the famous *Mahrousa*, the first boat to cross the Suez Canal at its inauguration, would return to Egypt after dropping the king in Capri. While in exile, Farouk continues living the way he always has—from casinos to high-end restaurants, from nightclubs to palaces. He will die at forty-seven years of age, weighing over 120 kg, in the company of a twenty-two-year-old Italian singer, after a gargantuan meal at the Ile de France restaurant in Rome.

The king's body, wrapped in a brown wool abaya

When History Cries

The king of Saudi Arabia, Faisal bin Abdul-Aziz Al Saud, is assassinated in 1975 by a young nephew back from the United States, for reasons that are still unknown to this day. Upon Nasser's death, Faisal takes over as Arab leader in place of his fiercest rival. He is also an authentic champion of the Palestinian cause and tries to use his influence with the Americans on that front. To halt the increasing assistance given to Israel by the United States under Kissinger, he uses oil as a weapon, causing the first oil shock during the October War in 1973. One year later, he is on the verge of securing a firmer position on Israel from Nixon when the Watergate scandal forces the American president to resign. Nixon's successor, Gerald Ford, is quick to officially recognize Jerusalem as the capital of Israel. This unilateral decision, which flouts the UN resolutions, elicits the anger of King Faisal. In August 1974, he decides to reduce oil production once more and withdraw the Saudi gold reserves stored in the USA. A few months later, he is assassinated. His successor, his brother Khalid, does not express any interest for the Palestinian cause during his reign, does not attempt the slightest intervention during the war that ravages Lebanon from the year he ascends to the throne, will be incapable of preventing Sadat from signing a separate peace agreement with Israel—which Faisal had managed to do—and aligns himself completely with the United States.

Faisal bin Abdul–Aziz Al Saud, the only Saudi Arabian king to be worshiped in the Middle East. "When history cries," reads a newspaper headline upon his death

The Elegant Portraits of His Majesty Hassan II

In the series of Arab monarchs of authoritarian pro-Western regimes, we now turn to Hassan II, King of Morocco. But Hassan II benefits from the indulgence of the Middle East. Because of his geographical distance from the center of the conflict, he is held less accountable for his ambiguous stance regarding the Palestinian cause. After all, Morocco is much closer geographically to the Champs-Élysées than to Al-Aqsa. The king speaks better French than Arabic, an elegant, sophisticated, scathing French. His repartee delights even those who do not support his policies or his dictatorial regime. It's worth noting that Hassan II has escaped more than one attack on his life, so it is only natural that he would be so ruthless! His position on Israel is well known. During a summit of the Arab League in Rabat, he secretly authorizes Israel's presence. Later, it will come out that the League meetings were recorded, and that Ben Barka was apparently murdered by Mossad in exchange for the tapes… True or false, Hassan II is untouchable.

You lived in Casablanca not long after the king's death. His portrait was still displayed in every boutique, every café, every office. You were fascinated by these photos of His Majesty; he was always depicted so elegantly, and was so excessive in his clothing choices. These portraits were all the more alluring because they were always in keeping with the place in which they were displayed. In a patisserie, the king would be eating a cake, in a café, the king would be drinking a cup of tea, at a fishmonger's, the king would be on his yacht, at a mechanic's, the king would be leaning on his beautiful Mercedes! You managed to find the official photographer of the king, the same one who provided the country with these magnificent icons, which were gradually replaced by the far less captivating portraits of Mohamed VI. You bought several photos from him, including one that he made you swear never to show anyone. You won't break that promise with this book.

One of the most popular portraits of Hassan II, once found in cafés, tea rooms, patisseries, and orange juice stalls

In Martyrs' Square, overgrown with vegetation, not long before the end of the war

Georges Semerdjian, the martyr-photographer

At the opposite end of the spectrum from the Moroccan king's photographer is a photographer who was also a martyr. Georges Semerdjian photographed the glory days of Martyrs' Square and of the rest of Lebanon: the frivolity, the heady pleasures, the high life. At the beginning of the Civil War in 1975, he became the primary witness of the great tragedy. His snapshots are among the most famous, the most emblematic, and the most enduring of those dark years. He photographed fifteen years of conflict from within the battles, massacres, and horrors, from as close as possible. He died in the last year of the war, while aiming his camera at the canon of a tank advancing menacingly...

A few of his famous photos: a female Christian combatant, a militiaman playing the piano

He photographed the era when it was easier to reach paradise than the end of the street

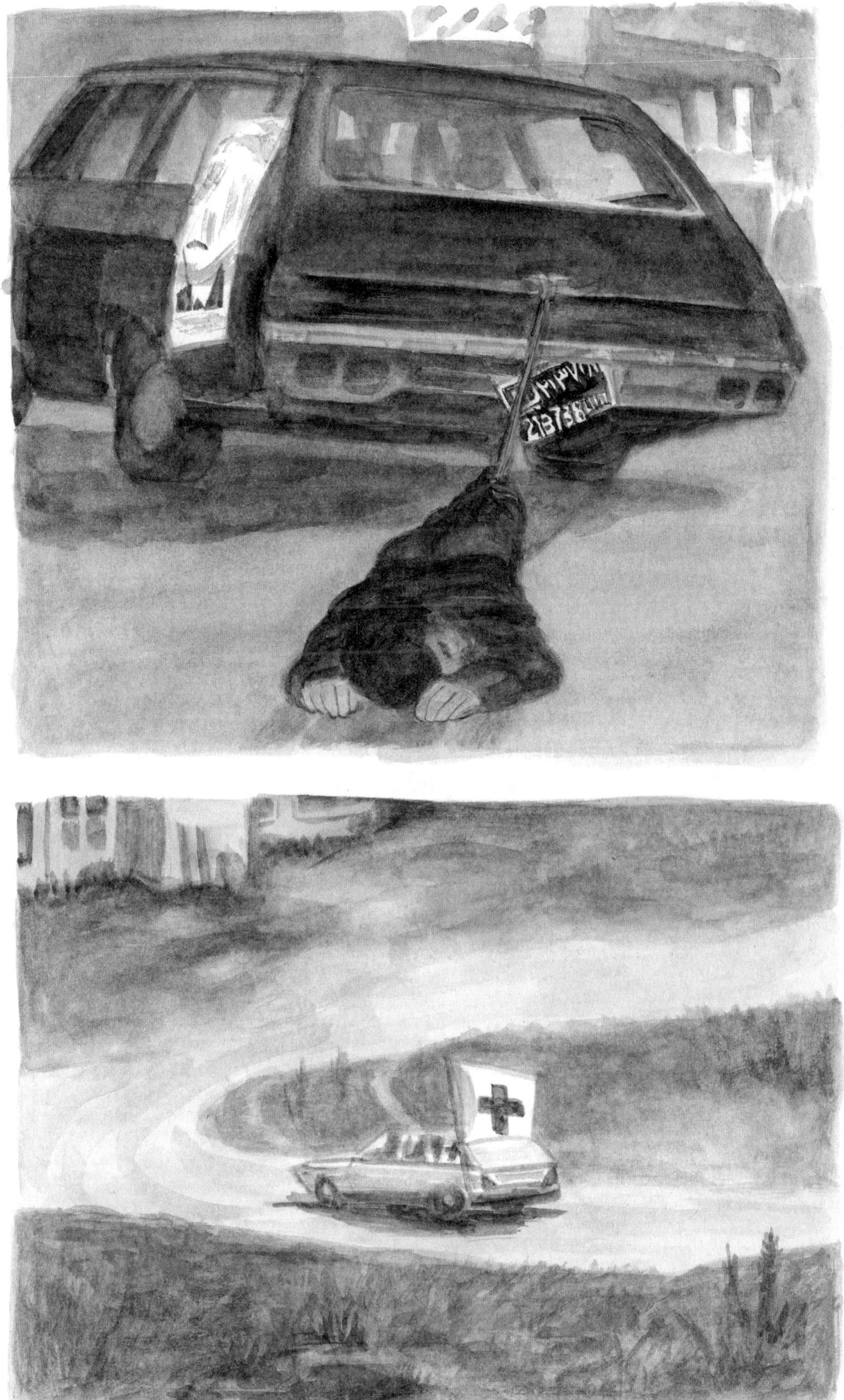

A famous photograph: a coffin containing a corpse, meant to be transported by foot from East Beirut to West Beirut, where it would be buried, instead abandoned on the side of the road by its carriers when a bombing began

A photo of the corpse of Kamal Jumblatt, assassinated alongside his chauffeur and bodyguard
This is the first of a long series of assassinations that will include presidents, ministers, deputies,
journalists...

The Murdered Mufti

And then, one day in May 1989, Sheikh Hassan Khaled, the Grand Mufti of Lebanon, is assassinated. The country is in shock. That upstanding, honest, selfless, moderate, and tolerant man has worked from the beginning of the war to achieve reconciliation among the Lebanese communities, national harmony, and an easing of tensions.

At a certain point, Sheikh Hassan Khaled is no longer content merely to refuse Syrian demands but decides to go against the Damascus regime with determination. The Syrians use every means available to put pressure on him. West Beirut is bombed, the mufti's residence is impacted. He is closely surveilled by Syrian agents who have infiltrated his entourage. Syrian intimidation continues in the form of an official invitation from Hafez al-Assad to come to Damascus to participate in the last iftar of Ramadan. The mufti declines the invitation, and gives the Syrian colonel who brought it to him shrapnel from the bomb that damaged his home, asking him to return it to Assad. For the Syrians, this is a step too far. A sizable load of explosives pulverizes his armored car, killing twenty-one other people and seriously wounding more than a hundred. The sight of the scene of the crime is among the most apocalyptic that Beirut has ever seen. It's like the gates of hell have been opened. The horror is beyond measure.

The bells of West Beirut sound the death knell on the day of the funeral. The shops, offices, and civil services in East Beirut, the Christian neighborhood, close to join in mourning with the Sunni community. The Christian region has been subjected to a ruthless Syrian blockade for two months under a deluge of bombings. It is completely impossible for its political and religious leaders to get to West Beirut to attend the funeral. The Maronite patriarch then takes an absolutely unprecedented initiative: condolences in homage to the mufti will be received at the patriarchal seat.

In West Beirut, the funeral takes place in a heated environment of uproar and fury. Sirens, gunshots, shouting, an enraged crowd, a violent clamor, a frightening tumult. After the official honors, the coffin is carried through a chaotic crowd amid screams, jostling, and the roar of gunfire in several neighborhoods of the city. Beirut has had enough, Beirut explodes. Beirut, the capital of grief for too long. The mufti's turban is brandished above the crowd. His eldest son, in tears, standing on the roof of a car surrounded by his brothers, presents it to the howling crowd.

The Grand Mufti of Lebanon, Sheikh Hassan Khaled, a martyr

The detonation rattles Beirut
Shock consumes the country when the identity of the victim is revealed

An upstanding, honest, selfless, moderate, and tolerant man

In the living room of his home in Aramoun, he was host to the most influential figures of Lebanon

The mufti preaching

His turban is brandished by his sobbing sons over the frenzied crowd, full of rage and grief

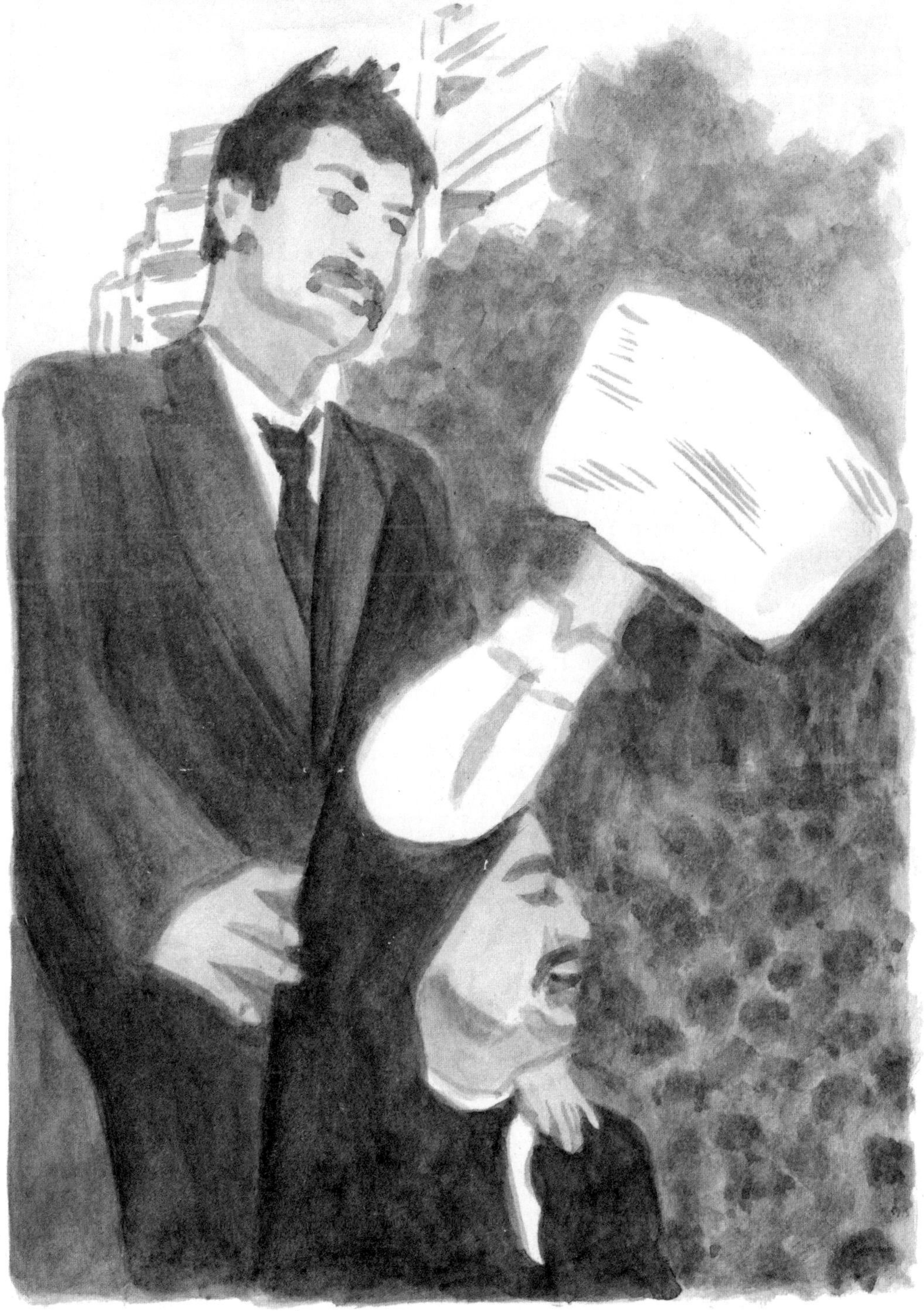

The vanished imam and the murdered mufti

Musa al–Sadr's smile and gaze contributed to his legendary status

The Vanished Imam

Eleven years earlier, another religious man was eliminated from the Lebanese political scene. The time has come to talk about Imam Musa al-Sadr. A living legend, his sudden and silent disappearance, shrouded in the darkest mystery, turned him into an eternal mythic figure. Musa al-Sadr vanished into thin air in August 1978 during an official trip to Libya to meet Gaddafi, and to this day no one knows what happened to him. His worshipers, and there are many of them, still await his return, seeing him as the incarnation of the Twelfth Imam, the one they call the Occulted Imam, or the Mahdi, who is supposed to reappear among men at the end of time. If such fantasies have arisen since his absence, it's because, while he was alive, Sayyed Musa was a god, the god of the "dispossessed."

His charisma was captivating

Born in Qom, Iran, Musa al-Sadr is the son of an important ayatollah from an illustrious political family of Shii ulema originally from Lebanon. From Tyre, to be precise. In Tehran he complements his theological studies in Islamic jurisprudence with academic studies in law and economics at the university, something completely unprecedented for a religious figure. He graduates top of his class and returns to Qom, where he studies Islamic philosophy before returning to Najaf to complete the most important level of Shii religious teaching, which will allow him to interpret a sacred text (*ijtihad*). He is distinguished by his dazzling intelligence, his extraordinary intellectual capacities, his curiosity, his modernity, and his great open-mindedness, as well as his tall stature and good looks, which earn him the admiration of his teachers and fellow students. In 1959, convinced that the moment has come to bring his studies to a close and live among men, he decides to move to Tyre, answering the call of his relative, Imam Sharafeddine, who wants to make him his successor. Determined to work for the betterment of the Shii community, the largest but most destitute and disadvantaged group in Lebanon, he goes about it in a very different way from previous religious leaders, both Christian and Muslim.

Venerated by everyone from the most humble to the most prestigious

Rather than waiting for men to come to him, he goes out to meet them. He preaches in markets, in stadiums, and in universities, since the youth are not going to mosques at the time. He opens schools, free clinics, clubs, associations, workshops. The results are rapid and positive. His rise is spectacular. The imam captivates people with his charisma. A man of action and a reformer, he earns respect through his moderation, his tact, his desire for social justice and dialogue. The entirety of the country's political class, supporters and adversaries alike, recognize his qualities.

He founds the Supreme Islamic Shia Council to offer his community the political weight that it has been deprived of within the government, and to fight for more civil rights. He then creates the "Movement of the Dispossessed" (Amal), whose mission is to rectify the underdevelopment impacting the inhabitants of the South. He insists that the movement be composed of 50 percent Christians. He holds large meetings where it is difficult to know what faith he belongs to when he preaches.

His face, marked by great kindness, betrayed a certain melancholy

He seemed to come out of nowhere

Working closely with the most impoverished, he aims to restore their confidence in themselves. The love that they have for him increases, along with his legendary status. Literary salons and intellectual, political, and journalistic circles fight over him—he is everywhere. According to the journalist and politician Ghassan Tueni: "His in-person meetings were a ritual of seduction... When he humbly opened the door of a modest office or an ordinary living room in a house he was staying in, you would ask yourself what that man was doing there and how was it possible that such a mythical person could seem so familiar to you. Then, like a Persian miniature, you sat at his feet to understand the master's teachings before leaving with more questions than you had when you arrived."

While still fighting for Muslim–Christian reconciliation, in January 1975 the imam announces the creation of the Amal militia to defend the Shii population of the South, which has been a victim of not only Israeli but also Palestinian violence.

The Final Voyage

In February 1975, he inaugurates the Lent sermons in Saint Louis church in Beirut, in front of a crowd of Christians and Muslims. An unprecedented symbolic gesture that will not be enough to prevent the war, which begins just two months later. The imam refuses to take part in it, mediating between the sides and going on a hunger strike to stop the canons. He advocates for contemplation, convinced that the use of weapons does not resolve conflict but merely aggravates it. Every community sends delegations to support him. Former presidents, intellectuals, businessmen, bishops, sheikhs, women... Everywhere in the country people join him in his fast. But it's too late, the machine is already in motion. The country is handed over to bloodthirsty hounds led by warlords. The imam is not one of them and will be the only great leader of a militia not to enter the game. He orders his supporters never to open fire on anyone and not to use their weapons except in self-defense. Difficult instructions to accept, but he is obeyed—until the day when, in the Bekaa, Shii villages threaten to attack the few surrounding Christian villages. The imam hurries to the scene, where he gives his famous televised call: "...I tell you that any shot fired at Deir al-Ahmar, or Qaa, or Sharifa[17] is a shot fired at my house, at my heart, and at my children. And that each person who tries to calm the escalation and put out fires helps to keep those fires away from me, my house, my mihrab and my minbar. I am telling you the truth, with no exaggeration."

---

17   Deir al-Ahmar, Qaa, and Sharifa are Christian villages.

During the Lent sermon, in the Saint Louis church.
Previous page: During his hunger strike, at the mosque

His turban, always knotted with a hint of negligence.
Melancholy...

His eloquence is also evident when he expresses his hostility for the Palestinian stranglehold on Lebanese affairs. Directly addressing Arafat, who is seated opposite him during one of his speeches, he says: "You fear your enemies and you are right to do so. But know that it is not your weapons that will protect you from them, but my abaya," accompanying these words with a great theatrical gesture in which he opens the abaya he is wearing on his shoulders as if providing shelter.[18]

After the Israeli invasion of South Lebanon in 1978, at the peak of his popularity, he makes a series of official visits to several Arab countries to call for an urgent summit. Syria, Jordan, Saudi Arabia, Algeria... He will never return from Libya. Accompanied by two close collaborators, the young Sheikh Muhammad Yacoub and the journalist Abbas Badreddine, Musa al-Sadr will be seen for the last time, along with his companions, on August 31, 1978. Lebanon, in a daze, has lost its conscience.

---

18   An abaya is a long, open, loose-fitting outer garment.

Yasser Arafat and Muammar Gaddafi...

On whose behalf did Gaddafi kill the imam? Numerous theories have been formulated. One is that the friendship between Gaddafi and Arafat, and Arafat's hostility toward the imam who impeded his dealings in Lebanon, was involved in Musa al-Sadr's monstrous disappearance.

The little girl in her father's arms

The Immolated Child

Since the end of the 1970s, there have been so many car bomb explosions in Lebanon that every Lebanese person, or at least everyone in Beirut, can say that one day they passed by a place five minutes before a deadly explosion occurred. For you, it was on February 23, 1980. You are twelve years old and coming back from school. The school bus drops you at the corner of your street and Talaat al-Akkawi. With your school bag on your back, you walk to your building, the second one on the street after a villa on the corner. You go upstairs; you live on the second floor. Just as you enter the apartment, a terrifying explosion shakes the earth and sky. The glass shatters and the windows come off their hinges. At the end of the street, all hell breaks loose.

The explosion took place at the exact spot where the bus dropped you off, on Talaat al-Akkawi, between the Ministry of Foreign Affairs and Villa Asmahan. Bashir Gemayel was the target, and his convoy had just driven by. But he is safe and sound, he was not in the Mercedes that has been reduced to crumpled smoking sheet metal. It's his daughter Maya, one-and-a-half year old, who was inside. Gemayel's chauffeur and bodyguards were bringing her to spend the afternoon at her grandmother's house.

Bashir, his wife Solange, and their first child, Maya

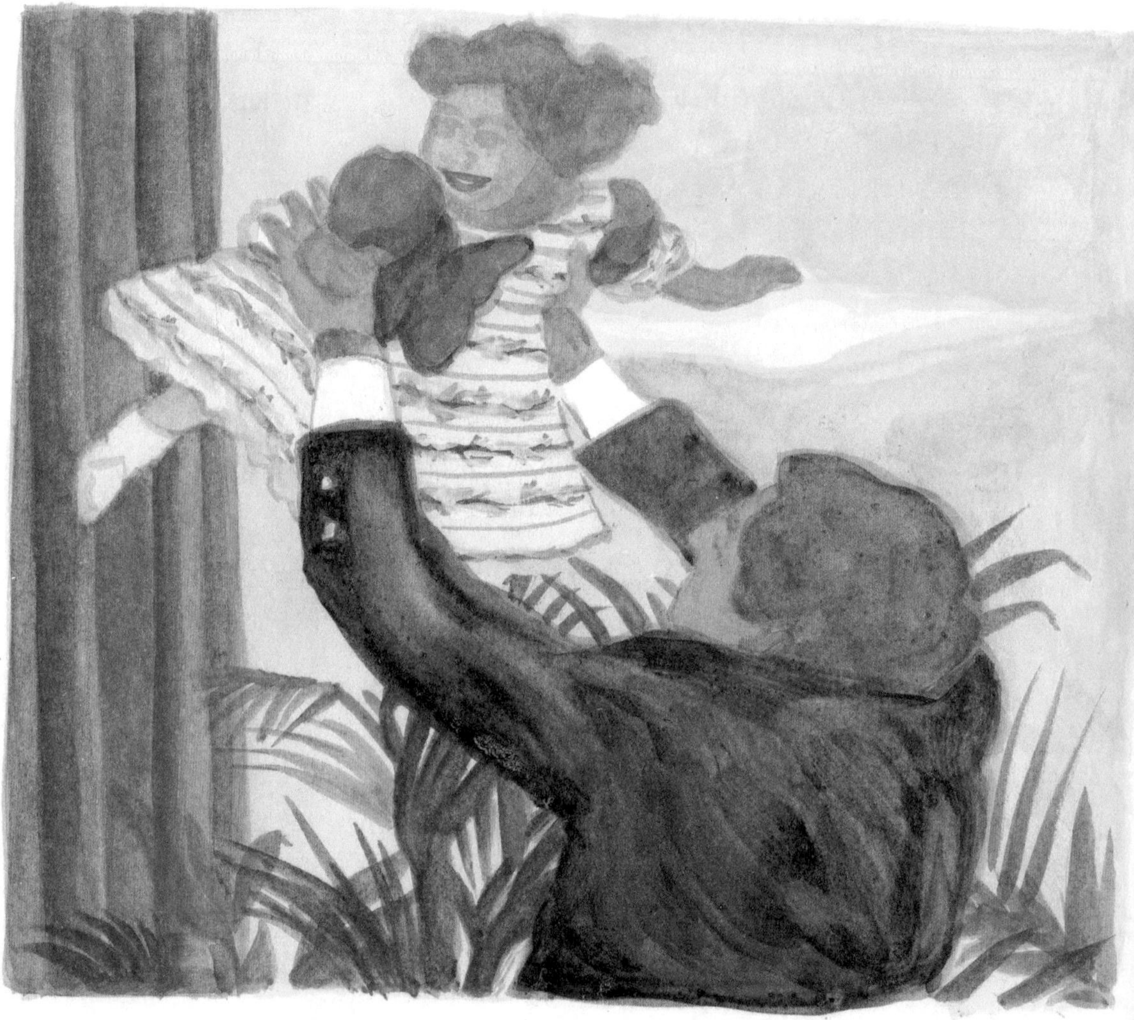

Times of joy…

The times of the militia...

*But this time will pass, and then there will be the time of the presidency,
the time of martyrdom...*

The Feast of the Cross

It's the day of the Feast of the Cross. Bashir Gemayel is a young man.
He was elected president of the Lebanese Republic twenty-three days prior
but has not yet taken office. For many, he is a mere clan leader, one of the
warlords with the dirtiest hands, the instigator of a number of merciless
massacres. However, since his election—which was only possible thanks to
the invasion of Lebanon by the Israeli army which by that time had reached
Beirut—the young man has changed. He is no longer the same. The sectarian,
partisan, intolerant man has become the leader of all the Lebanese people,
all faiths combined. He wants to dissolve the individual militias and create
a strong national army, he wants the retreat of all foreign armies from the
country, not only the Syrians but also the Israelis. This is what he declares to
the microphones and cameras of the entire world, which have been focused
on him since the election. Now in the supreme leadership position, he
seems to want to abandon the dubious means that have put him there, and
instead, to everyone's surprise, take on the new role of a determined unifier.
Allegedly, he who has received Israel's support to become the champion of
the partition of Lebanon and the end of the Muslim–Christian agreement is
now challenging the Israelis, and his last secret interview with Begin, which
took place in Israel, degenerated into a serious argument that ended badly.
Bashir, who had refused for his militia to take part in the fights against
the Palestinians and their allies at the time of the invasion, now refused to
sign a peace treaty with Israel without consulting the Muslim forces of the
country. Faced with injunctions and threats from Begin, Bashir apparently
declared, extending his arms: "Pass me the handcuffs!" before adding: "I am
not your vassal!" Even the most skeptical allow themselves to dream.

So it is September 14, 1982, the Feast of the Cross. Bashir Gemayel, in
a sky-blue safari jacket, goes to Deir al-Salib, the Monastery of the Cross,
for a meeting with religious figures and prelates on the occasion of the feast.
During a lunch in the convent refectory, he gives a speech. His last speech.
An hour and a half later, he will be torn to pieces in the explosion that
blasts the three-story building where his headquarters is located. "I am the
president of all of Lebanon, responsible for all Lebanese people who live
on this country's soil and for all the country's institutions, which are
neither Christian, nor Muslim, but Lebanese... Today I ask each Lebanese

Images of this last meal evoke the Last Supper

citizen to resist every foreigner, every oppressor, every aggressor, who tries, from near or far, to denigrate the symbols of civilization, heritage, values, and beliefs of Lebanon…"

The cadaver is unrecognizable. But there is no doubt about its identity: in the pocket of the safari jacket, they will find a holy card given to him by the nuns of the Hospital of the Cross to guarantee the Virgin's protection. Israel uses this tragedy as a pretext to enter West Beirut. "To maintain order and security." The following night, the massacres of Sabra and Shatila begin. They last for about thirty-six hours.

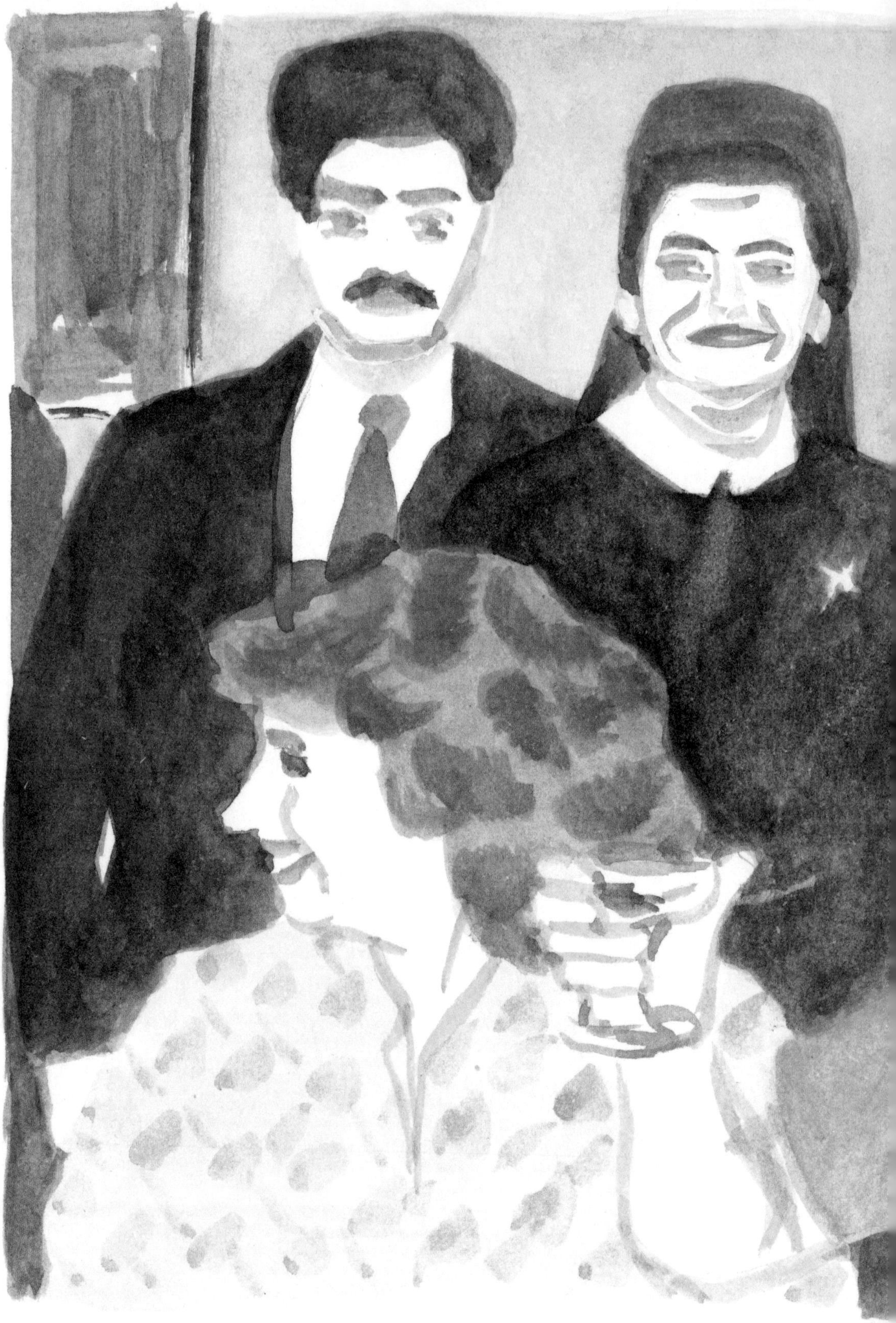

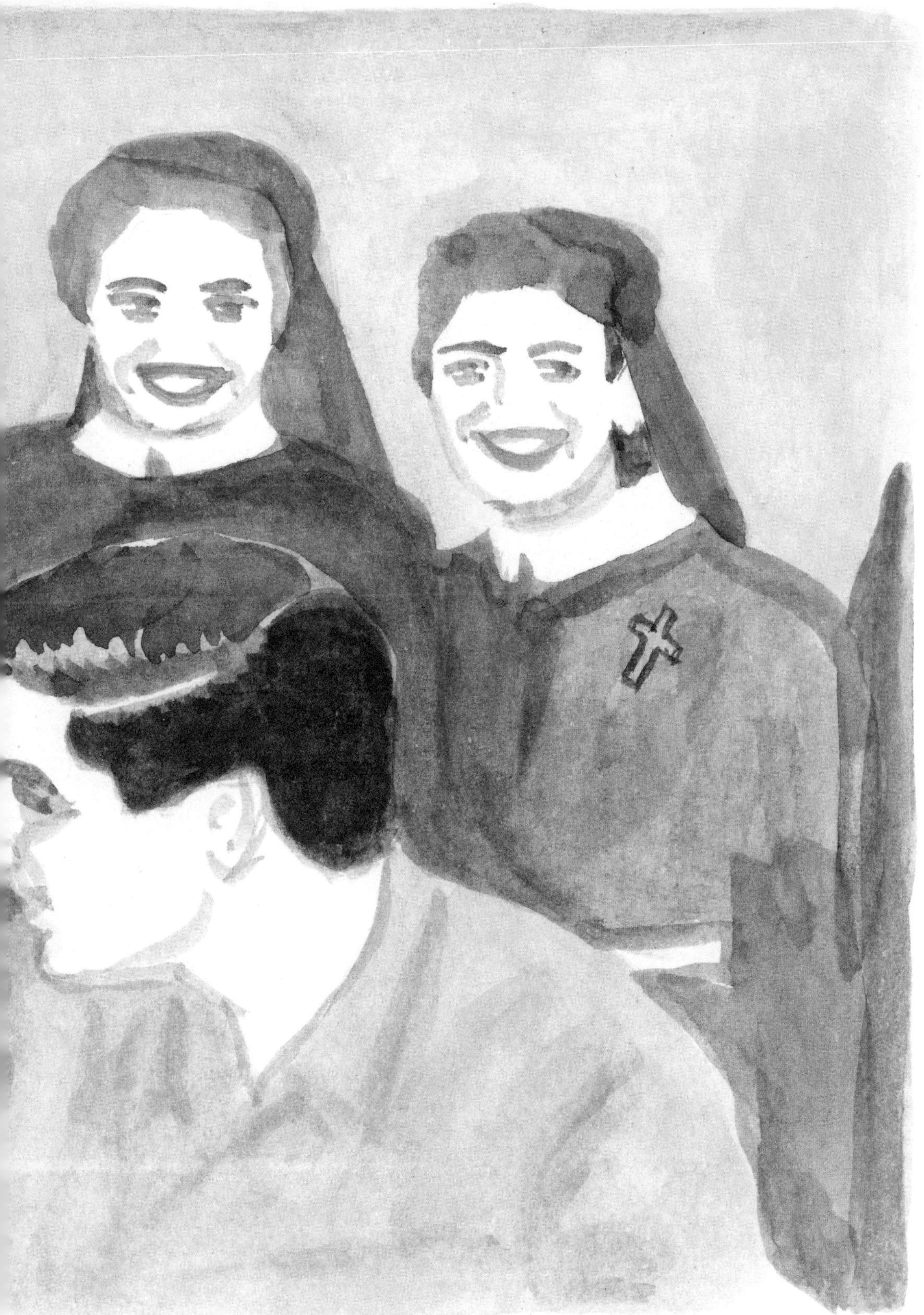

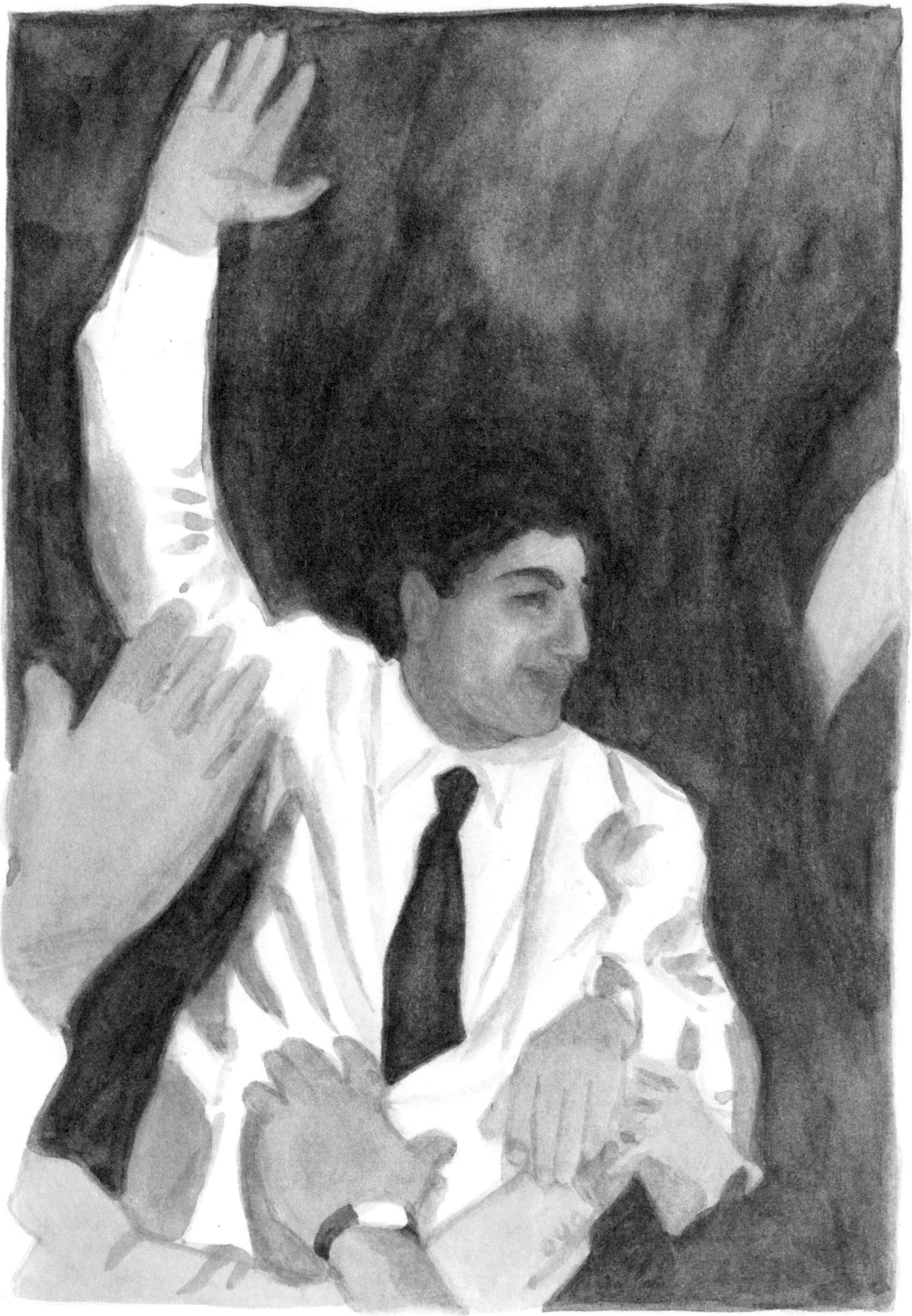

The time of victory... the time of funerals...

The Sabra and Shatila massacres…

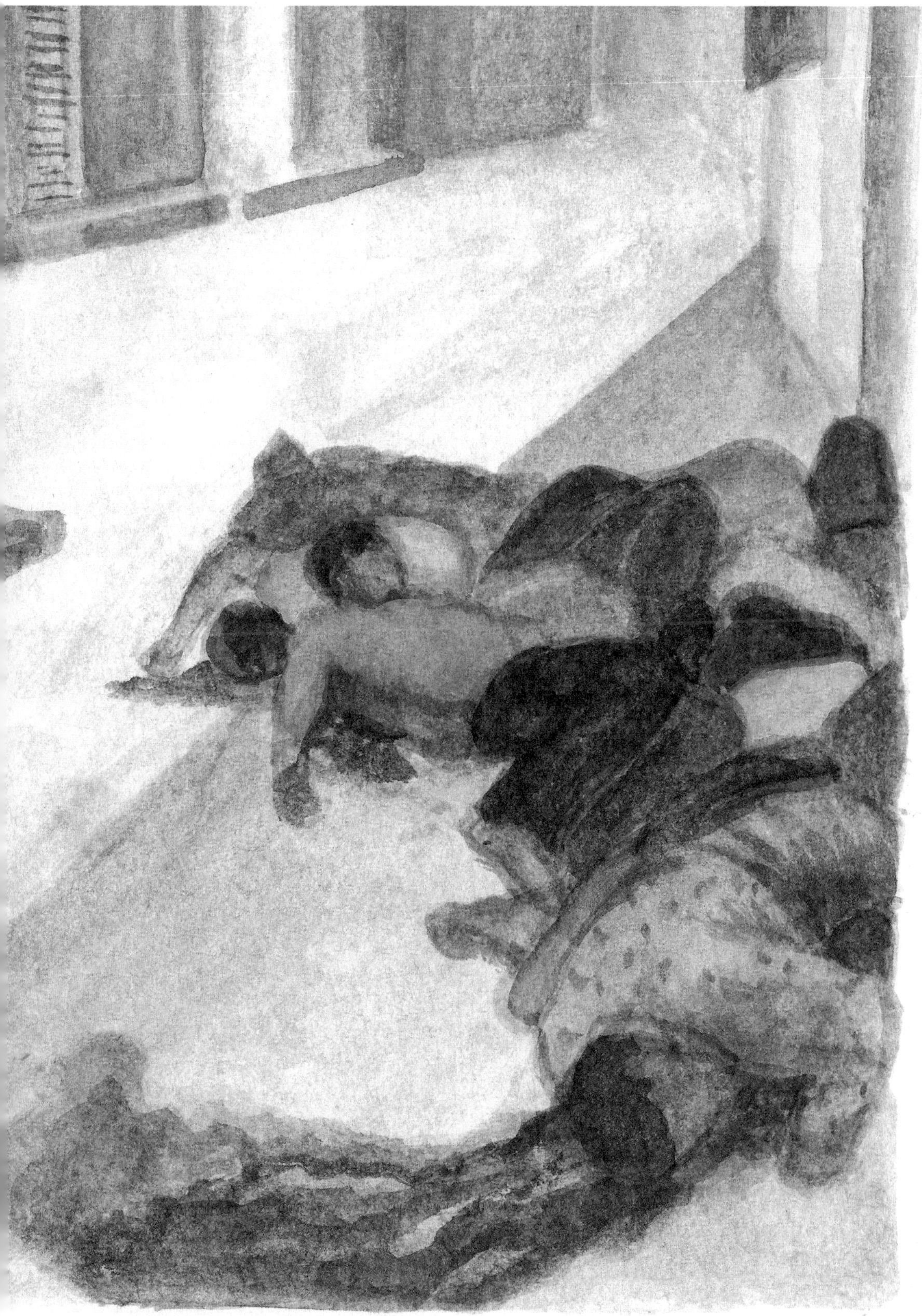

...last thirty-six hours

Empress Helena and the True Cross

The history of the Feast of the Cross is too beautiful not to recount it in the way it's told in Lebanon. On a pilgrimage to the Holy Land, the very Christian Roman empress Helena (future saint, mother of Constantine I), establishes the Church of the Nativity, discovers the sacred relics of the passion of the Christ, and knocks down the temple of Venus built on the site of the Church of the Holy Sepulchre, but does not have time, before leaving Jerusalem, to find the cross upon which Jesus died. She gives this task to her troupe that remains there, giving them instructions to light a bonfire to announce the news once the cross has been discovered. When they finally find the three crosses, Helen's emissaries cannot distinguish between the true cross on which Christ was crucified and those of the two thieves who were crucified at the same time. The inscription "Jesus of Nazarene, King of the Jews" has disappeared, there is no longer a way to discern the Holy Cross. They bring a paralytic woman to the site and have her touch the three crosses, counting on her being miraculously healed when she touches the cross of Jesus Christ—which is precisely what happens. A fire is lit on a hill in Jerusalem. It's relayed by other fires, from hill to hill, through all of Palestine, Lebanon, Syria, and Turkey, until it reaches the convoy of the empress who is traveling to Constantinople. Still today, on the night of the Feast of the Cross, bonfires are lit in all the Christian villages of Lebanon, to the delight of the children. The subterfuge used to distinguish the true cross is the origin of the expression "touch wood."

371

Riad Al Solh and Bechara El Khoury,
champions of independence and authors of the National Pact

Riad Al Solh and the National Pact

The Sunni mufti, the Shii imam, the Christian president, the Druze leader... Despite themselves, the assassins help to promote the Lebanese miracle of coexisting communities and denominational equilibrium— even among martyrs! It is neither a myth nor a fantasy, but an appalling reality: the impartiality of killers reflects the wonder of this small country and its "National Pact." The National Pact is not written in the constitution or recorded on any piece of paper. It is an oral agreement made between two men in 1943, during their battle against the French for Lebanese independence. The essence of this agreement has never been called into question by the successors of those two men, despite fifteen years of war and a continually explosive situation. It is the founding principle of Lebanon: the country must be led by Christians and Muslims conjointly, by an equitable division of government offices and political functions between the different

Riad Al Solh: cunning politician, loyal patriot

Lebanese communities, which must remain free from all foreign influence, whether Arab or Western. These two men are Bechara El Khoury, then President of Lebanon, and Riad Al Solh, President of the Council. Their imprisonment in the Rashaya Citadel by the French and the independence they have managed to wrest from them make them into heroes in an Arab world still entirely under foreign domination. One of these two heroes, Riad Al Solh, will be assassinated a few years later, in 1951. It is the first political assassination in Lebanon, the first of such importance in the Middle East, the first of an endless succession... But the man targeted is not just anyone, he is the living symbol of the coexistence of communities. It is this miraculous equilibrium that the murderers targeted. With this assassination, violence makes its entrance into Lebanon, and throughout the Middle East...

The three daughters of Riad Al Solh

Three young girls walk at the head of the procession. It is the first time that women have participated in a Sunni funeral procession. An impressive cortège, which includes, in the first row, the most eminent figures of the country, starting with Bechara El Khoury, the Lebanese president himself, who is visibly emotional. It is a national funeral. The girls insist on being present, against the wishes of the heads of the family. They are bare-armed and their hair is down, flowing over their shoulders, a thin white veil resting untied on their heads. Young modern girls. The daughters of Riad Al Solh. Their father's prestige is so great, not only in Lebanon, but throughout the Arab world, that one of them would go on to marry the son of the king of Morocco, and another the son of the king of Saudi Arabia. The procession follows the coffin, covered with the national flag and placed on a cannon. There are to be three days of mourning. Riad Al Solh was assassinated in Amman, where he had gone to meet King Abdullah and confront their differing views on the position to adopt toward Israel. His death is still shrouded in mystery to this day. He was gunned down by a member of the SSNP, whose founder, Antoun Saadeh, he had sentenced to death a few months prior, but there are also theories of Israeli involvement. His assassination came three days before the assassination of King Abdullah, killed by a Palestinian nationalist in front of Al-Aqsa Mosque.

The statue of Riad Al Solh is still standing today, at the most prestigious location in Beirut

A statue of Riad Al Solh still presides over the square that bears his name in Beirut, at the foot of the seraglio, in the most prestigious location in the city. The statue has survived fifteen years of war and the destruction of Beirut. One other statue has survived, on Martyrs' Square, which itself no longer exists. The statue is still standing but mutilated and riddled with bullet holes. And isn't this in fact the best thing that could happen to a statue of martyrs? You find it very beautiful that it's peppered with chips and shards that let the light through... like a constellation, a little gleam for each martyr. After all, it is the attraction of the stars that makes the world go round, and what brings down heroes. Your sky is strewn with martyrs... you offer them a sepulcher worthy of a kingdom. You are going to photograph the statue; this will be the final stop of your stroll among the tombs. You will end your macabre dance there. What better place than Martyrs' Square in Beirut?

But wait just a moment, you will not bring your funereal wandering to a close so easily... not before you have recounted your final journey to Cairo and your obsessive quest through that city which is the most famous in the world for its tombs. Though it was not the tombs inside the pyramids that interested you on that day...

During the dark years, in the shadow of Riad Al Solh

Mutilated and riddled with gunshots, the statue from Martyrs' Square is still standing

The Tomb of Gamal Abdel Nasser

In Cairo, the first taxi driver you ask to take you to Abdel Nasser's tomb asks: "Who, Abdel Nasser the president?" You are taken aback that he could think you would want to visit the tomb of a different Abdel Nasser in Cairo. But that's nothing compared to your surprise when he says to you, once you have confirmed that it is in fact Gamal the president whom you want to see, that he doesn't know where his tomb is. This scenario repeats itself three or four times—with a few minor differences—before you give up and ask the fifth taxi driver to take you to the pyramids instead. On the drive, you try to understand, you are in disbelief... A man whose funeral procession was attended by 5 million people, setting a record for the first or second most-watched funeral in history, and no one in his own city knows where he is buried. "If you want, I can take you to the Shah of Iran's tomb," your driver says pitifully, "or the tomb of King Farouk..." You had forgotten that the Shah was buried in Cairo. "What about Umm Kulthum," you ask, "do you know where Umm Kulthum is buried?" The poor man doesn't dare say no, but he's not sure. It's clear that he is mad at himself, most of all because he has never even asked himself that question. When you ask him if he knows where Asmahan, Farid al-Atrash, and Mohammed Abdel Wahab are, you feel as if you're torturing him and decide to stop. But you are determined not to leave Cairo without seeing the mausoleums of the heroes of your last book![19] You complete your tour of the pyramids and visit the small mortuary temple at the foot of the Sphinx where they embalmed the dead. It's a feast for the eyes, each visit to the pyramids as marvelous as the last. Finally you return to the car waiting for you and your driver welcomes you proudly: "I can take you to see the tomb of Abdel Nasser," he says, "I found out where it is." "And Umm Kulthum?" "No one knows," he says. "She might be buried in her village, in the delta." "No," you say, "she's in the City of the Dead, in Cairo. Four million people followed her coffin to her tomb!"

You arrive at Nasser's mosque, far from the city center, squeezed between two very large main roads. It's impossible to park, even far away, it's a completely military zone. The taxi driver isn't allowed to wait for you, instead he must drive around in circles until you come out. And you come out very quickly, because you cannot enter to begin with—it is closed in the

---

19   Lamia Ziadé, *Ô nuit, Ô mes yeux: Le Caire/ Beyrouth/ Damas/Jérusalem* (Paris: POL, 2015).

afternoons. Oh well, you'll come back tomorrow! Now that you know where it is... The next day, you arrive around 11am. There is absolutely no one else there. The caretaker lets you into the official rooms. He asks you if you're Lebanese. You ask how he guessed. "Only Lebanese people come to visit this tomb," he says. You blush with pride. You believe him, even if you think that it was probably your accent that tipped him off...

Abandoned tomb... abandoned pride... buried era... forgotten hero... you are the only visitor

The Last Tomb

They say that 4 million people took to the streets in Cairo for Umm Kulthum's funeral. When you watch films from that time, you have absolutely no doubt. Today, no one in town is able to tell you where in the City of the Dead her tomb is located. And you had thought her mausoleum would be a pilgrimage site with a dedicated cult! You finally manage to figure out which area of the gigantic cemetery you have to look in, but your quest is far from over. You have to ask no fewer than thirty people who live among the tombs before you finally reach your destination. At last, there she is. You are shocked. Her tomb is more impressive and opulent than all the other tombs around it, but it is also in a state of unbelievable dilapidation and abandonment. It looks like a dump. A destitute family that lives in the shade of another tomb a few meters away approaches you. A young woman in rags, toothless and barefoot, two young children also in rags, an elderly man, and a young man surround you. You have never seen so much misery. They look exhumed. They offer to open the tomb for you. The portal that opens onto the street is ajar, and the garden that surrounds the mausoleum has become a sort of wasteland where dead plants, plastic bags, and other trash like beat-up armchairs and machine carcasses serve as decor. The young woman opens the door to the tomb. On the inside are a couch, a few armchairs, an old rug, and a dim chandelier, all completely faded and dusty, but still there, while you sense that other objects and paintings have disappeared. On the slab under which Umm Kulthum rests is an old, dried bouquet. The desolation of the site fills you with gloom. But after all, it is the City of Dead, isn't it? Not every cemetery can be as paradisiacal and joyous as the one in Tyre. The more you think about it, the more you are struck by the contrast between the tragic, violent deaths of the majority of those buried in Tyre with their graves full of flowers, in the sun and by the sea, and this tomb, so dreary, of the Star of the East...

A little girl in rags dances in the dinghy mausoleum of Umm Kulthum...

Beneath this slab rests the Star of the East

Along the outside wall, a dump, as in the rest of the City of the Dead...

Your pilgrimage of sorts through Cairo continues in this way. You go from devastation to dismay... You went to see the Umm Kulthum hotel, which replaced her razed villa in Zamalek, the eight-story parking lot that replaced the Royal Opera House, the mall that replaced the mythic Casino Badia... Passing in front of a large carcass on the edge of the Nile, at the southern tip of Zamalek, you have the feeling that you've seen this building before in photos, or in a movie. The taxi driver tells you that it's the head office of the Revolutionary Command Council, where Nasser's funeral procession began. He says it will be restored soon—to become a five-star hotel. But it's in Alexandria, where you spend two days, that you experience the most intense shock. When you ask your hosts to show you the balcony where Nasser gave his famous Suez Canal speech, they look at each other, embarrassed, and tell you that it no longer exists. The building, the Alexandria Bourse, caught fire a few years ago and was razed to the ground. In its place today, a miserable parking lot.

With a heavy heart, you think of Rivoli...

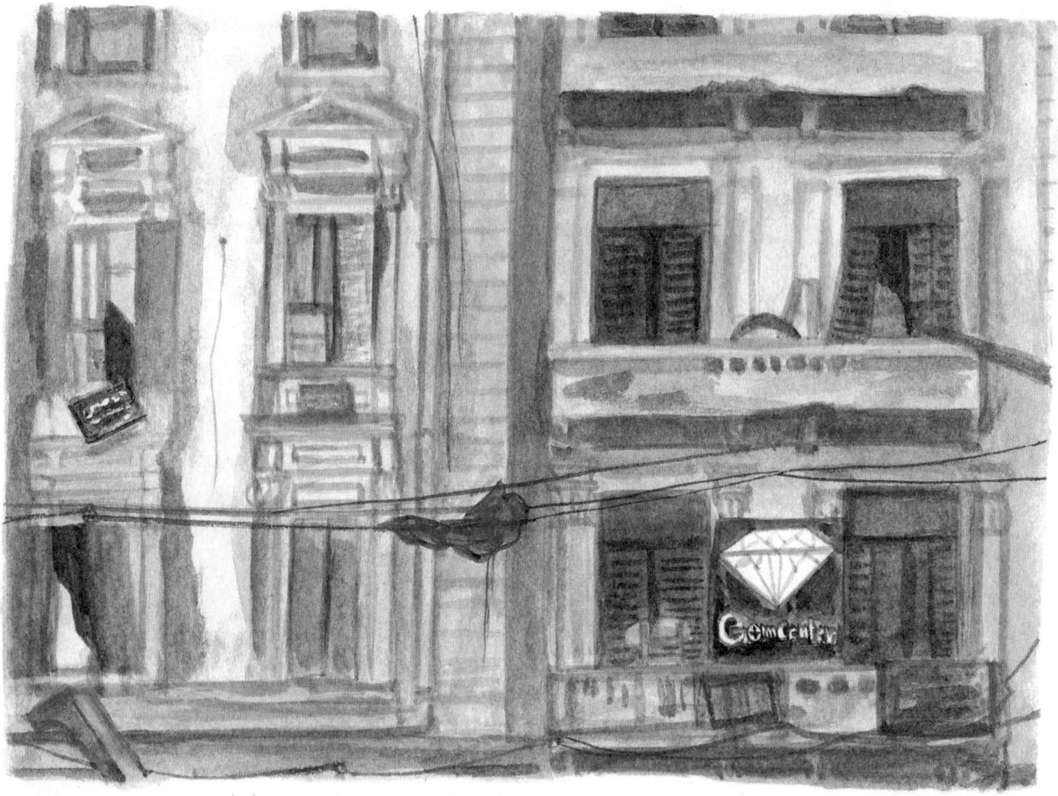
Gem Center

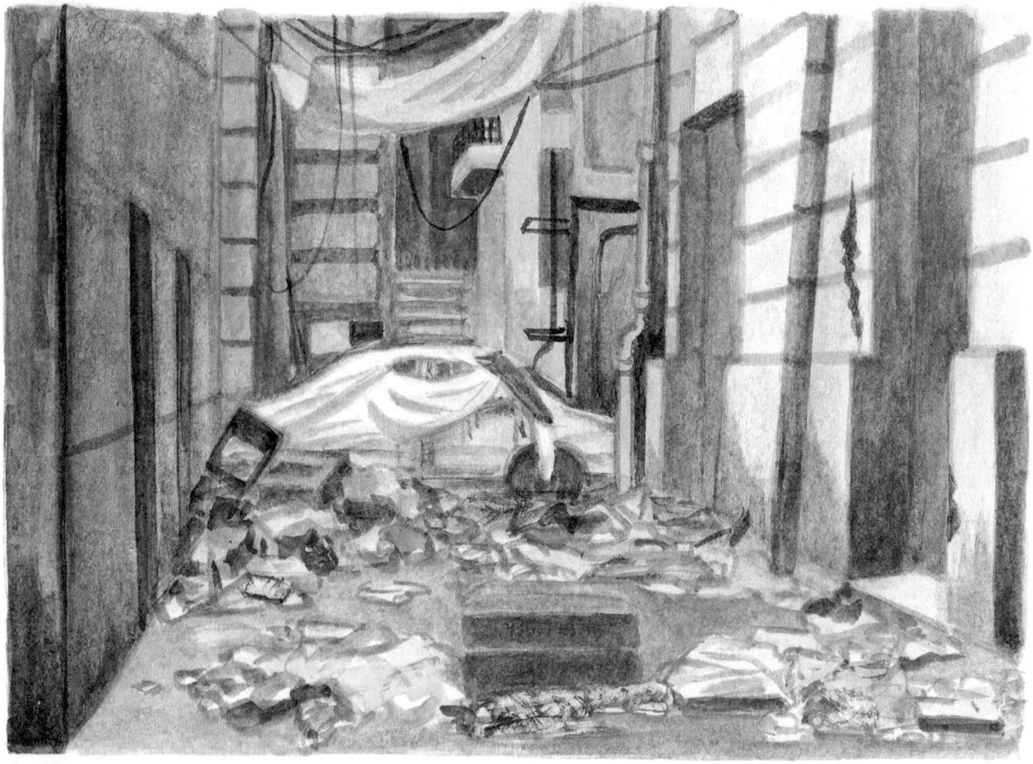

The building from which Nasser gave his legendary speech was razed. Mohammed Ali Square, where the building was located, is in a state of dilapidation and abandonment that you see as the reflection of your soul, and that of millions of Arabs... the time of stars is over... everyone has forgotten

Back in Martyrs' Square...
the statue is still there. The bullet holes create a constellation of martyrs,
a small light for each heroic soul...
Stars don't die... you can no longer resist the allure of the stars... des astres... désastres... disasters.
You think, your heart heavy, of the Rivoli, the other monument on the square, a cinema...
It enclosed the part of the square closest to the sea with its famous ORIENT sign, a watch brand...
After surviving fifteen years of barbarism as best as it could,
it was simply and completely razed at the end of the war,
in an apocalyptic implosion that you cannot, today,
see as anything but prophetic...

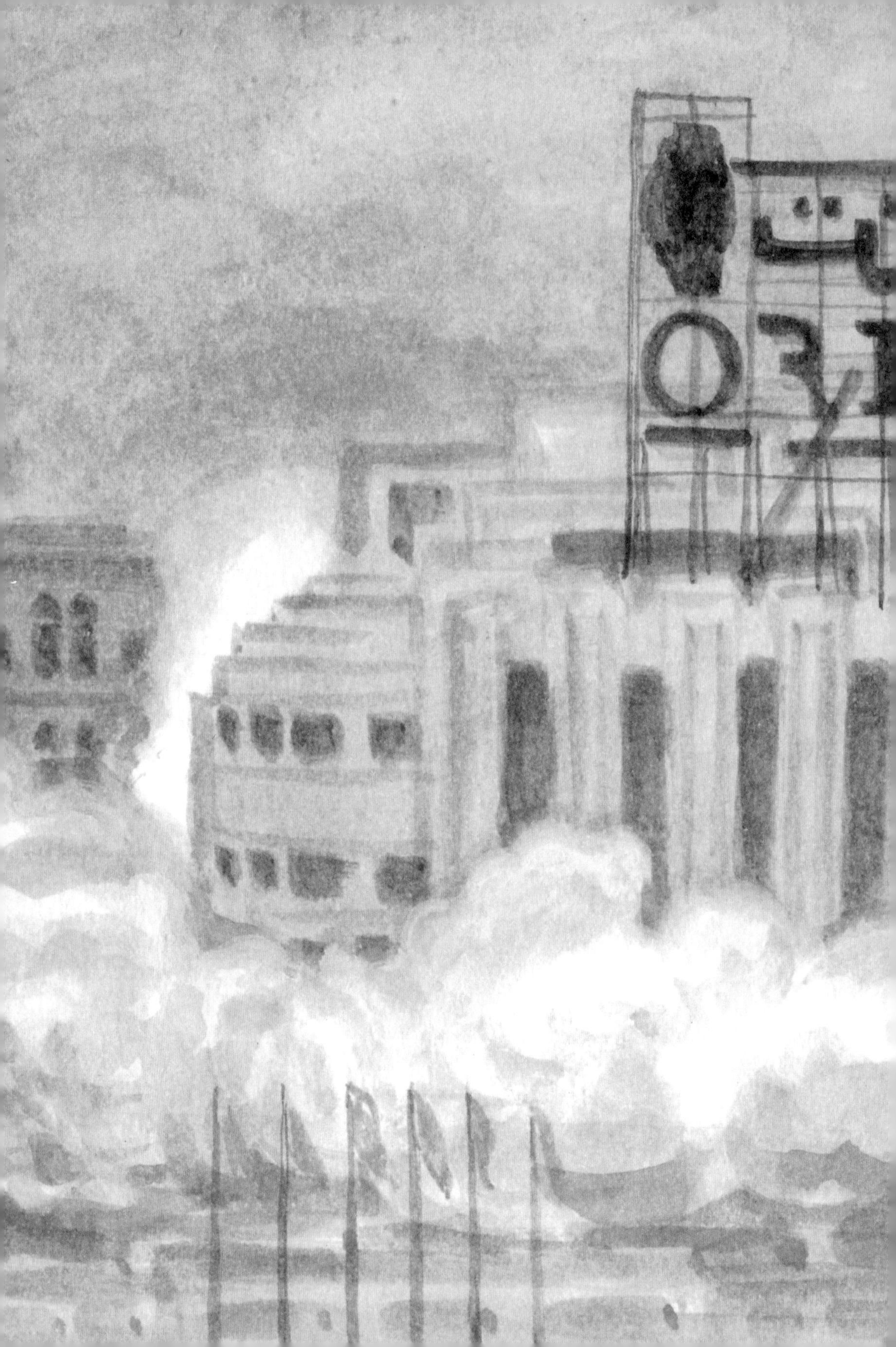

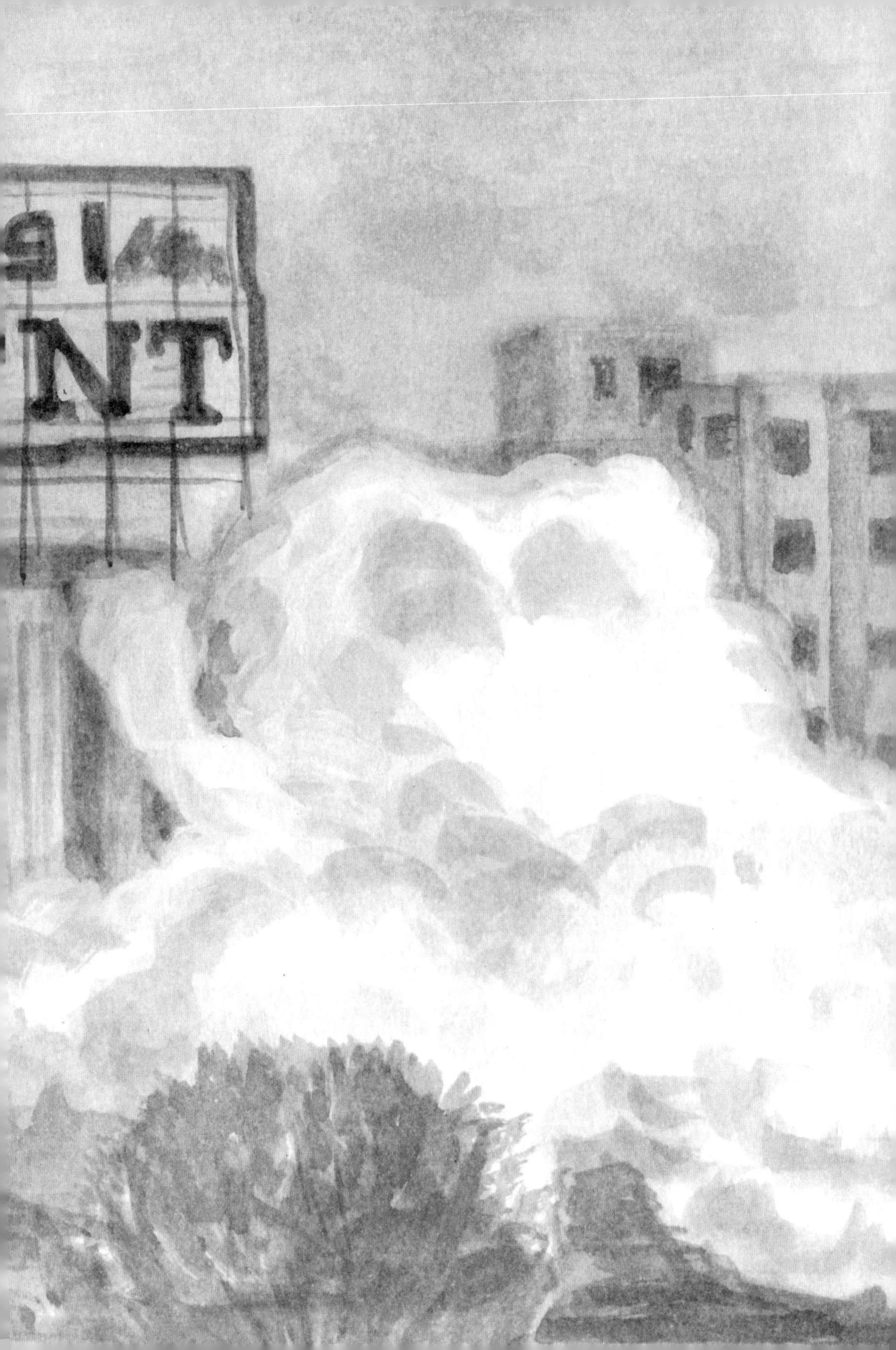
NT

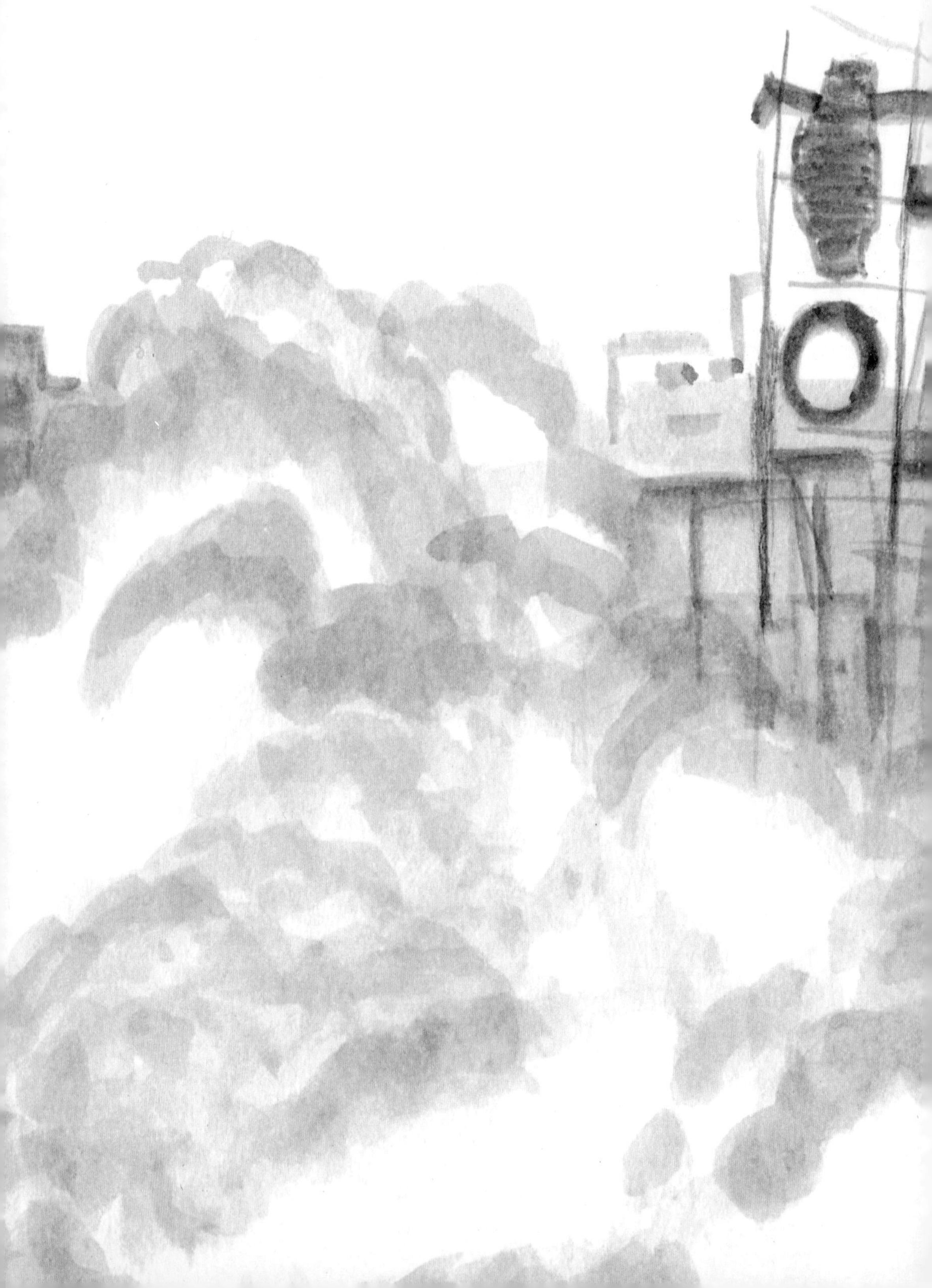

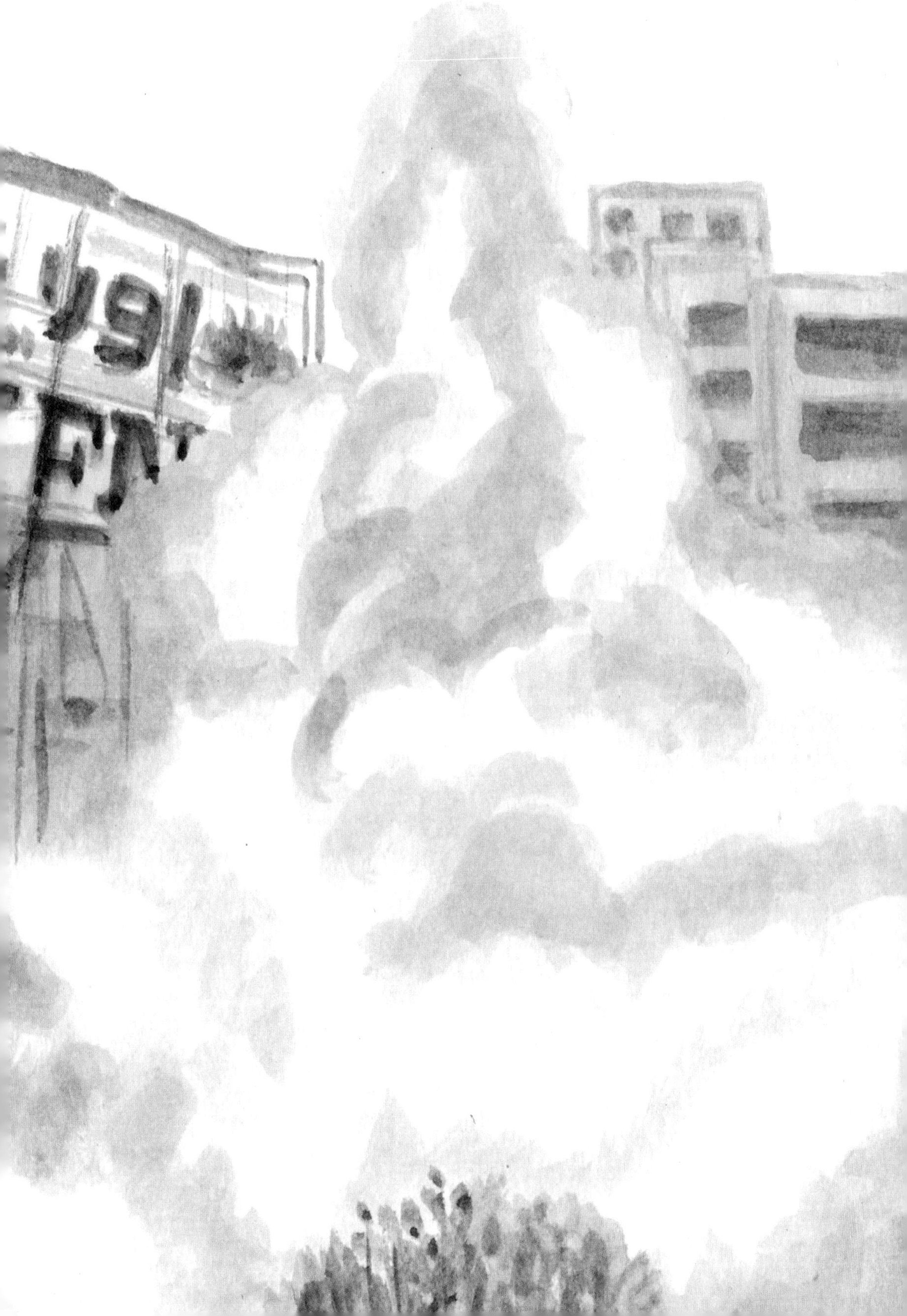

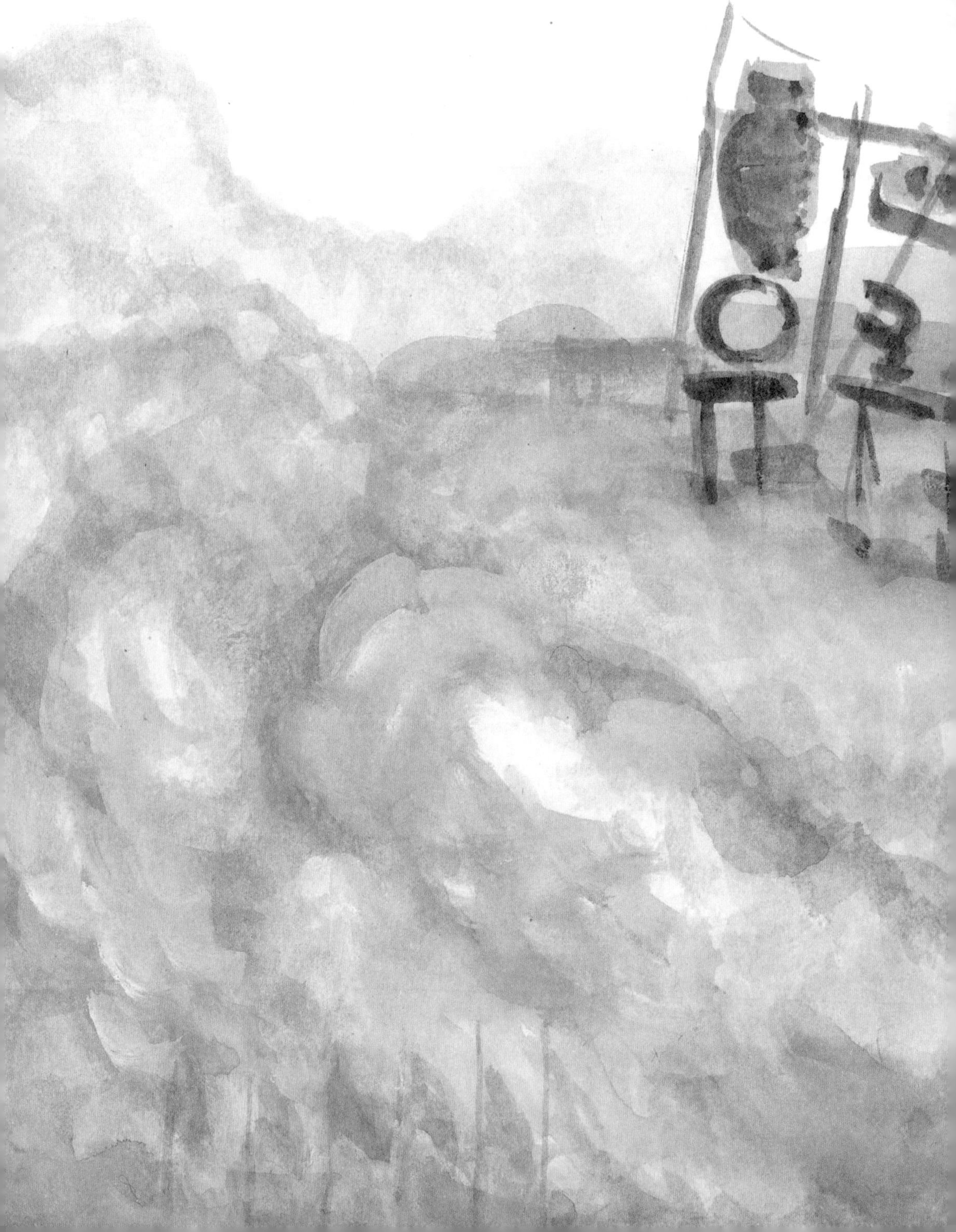

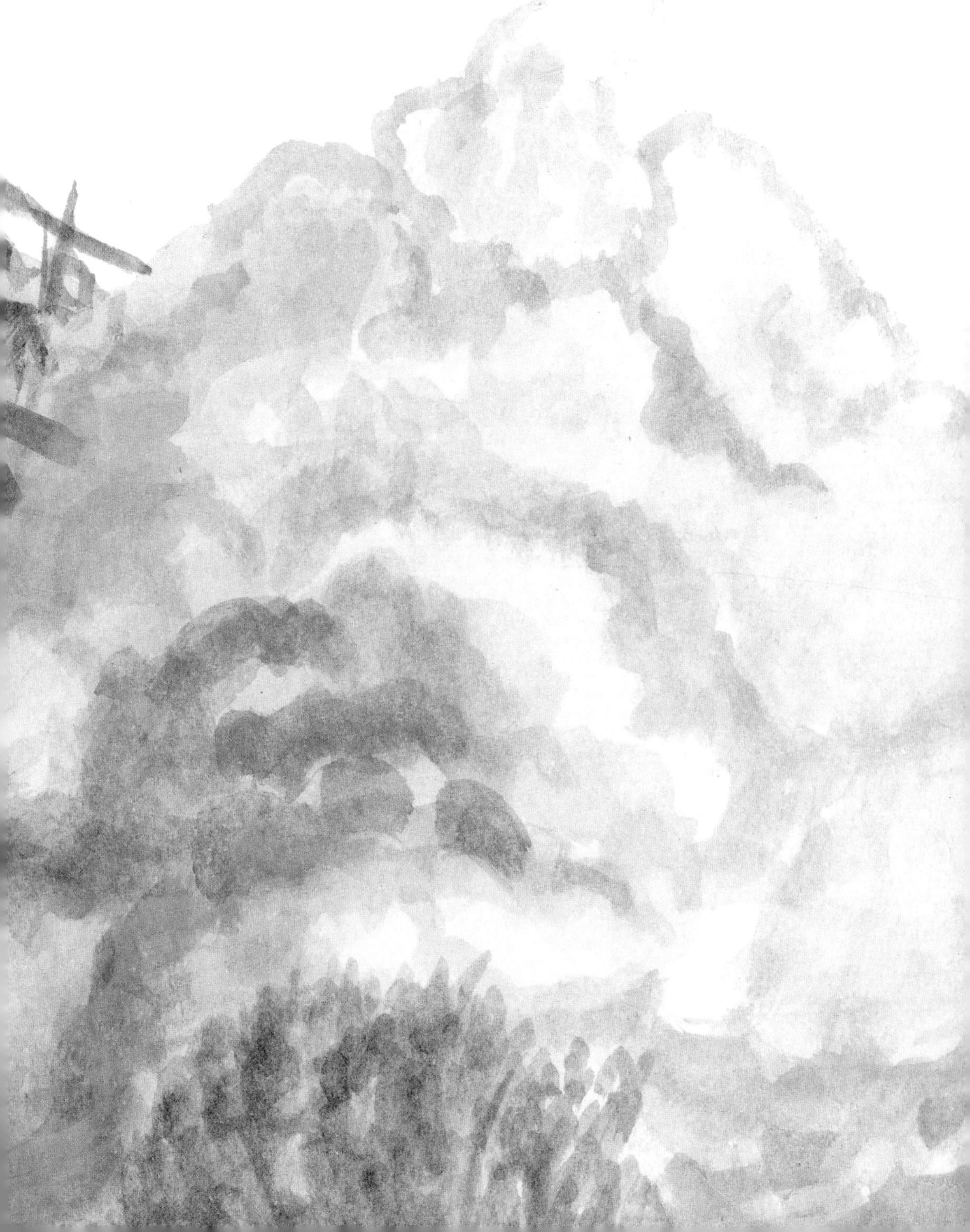

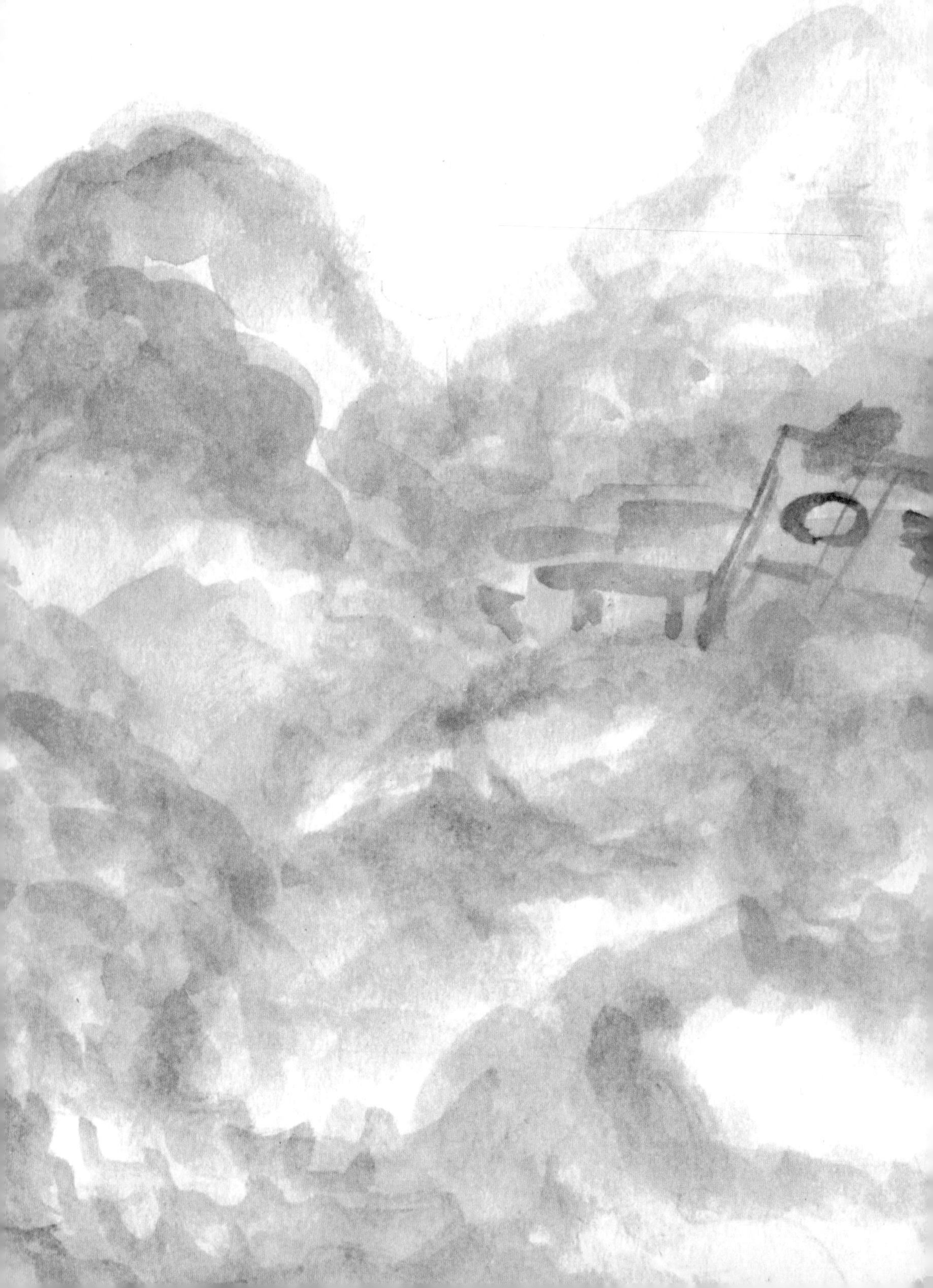

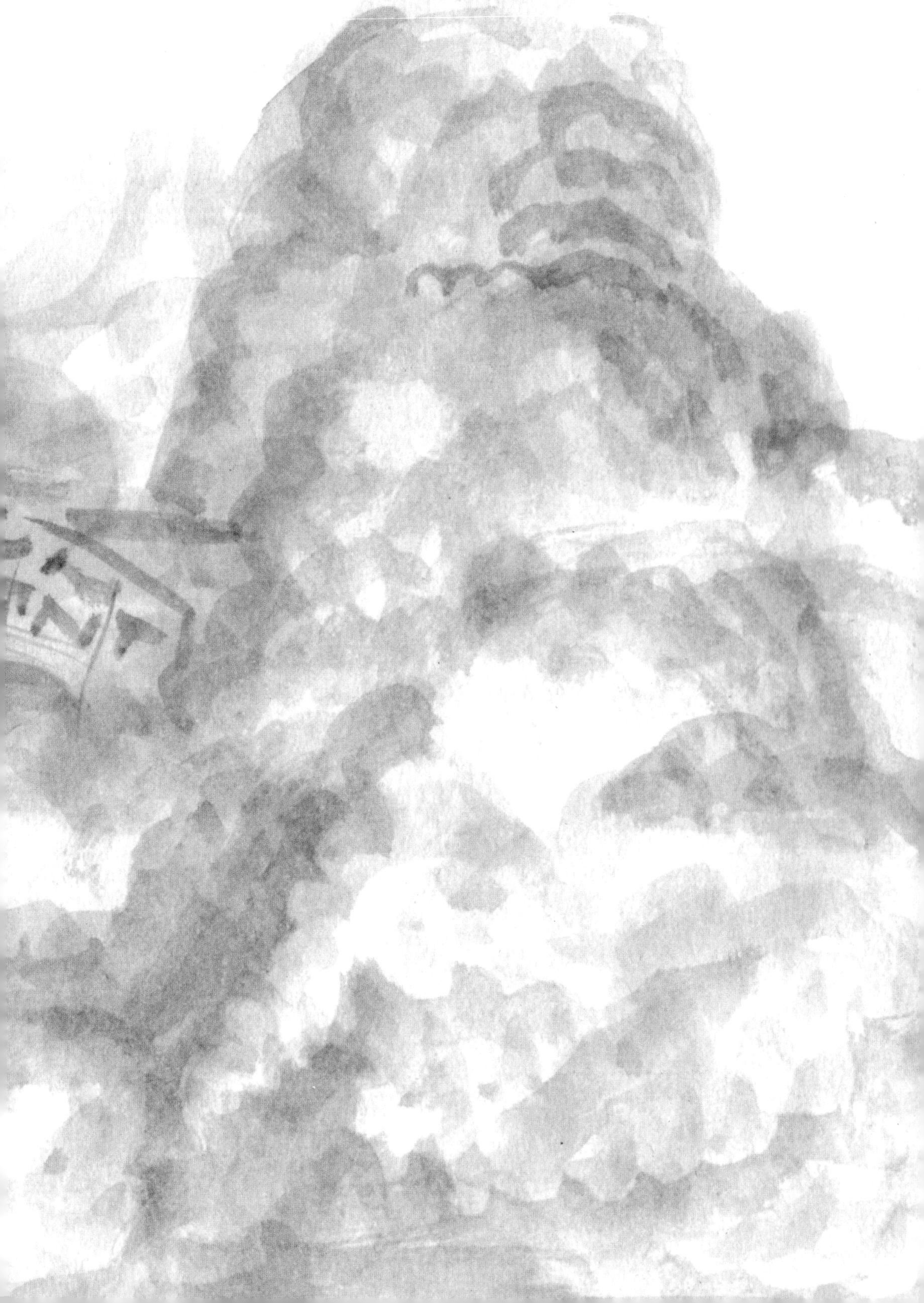

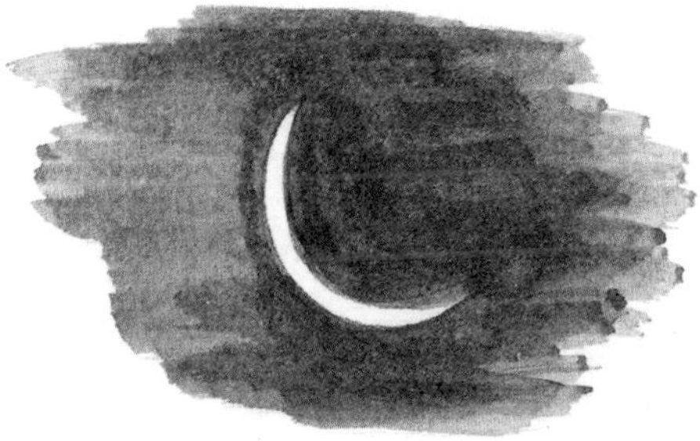

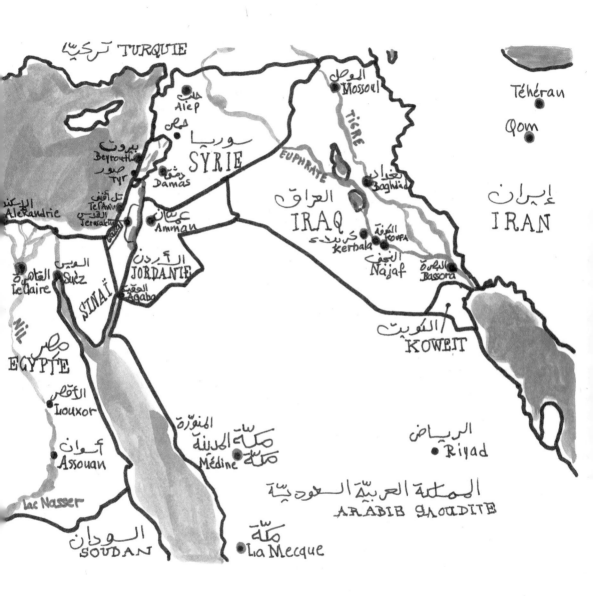

The major cities of the Middle East visited in this book

Above: Map of the places in South Lebanon visited during this pilgrimage
Below: A cursory map of Tyre

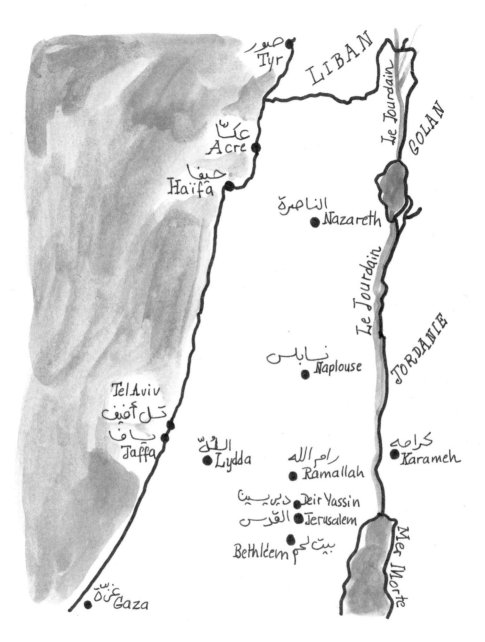

The major cities of Palestine/Israel mentioned in this book

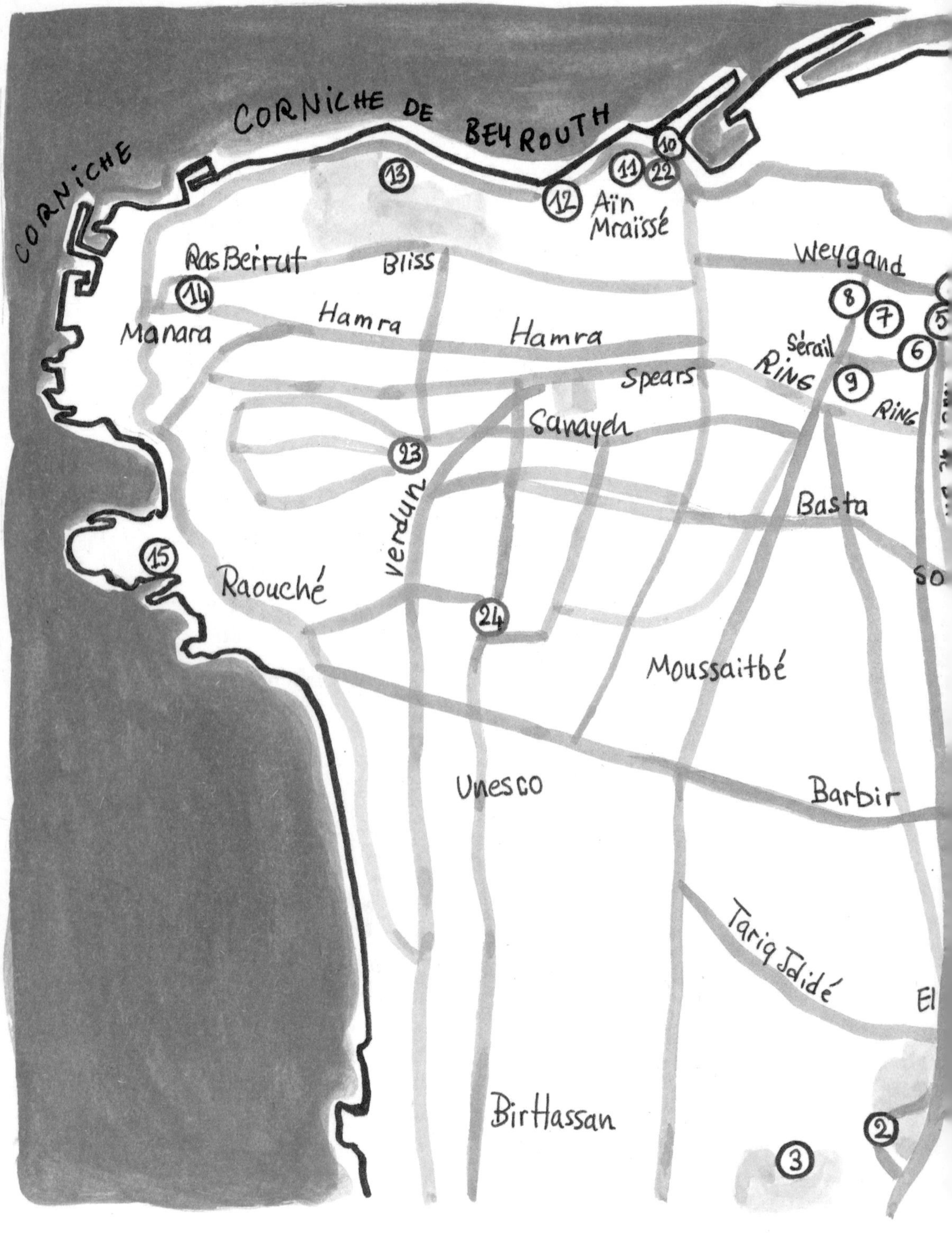
CORNICHE
CORNICHE DE BEYROUTH
Aïn Mraïssé
Ras Beirut
Bliss
Weygand
Manara
Hamra
Hamra
Sérail
Spears
RING
RING
Sanayeh
Basta
Verdun
Raouché
Moussaitbé
Unesco
Barbir
Tariq Jdidé
Bir Hassan
13
12
11
22
10
14
8
7
5
6
9
23
15
24
2
3

Map of Beirut

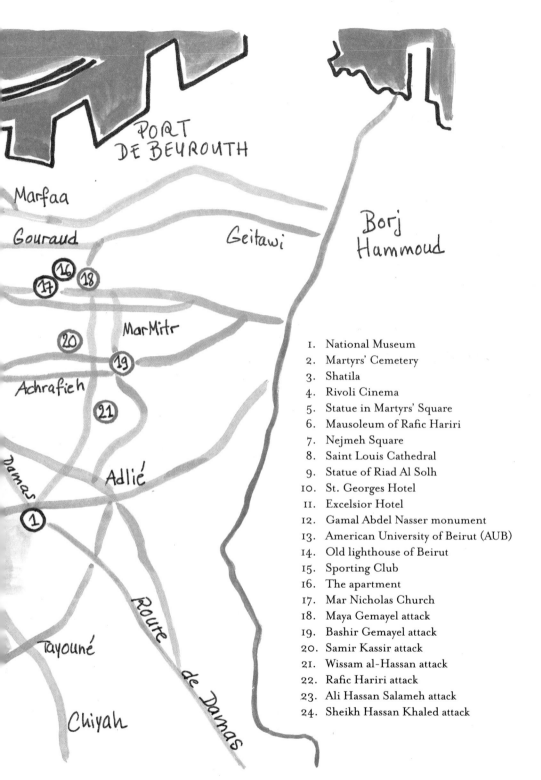

PORT DE BEYROUTH

Marfaa

Gouraud

Geitawi

Borj Hammoud

⑯ ⑰ ⑱

MarMitr

⑳

⑲

Achrafieh

㉑

Damas

Adlié

①

Route de Damas

Tayouné

Chiyah

1. National Museum
2. Martyrs' Cemetery
3. Shatila
4. Rivoli Cinema
5. Statue in Martyrs' Square
6. Mausoleum of Rafic Hariri
7. Nejmeh Square
8. Saint Louis Cathedral
9. Statue of Riad Al Solh
10. St. Georges Hotel
11. Excelsior Hotel
12. Gamal Abdel Nasser monument
13. American University of Beirut (AUB)
14. Old lighthouse of Beirut
15. Sporting Club
16. The apartment
17. Mar Nicholas Church
18. Maya Gemayel attack
19. Bashir Gemayel attack
20. Samir Kassir attack
21. Wissam al-Hassan attack
22. Rafic Hariri attack
23. Ali Hassan Salameh attack
24. Sheikh Hassan Khaled attack

Major sites mentioned and the locations of a few of the countless attacks that took place in Beirut

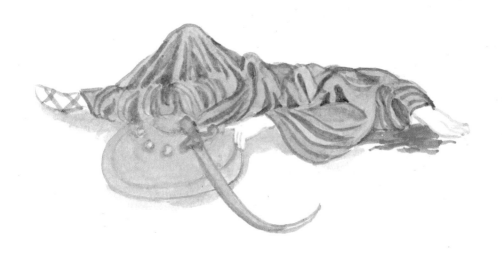